BUTCHERED!

As she walked toward the barn, following the light source, Ellingsen felt ill—either from the excessive drug use that night or the sickening odor that hung in the night air, which grew stronger as she reached the barn. She cautiously pushed open the barn door a bit when, suddenly and without warning, Willie Pickton, covered in blood, reached out and grabbed her, pulling her inside the barn. He pulled Ellingsen over to a table and forced her to look at the dead woman, naked and hanging from a hook. The woman, Georgina Papin, was just hanging there, covered in blood. Willie had placed her on a hook in the same manner that he always hung up the pigs that he was going to slaughter. The victim's feet, whose toenails were painted red, were at Ellingsen's eye level. On a "shiny table" next to the hanging body, Ellingsen saw long black hair lying there, Georgina Papin's hair, and a lot of blood. She also saw two bloody knives. It looked to her like Willie had skinned Papin, and was preparing to butcher her like an animal.

Willie told Ellingsen that if she told anyone anything about what she had seen that night, the same thing would happen to her.

Also by Gary C. King:

BUTCHER

GARY C. KING

PINNACLE BOOKS
Kensington Publishing Corp.
http://www.kensingtonbooks.com

Some names have been changed to protect the privacy of individuals connected to this story.

PINNACLE BOOKS are published by

Kensington Publishing Corp.
850 Third Avenue
New York, NY 10022

All Kensington Titles, Imprints, and Distributed Lines are available at special quantity discounts for bulk purchases for sales promotions, premiums, fund-raising, and educational or institutional use. Special book excerpts or customized printings can also be created to fit specific needs. For details, write or phone the office of the Kensington special sales manager: Kensington Publishing Corp., 850 Third Avenue, New York, NY 10022, attn: Special Sales Department, Phone: 1-800-221-2647.

Pinnacle and the P logo Reg. U.S. Pat. & TM Off.

ISBN-13: 978-0-7860-1934-2
ISBN-10: 0-7860-1934-4

First Printing: April 2009

10 9 8 7 6 5 4 3 2 1

Printed in the United States of America

This book is dedicated to the memory of the victims . . .

Acknowledgments

I would like to thank the following people for their support and assistance during the writing of this book: First and foremost, my wife, Teresita, for her endurance and months of essentially living alone while I barricaded myself behind closed doors and confined myself to the computer, telephone, and, of course, my "big-boy" office chair, which I rarely left—three major, and necessary, tools of the trade! I couldn't do it without her love, cooperation, and understanding. I am also very grateful to Kirsten and Sarah, as always, for helping out when needed during such a time-intensive and grueling project. Thanks to all of you for always being there.

I am also forever grateful to Michaela Hamilton, editor-in-chief at Kensington Publishing Corporation, for her keen insight, sharp red pencil, and the clear vision for having seen the importance and magnitude of doing a book about the Robert Pickton case, clearly one of the worst serial murder cases in history. I'm also grateful to Mike Shohl for his suggestions to improve the manuscript, and am equally grateful to everyone else at Kensington who work in the forefront as well as behind the scenes to make these books happen.

Thanks also to my longtime agent, Peter Miller, of PMA Literary & Film Management, Inc., for his support and show of confidence throughout the years, and to his assistant, Adrienne Rosado, who keeps everything fine-tuned and in great working order, and for her patience during those times when I become a nuisance. A writer couldn't ask for better representation when the best is already there!

I would also like to acknowledge the work of the numerous dedicated members of the Royal Canadian Mounted Police and the Vancouver Police Department for their tedious work in gathering the tremendous amount of evidence that it took to bring Robert Pickton to justice after they realized they had a serial killer at work in their midst.

Thanks also to Jorge Jaramillo at Newscom and to Kimberly Waldman at Associated Press for their assistance in helping locate photographs appropriate for this book.

A very special "thank-you" to copyeditor Stephanie Finnegan whose efforts and professionalism in literally working over my manuscript have resulted in a more readable final product.

Author's Note

The contents of the book that you now hold in your hands is that of an often complicated story of missing women, torture, mutilation, and dismemberment involving one of the most horrifying cases of serial murder in modern history. I have been following the case in varying degrees since it first broke with Robert Pickton's arrest in February 2002, and the depiction of the events herein is based on hundreds of hours of research of more than yearlong trial accounts, telephone calls, and e-mails with those who were willing to discuss the tragic events following the trial, as well as a careful analysis of statements that Pickton made to an undercover police officer and others after his arrest. For purposes of clarity, every attempt has been made to present the story in the order that it unfolded, from the time that it was first noticed that women from Vancouver's "Low Track" area began disappearing, through the investigation after the police were convinced that they had a serial murderer on their hands, and on through the trial. Even though backgrounds of the women who disappeared during "Uncle Willie's" reign of terror will be presented, the primary focus of this book is on the victims whose deaths Pickton was actually charged with and those women of which he was convicted of murdering.

No attempt has been made to fictionalize any aspect of this sad story—every incident portrayed herein is based on the facts as they are known—and none of the characters portrayed are fictional or are composites of my imagination. Portions of the story were related to me by family members and friends of the victims, and portions were taken from the various public information sources that became available following Pickton's trial. A gag order had been in effect prior to the outcome of the trial, and during the trial only selected information releases to an equally selected media were authorized by the Canadian government.

Nonetheless, every effort has been made to portray the victims of Vancouver's Downtown Eastside as the living, breathing human beings that they were, and it is my hope that they are not further objectified. These women, whose lives on the streets were tragic enough before Robert Pickton came along, deserve the honor, respect, and commemoration that Pickton took away from them and their families.

—G.C.K.

The angels all were singing out of tune,
And hoarse with having little else to do,
Excepting to wind up the sun and moon,
Or curb a runaway young star or two.
—Lord Byron, *The Vision of Judgement*

Ye are of your father the devil, and the lusts of
your father ye will do. He was a murderer from
the beginning, and abode not in the truth, because there is no truth in him. When he speaketh
a lie, he speaketh of his own: for he is a liar, and
the father of it.

—John 8:44

Prologue

Summer was still barely hanging on when Lillian Jean O'Dare, thirty-four, disappeared without a trace from the rough-and-tumble streets of East Vancouver, British Columbia, on September 12, 1978. The temperature was still in the low-sixties during the day, but the nights were becoming somewhat chilly with the mercury hovering in the mid-to-upper forties, cold enough to bring out the onset of autumn colors and to necessitate the wearing of warm clothing in the evening. With a light breeze comprising variable minor gusts and occasional fog during the early-morning hours, and with scattered clouds throughout much of the rest of the day, Vancouver was free of precipitation as Lillian walked the streets of "Low Track," a high-vice area that is home to prostitution and drug addicts, where overdosing had become a regular occurrence. Low Track is known for having one of the highest HIV-infection rates in North America, and would eventually become the focal point of a prolific serial killer bent on snatching unsuspecting prostitutes off its seedy streets with promises of drugs and money. Of course, when Lillian O'Dare vanished, no one had a clue, yet, of what was to come.

Although little was known about the average-built Caucasian woman, with short reddish blond hair, who stood five feet six inches tall, Lillian was reported missing on the same day that she seemingly vanished. Years later, in 2002, when the Joint Missing Women Task Force began compiling names and backgrounds of the women who had disappeared from Low Track, Lillian's case would become the oldest of the sixty-five women that would eventually make the list.

The ensuing missing person investigation at first failed to turn up anything significant about Lillian. In fact, it would be nearly eleven years before any new clues turned up in what had quickly become a cold case. As it turned out, the resident of a rental house, located in the 900 block of Salsbury Drive in East Vancouver, provided the first clue to Lillian's whereabouts when he found a human skull in a crawl space inside the dwelling, on April 22, 1989. After summoning the police, the rest of the skeleton was found in the house that had, at one time, been occupied by a motorcycle gang. According to Royal Canadian Mounted Police (RCMP) constable Annie Linteau, all the police knew at that time was that the skeletal remains were that of a female. Despite an intensive investigation in which detectives suspected foul play, it would take an additional thirteen years before positive identification would be made, due, in part, to the limitations of DNA testing at that time.

Nonetheless, the skeletal remains found at the Salsbury Drive house were positively identified as Lillian O'Dare's in 2002, nearly twenty-five years after she disappeared from Vancouver's unflinchingly mean

Downtown Eastside. There had been no evidence to indicate that she was residing at that location when she disappeared. By 2002, the police realized that they had a huge problem on their hands, and they placed Lillian's information on the Joint Missing Women Task Force list, as well as the official poster, after determining that her background was similar to other missing women on that list who had some degree of involvement in prostitution and/or drug use, according to Vancouver police sergeant Sheila Sullivan. Unfortunately, the task force had been unable to immediately locate any of her relatives, and it wouldn't be until August 2007 that authorities were able to track down her next of kin and inform them of what they knew—little as it was—regarding what had happened to Lillian. Basically, all that they had been able to accomplish in nearly twenty-five years was to put a name to a skeleton, thanks, in part, to new DNA technology that had been refined over the years since Lillian had gone missing. The new technology was called miniSTR (mini-short tandem repeat), and it provided investigators with the much-needed ability to extract and refine much smaller DNA samples. It would be used extensively in the case that they didn't know existed, yet.

At one point a photograph of Lillian and another woman, known only as Diana, surfaced as detectives continued in their efforts to solve her murder. Investigators circulated the old, faded photo in an attempt to generate new leads in the case, but, unfortunately, no one came forward with information. Lillian O'Dare, of course, was only one of many women that Vancouver police and, later, the RCMP investigators were faced with the overwhelming task of determining what had become of them. By the time the police had a suspect to focus on in what was beginning to look like a massive serial murder case, the list of missing women had topped out at sixty-five, after four women were found alive and removed from the list. With literally dozens of cases and volumes of leads to follow up, the task force had its work cut out for it—and then some.

Although the families of the sixty-five missing women were naturally frustrated and angry at the police for what they perceived as having their pleas for help in finding their missing loved ones ignored, it should be pointed out that the police truly had no idea what they were dealing with here. Although they could not possibly feel the hurt, pain, and anguish that the family members of the missing women were feeling, the truth of the matter is that the police were bewildered, puzzled, and taken aback at the overwhelming prospect of finding out what had happened to the women. Many family members of the missing women felt that the police looked at their loved ones as criminals first, and humans who had been victimized second.

"In the case of these missing women, we don't have a suspect," Vancouver police constable Anne Drennan said in April 1999. "In fact, we don't have a crime."

Nor did they have any crime scenes with which to work, Constable Sarah Bloor said two years later as the police continued their search for clues that could help them determine what had become of so many women. "We don't have any leads like crime scenes or anything like that to help us uncover more facts."

"These women frequented the Downtown Eastside of Vancouver, they had dependency problems, either with drugs or alcohol or both," said Constable Catherine Galliford, spokesperson for what would become the joint RCMP-Vancouver City Police Task Force.

Unfortunately, the cases of many of the missing

women would never be officially solved, and their families would be left forever wondering what had become of their loved ones. Some degree of closure had been attained for the families of six of the missing women with the conviction of a man who was found guilty of their murders and who remains charged with the murders of twenty others in a case that might not ever make it to trial, and only an aura of bewilderment about what had become of the remaining women on Vancouver's list of missing women lives on.

March 1995

While looking for a place to set up shop for the day near Highway 7, also known as the Lougheed Highway, at a location approximately seven kilometers, or roughly 4.3 miles, from Port Coquitlam, near the community of Mission, British Columbia, a roadside merchant ambled about near a boggy area in close proximity to a creek that empties into the Stave River when he made a rather unexpected, and macabre, discovery by nearly walking upon what looked like a portion of a human skull. Somewhat unnerved, he called the local police to inform them of his finding.

A number of police officers were dispatched to the site, along with search dogs and a crime scene investigation (CSI) expert, who collectively made a thorough search of the area. When it became apparent that little else of significance could be found on the marshy land, divers were brought in to search the Stave River. Although nothing else was found at the site, forensic experts were able to determine that the skull belonged to the right side of a woman's head, which, they believed, had been neatly bisected, literally sawed in half vertically, front to back. Although a number of theories as to how the skull came to be at that location were considered, including that it may have come from an indigenous burial site that had been disturbed or perhaps had been carried there by the nearby river during a high tide or flood, the investigators never came up with a satisfactory explanation for its presence, nor were they able to ever identify it. Nonetheless, it was a discovery that CSI expert Tim Sleigh would never forget. After all, it wasn't just any skull—it was a skull that had been neatly cut in half, proving, in his mind, that such a precise cut could be far from accidental. His gut told him that not only did the grisly discovery mean that someone had died, but that the person likely had been murdered. With nothing else to go on, however, it would be years before Sleigh would understand the magnitude of what he had been called out to investigate that day in March 1995.

March 23, 1997

It was a cloudy, chilly evening when sex-trade worker and drug addict Wendy Lynn Eistetter hit the streets of Vancouver, British Columbia's Downtown Eastside, sometimes referred to as "DES," to try and earn a few bucks to support her habit. Sometime before midnight a light breeze blew in off the Pacific Ocean, at perhaps six miles per hour, and made the late-night temperature seem even colder than the present forty-three degrees. Nonetheless, Wendy flitted up and down the boulevard in the vicinity of Main Street and East Hastings, hopeful that another trick would come along soon. As it turned out, she didn't have to wait very long.

Robert "Willie" Pickton, forty-seven, a smelly little man who always wore gum boots, turned the corner and pulled to the curb, where he stopped and beckoned Wendy over to the car. He told her that he had crack cocaine and marijuana, and would pay her whatever her going rate was if she would accompany him back to his trailer, located just outside of town in nearby Port Coquitlam.

Wendy, glad to get out of the cold night air, didn't hesitate or quibble about his offer as she climbed into the passenger seat of Pickton's vehicle. Pickton's unkempt, dirty appearance and hygiene hadn't deterred her, either. As she viewed the man with the scraggly beard and long hair, which had been pulled back into a short ponytail, Wendy knew that she had been with worse—she just couldn't remember when.

It became darker as they drove out of the city, past New Westminster and onto Lougheed Highway. During the drive Pickton told her how he operated a pig farm, and they smoked crack cocaine along the way and made small talk, which didn't seem to matter to either of them. The cloud cover made it seem eerie as they turned off the highway and drove down Dominion Avenue, eventually approaching Pickton's pig farm, but Wendy paid little mind, at that time, to her surroundings. After driving through the metal gate at the entrance to the farm, which resembled a desolated industrial area during the day, Pickton parked just outside his trailer, which was situated adjacent to the slaughterhouse. The two of them stumbled up the three short steps onto the porch and went inside, crack and crack pipe in hand.

The interior of the trailer was filthy. It appeared nearly uninhabitable, with clothing, much of it women's, scattered about, and occasional women's accessories lying here and there amid the trash that looked like it had been there for a long time. The trailer also stank badly with an odor that Wendy could not discern, and she soon found herself wishing that she hadn't gone there with Pickton. But it was too late now, and she realized that she would just have to make the best of it, get it over with, and then have Pickton drive her back to town.

They turned left in the hallway near the trailer's entrance, and passed by a room that Pickton used as an office. It was also filthy and in disarray. The desk was cluttered, and a stuffed horse's head hung on the wall behind a watercooler off to one side. They passed a stereo located near the trailer's entrance, and Pickton paused for a moment to turn it on, with the volume loud, as they made their way toward the bedroom. There were large, dark stains embedded into the badly soiled carpet at various locations, but Pickton didn't seem at all concerned about showing his guest how filthily he lived. Once they reached the bedroom, they removed their clothing and began various forms of sex play; at one point Pickton bound Wendy with a pair of fur-lined handcuffs. Afterward, satisfied that he had the young woman under his control, the sex play began to turn somewhat rough. But that's what Wendy was there for, and at first she didn't mind too much.

A little later, however, after releasing Wendy from her much-used bindings, Pickton became even rougher, and his demeanor turned maniacal. Out of seemingly nowhere he pulled out "a brown-handled knife," and Wendy suddenly became horrified at the sight of the knife's blade. She began screaming. Out in the middle of a several-acre farm, and inside a trailer where the music was blasting, no one could hear her—and she knew it. Pickton seemed to revel at her obvious fear, and he began stabbing her repeatedly with the knife. Pickton's voice became elevated and eerily shrill, which served to terrify Wendy even more. At one point, after sustaining several serious stab wounds, some of which were to her abdomen, Wendy managed a show of strength and broke free from Pickton's grip, mustering enough energy to turn the tables on her attacker. After a violent struggle she wrested the knife away from Pickton and stabbed him with it. Satisfied that she had bought some time for herself, Wendy, half-naked, staggered out of Pickton's trailer and made her way toward Dominion Avenue.

It was about 1:45 A.M. when Wendy reached the street, blood gushing out of her stomach wounds. According to a police report taken later, Wendy was picked up by a couple driving along the dark road. After loading her into the backseat, minutes later they flagged down a police officer who arranged to have the injured woman taken to the Royal Columbian Hospital in nearby New Westminster, a Vancouver suburb, where she was treated for deep stab wounds to her torso. Similarly, Pickton drove to another hospital, where he was treated for the stab wound inflicted by his victim.

Fortunately, Wendy Eistetter survived her violent encounter with Robert Pickton. She had been one of the lucky ones—many others were not. Pickton also survived, both medically and legally. Although Pickton had been charged with attempted murder by the Crown after the attack on Wendy, he hired big-time Vancouver lawyer Peter Ritchie to represent him. The charges were later dropped when Wendy did not show up to testify against him—despite the fact that the police knew that he had been the person who had provoked the attack by stabbing Wendy first. It seemed just as well from the Crown's viewpoint— Pickton had hired a private detective for $10,000, according to Pickton, to investigate Wendy's background, leaving prosecutors believing that they would have had a tough time convincing a jury that a millionaire pig farmer had tried to kill a hooker who was also a junkie. The incident should have been one of the first clues that something very wrong may have been going on at the Pickton farm, but it seemed to just fly right over the heads of the local police, who chalked it up as an isolated incident.

Part 1

The Missing Women

1

The city of Vancouver, British Columbia, with a metropolitan area population of 2,249,725, is the largest metro area in the western part of Canada and the third largest in that country. Located along the coast and sheltered from the Pacific Ocean by Vancouver Island, the major seaport is ethnically diverse, with 43 percent of the area's residents speaking a first language other than English, and is ranked fourth in population density for a major city on the North American continent, behind only New York City, San Francisco, and Mexico City. Because of its rapid growth, it is expected to take over the number two spot by 2021. Idyllic in appearance because of its surroundings of natural beauty, Vancouver is repeatedly ranked as one of the world's most livable cities. In Canada it is among the most expensive places in which to live. But Vancouver is a major city, and with that distinction comes the grim reality that, like all major cities, it has a dark side that most tourists rarely get, or even want, to see.

One of Vancouver's unpleasant sides, an understatement to be sure, is its Downtown Eastside, also known as Low Track, long recognized as the poorest neighborhood in all of Canada. Rife with heroin addicts and prostitutes, Low Track is an area of Vancouver where misery and despair rarely—if ever—subside. The area abounds in grubby tenements, some of which are not fit for human habitation, rundown hotels that can easily be described as flophouses, and many of its back alleys and some of its streets are just plain filthy. Cigarette butts, used hypodermic needles discarded by addicts, and empty liquor and beer bottles are strewn about and broken. Discarded articles of furniture, such as sofas, chairs, and mattresses, which some of the homeless use to sleep on, can be found without having to look very hard. The smell of urine and vomit is often overpowering, and used condoms discarded by hookers or their johns are a frequent sight. The sounds of emergency vehicle sirens are frequent, day and night—the police are either making drug busts or other arrests, or medical teams are rushing to the scene of daily drug overdoses. It is also known as the place where many of the resident prostitutes began disappearing in the late 1970s and continued vanishing past the turn of the century. Few people would dispute that Low Track is aptly named.

A number of theories about what may have happened to the missing women have surfaced over the years and range from opinions that one or more serial killers were at work, such as a copycat of the "Green River Killer," to hookers who visited the freighters that docked in the city's harbor, only blocks from Low Track, and were kidnapped. The women were kept as sex slaves, only to be thrown overboard at sea when the sailors were finished with them.

Finding out what happened to the missing women has been especially troubling for the police who, according to Vancouver police constable Anne Drennan, had few leads with which to work because in most cases the police didn't even know where the women came from. Were some of the women following the prostitution circuit along the West Coast—Los Angeles, San Francisco, Portland, Seattle—only to end up in Vancouver? No one knew, and guesses weren't good enough to move the investigation forward. For a time the freighter theory seemed viable because there were stories being told among the city's hookers about women visiting a number of the ships and not returning. Even though such leads were followed up, the police could never find the evidence they needed to line up any suspects connected to the freighters. As a result, the disappearances remained a mystery—and the women continued vanishing without a trace.

Sometime on Wednesday, December 27, 1995, twenty-year-old Diana Melnick joined the ranks of many of the other women in the vicinity of the high-vice area of Hastings and Main who tried to earn enough money to maintain her drug addiction, and to pay for food and a place to sleep, by selling her body to men, many of whom she had never seen before. The brown-eyed young woman, with brown hair, stood five feet two inches tall and weighed barely one hundred pounds. She had been arrested four times during the preceding few months by police officers posing as johns, yet she continued returning to the streets. Even though information about her was limited, the police learned enough to know that she had friends, and she was described as a warm, kind person with compassion for others. She had apparently attended a private high school, and had not been fond of wearing the school's uniform. She liked to talk about boys, and always looked forward to going to school dances. Diana also liked to listen to heavy metal, and had a passion for horses, according to information that would surface years later.

She was also apparently a very trusting young woman, as evidenced by her desperation to make the money she needed for survival, because at some point that day she willingly slid into a vehicle driven by a man old enough to be her father and was never seen or heard from again. Diana was reported missing two days later from "the back-side alley of hell," which is how a friend would describe Low Track some six years later.

Diana Melnick had been the twenty-fifth woman to be placed on the list that would be compiled by the not-as-yet-formed Joint Missing Women Task Force. She would also be one of the victims that the police would eventually be able to attribute to the serial killer at work here, an unremarkable and otherwise trite forty-seven-year-old pig farmer named Robert William Pickton. Had he not been a violent "backyard butcher," from appearances alone, he would fit right in as one of the characters on *Green Acres* or *The Beverly Hillbillies*. However, because of his violent, predatory ways—along with his hillbilly appearance—he could more easily be compared to one of the murderous characters out of the cult horror film *The Texas Chainsaw Massacre*. While the first twenty-four missing women would remain among the vanishings that either remained unsolved or were among four out of sixty-nine women that would eventually be located—alive—"Uncle Willie," as Pickton was also known, was far from finished. In fact, his reign of terror had only just begun.

* * *

According to those who knew her, twenty-year-old Tanya Marlo Holyk got along well with most people, and easily fit in when new situations required it. Growing up, long-legged Tanya liked to play basketball, as well as other sports. She also liked to read, and enjoyed doing book reports in school. But influences at home were less than ideal. Her mother, Dixie Purcell, had been a party animal and was known to have brought men, as well as drugs and alcohol, into their home while Tanya was still quite young. Her father had been out of the picture for quite some time, but he was believed to have resided somewhere on Vancouver's Downtown Eastside. A few years before Tanya was born, her mother had given birth to another daughter with another man, but she had given her up for adoption when the girl was only two years old. Dixie had never told either girl that each had a half sister until much later, and the meeting took place at Vancouver International Airport at the same time that Dixie and her first daughter were reunited.

Although her mother claimed to have loved her very much, Tanya spent considerable time living with a cousin in an apartment in downtown Vancouver during her preteen and teenage years. Even though Tanya was three years younger than her cousin, the two got along well together and lived like sisters.

"She taught me lots of things," Tanya's cousin said about her. "Some of them good things, some of them not-so-good things. But they all stayed with me."

At one point Tanya left Vancouver to live with her half sister and her family in the small community of Klemtu, located on Kitasoo Indian Reserve on Swindle Island. As could be expected, Tanya adjusted to the new environment and seemed to enjoy her new life there. She helped out with family chores around the house, and sometimes babysat her half sister's child. But as she began growing older, Tanya became difficult to handle. Things eventually became so unpleasant that Tanya was sent back to Vancouver.

At one point Tanya became pregnant, and gave birth to a baby boy, the product of a purportedly abusive relationship in which she had gotten hooked on drugs. But Tanya adored her son, opting to leave the relationship and to get clean so that she could properly care for her child. According to her cousin, Tanya moved into an apartment and managed to stay off drugs for approximately two months as she tried to put the pieces of her life back together. Despite her temporary accomplishment her desire for drugs was too much for her to handle.

"She had the access," her cousin said. "She could get the drugs, she could get the money. She had a friend who would drive her to Vancouver and back. An addiction is an addiction."

Tanya's half sister last heard from her when Tanya called her in August 1995 from a detoxification center, at which time she pleaded with her sister to allow her and her young son back into their home. She didn't want to return to the streets of Vancouver, and although a tentative agreement was made between her and her sister for Tanya and her son to return to her home in Klemtu, the plan fell through. Instead, Tanya went back to the drugs and the streets of Low Track, where, police believe, she met up with Robert Pickton sometime on Tuesday, October 29, 1996. Tanya was never seen again and her mother, Dixie, reported her missing on Sunday, November 3, 1996, a little more than a month before her twenty-first birthday.

Her mother said that she continually urged the

police to investigate Tanya's disappearance, but they didn't take her seriously.

"'Tanya was just out having fun,'" her mother claimed the police told her. "'Don't bother us. Don't waste our time. . . .' I just stood there with the phone in my hand for ten minutes, just looking at it."

She told CNN six years later that the police had chosen to ignore her, but she nonetheless persisted.

Though she knew that it was likely that her daughter had been murdered, probably by Robert Pickton, Dixie Purcell died in January 2006 without ever knowing the final outcome, nor that Tanya would be but one of twenty young women whose deaths might never be served by the scales of justice. In all likelihood, Tanya was butchered by Pickton in the slaughterhouse adjacent to his trailer following an evening of drugs and sex, and her body parts fed to Pickton's pigs.

2

The following year, 1997, proved to be a bumper-crop year for Canada's worst serial killer and the disappearances of Vancouver's street women. The residents of British Columbia—as well as the police—didn't have a clue about the bloody carnage that was occurring on a fairly regular basis at the nondescript pig farm in Port Coquitlam, where women were being slaughtered, literally butchered like animals, by a sadistic, maniacal pervert for his own unnatural pleasure. When his lust for pain, terror, and blood—elicited by his actions from his chosen victims—was finally satisfied, the victims were then dismembered, sometimes ground up or sawed into smaller pieces before being fed to his hogs and pigs. These swine would, in turn, and at the proper time, be slaughtered by the same man in the same slaughterhouse where he had butchered many of his human female victims. Then their meat, in the form of pork chops, roasts, loins, and sausages, would be given to unknowing friends and neighbors and sold to the public. Unlike most serial killers, who would dispose of their victims' bodies in a number of locations or cluster dump them in a single location, often far from the killer's home, Robert Pickton never even left home to get rid of his victims' remains. He would pick up his victims who, by the nature of their lifestyles, willingly but unwittingly accompanied him to his pig farm, and most would never leave—until it was time to butcher one of the hogs. Because bodies were not turning up anywhere, the police had little to go on except for a disappearance now and again, and many people merely assumed, including other prostitutes, that Pickton's victims had simply decided to pack up a small suitcase and move on to another location.

Between January and December 1997, no fewer than fourteen women would turn up missing from Vancouver's Downtown Eastside. All fourteen of the disappearances would be attributed to the still-unknown killer's handiwork, much later, of course, after a thorough investigation. When the police finally agreed that a killer was indeed at work, Robert Pickton would eventually be charged with the murders of six of those women. The list of Vancouver's missing women was an ever-changing one, with some of the missing taken off the list because they were either found alive or their bodies were found and the cause of death was attributed to something other than the work of the killer. But as names fell off the list, new ones were added to it. By the time the Joint Missing Women Task Force was finally formed, there were still sixty-five names on the list of missing women and one Jane Doe.

The work facing Vancouver's missing person investigator, Constable Al Howlett, was daunting, to say the least. It seemed like each day he had one or two new files added to the pile already on his desk, and although he and his team remained determined to learn as much as possible about each missing woman,

the circumstances of their shady backgrounds made
the team's work all the more difficult.

The neighborhoods where they had to go in search
of information didn't help matters, either. In fact, in
the area of Hastings and Main, where a blow job could
be bought for ten dollars or a fifteen-minute "suck-
and-f***" encounter could be had from any number
of working girls for twice that amount, Howlett's problems were compounded because, particularly in the
early days of the disappearances, the working girl's
subculture shied away from talking to the cops about
anything at all. At first, with little to build a case upon,
Howlett and his team had little choice but to treat the
disappearances as unrelated. In truth, it would be another two years before the cops began to put "two and
two" together and were able to see that something very
horrible was going on here. In the meantime, women
continued to disappear on a regular basis.

One of those women was street-tough, twenty-five-
year-old Cara Louise Ellis, who often went by the street
name of "Nicky Trimble." When Cara disappeared in
January 1997, she was barely three months away from
her next birthday. She looked older than her years,
and her face clearly showed the ravages of what living
on the streets can do to a person. Bisexual and carrying a $500-a-day heroin habit, Cara grew up in Alberta.
Cara was diminutive, at four feet eleven inches, and
barely weighed ninety pounds. Perhaps it was because
of her small stature that she liked to sport a "biker
bitch" persona. She also liked tattoos, and had one of
a rose on her left shoulder, a heart on her left hand,
and a Playboy bunny on her chest. She also had a considerable array of track marks, where she injected her

daily doses of heroin that kept her "well"—in other words, from entering withdrawal. She lived in Calgary for a while, where she was raped as a young girl barely into her teens, and where one of her friends, a young hooker, was beaten to death by a trick. It was shortly after those two experiences that Cara, forever a loner, decided to pack up her few belongings and move to Vancouver.

She only met one good friend after reaching Vancouver, and that friendship took a few months to find her, as opposed to her finding it. As it turned out, Cara met another young woman on the streets and the friendship began soon after they moved into a recovery center for women and became roommates. They occasionally worked the streets together, turning tricks to make enough money to keep Cara supplied with heroin and her friend with cocaine. Despite trying to kick their habits in the women's recovery center, neither had what it took to cast out their demons. The nausea, diarrhea, and severe joint and muscle pain, the effects of withdrawal, always brought Cara back to the heroin. Even a stint at a detoxification facility, Cara lasted only five days before heading back to the streets.

"Unfortunately, she was in a position where the drugs were speaking for her," said a family member after learning of Cara's disappearance. "She would basically prostitute herself in order to be able to get the next fix in order to be able to prostitute herself. It was a really vicious cycle."

Despite her addiction to heroin, Cara's friend described her as a person who made sure that she could take care of herself. And unlike many of the women in Low Track, Cara kept her clothes as clean as possible and bathed regularly. She also made certain that she had enough heroin on hand for a morning fix, which kept her from getting withdrawal sickness and enabled her to work as a prostitute. For reasons that were never clear, Cara chose to not have any contact with the family she left behind in Alberta, but her relatives never forgot about her.

"She was a great auntie," said a family member. "She absolutely love(d) my little daughter—she's not so little anymore. She was a kid at heart when I met her, just a really wonderful girl."

Although she had confirmed her bisexuality a number of times, Cara told her friend that she wanted a husband and hoped to have children someday. She wanted to be happy, and she wanted to have a better life, said her friend, but she didn't know how to attain those things. The last time her friend saw her, Cara was in a bad way, sitting in a niche off one of the main streets of Low Track, clutching her drugs in one hand. She smelled bad by then, and she had open sores on her body. She had lost a lot of weight, and her clothes were tattered and dirty. A short time later, on a cold January night, Cara had gotten into a car with an uneducated, but amiable, little man wearing nearly knee-high gum boots who drove her away, taking her from the mean streets of Vancouver—forever.

"Cara vanished," her friend said. "She just disappeared."

Over the next few weeks in January 1997, Marie LaLiberte, Stephanie Lane, and Jacqueline Murdock disappeared in a similar manner, although it was never known whether they had gotten into a car with Uncle Willie or not.

Many murders attributed to a serial killer are of the stranger-to-stranger type in which the killer has no known connection to his victims. In the case of Robert Pickton, the police would later learn that he had known or had dealings with at least some of his victims on prior occasions, perhaps engaging in sex with them or merely bringing them to his house trailer to party with him, giving them drugs and money, and then driving them back to Vancouver unharmed. This seemed like a reasonable explanation of why many of his victims felt a strong enough comfort level with him that they did not hesitate to get into his car and drive away with him. This could also, perhaps, help explain why he was able to get away with his cruel and vicious crimes for so long without arousing the curiosity of the community at large or of the police. No one, as will be seen, ever seemed particularly alarmed whenever Uncle Willie showed up in the vicinity of Main and Hastings—at least not at first. Few people saw the evil that lay beneath his skin—until it was too late. Another plausible reason for the lack of concern shown by the police, as well as by the residents of Low Track, at least for a time, when women left with Pickton and did not return, was because their bodies had not turned up anywhere. It seemed entirely possible that Pickton would have been looked at sooner as a suspect if at least some of the bodies of the missing women had been found.

At least one person, however, had seen the evil that lurked inside Robert Pickton. According to a Seattle, Washington, writer, Charles Mudede, and an article of his that appeared in a Seattle weekly called *The Stranger*, of which Mudede is associate editor, a longshoreman had gone to a Halloween party, perhaps as early as 1996 or 1997, at Pickton's farm in the 900 block of Dominion Avenue in Port Coquitlam, accompanied by a friend. The party was held inside a building on the farm that Pickton and his brother, Dave, called "Piggy's

Palace." It was a dark, rainy night when the longshore-man and his friend arrived. The parking area, filled with motorcycles and cars, was muddy. One of the first things the two visitors saw was a large pig being roasted on a spit, and children dressed in Halloween costumes were outside playing in the dark.

"There wasn't much light," the longshoreman said. "There were lots of women, who looked like hookers."

The party, he explained, was outside on the grounds, as well as inside the building and inside a trailer, where they were "doing the wild thing." People were not only having sex, but they were doing a lot of drugs. He explained that when it came time to eat the pig, he saw Pickton tear it apart with his dirty hands. The sight was sufficient to cause the longshoreman to decide that he wouldn't be eating anything that evening—at least not while at Pickton's farm.

He said that at one point he had walked past a shack where a low-wattage light burned dimly above the door, and he could hear machinery running inside. He wasn't sure what kind of machinery he had heard that night, but it had frightened him terribly.

"Here, I got a death chill," said the longshoreman. "The hairs raised on the back of my neck and my feet froze to the ground. I didn't want to be there any-more, so I left and walked home."

Another party attendee, a woman who said that it had been her first and last time to visit Pickton's farm, described the partygoers as raunchy, and claimed that a lot of cocaine was being passed around that evening.

"[There were] lots of really, really bad, badass people. . . . I did not want to be a part of it."

Piggy's Palace, however, was more than just a party place, as the cops eventually learned. It was listed in Canadian government records as a nonprofit organization under the name Piggy Palace Good Times Society, and it routinely raised money for any organization that its operators deemed worthy. Piggy's Palace was located in the 2500 block of Burns Road, adjacent to Pickton's farm on Dominion Avenue, but several acres away, and was built out of tin—basically it was an elongated tin shed. It was visited not only by many of Port Coquitlam's average citizens but by the town's civic leaders, including mayors, members of the city council, businessmen and businesswomen, and so forth. Functions, such as dances and concerts, were held there, the proceeds of which often benefitted local elementary and high schools. At nearly every function roasted pork had been served to the guests, whether they had been civic leaders or badass party animals. Truth is, although one wouldn't know it by looking at him, Robert Pickton had become a wealthy man, not so much from his commercial pig-farming operation but from the continually increasing value of the land that the pig farm was situated on. By 1996, he no longer needed the money. Although the land had been purchased in 1963 by his father and mother, Leonard and Louise Pickton, for a mere $18,000, it was valued at $7.2 million by 1994. When Leonard and Louise died in the late 1970s, Robert, his brother, Dave, and their sister, Linda, inherited the land. Robert and David remained on the farm, while Linda was sent off to boarding school.

In the autumn of 1994, the Pickton siblings sold off the first significant portion of their land to a holding company for $1.7 million, and town house condominiums promptly went up on the parcel. A short time later, the City of Port Coquitlam purchased another parcel of their land for $1.2 million and installed a park on it. The following year Port Coquitlam's school district purchased yet another parcel for $2.3 million, and constructed an elementary school on the land. By then, Robert was treating his pig-farming operation more as a hobby than as an income-producing business, and he often merely sold the meat it produced to friends and neighbors, or gave the butchered meat away by holding wild parties. It was also about that time that Pickton's generosity was becoming known in Low Track—and when people began to notice Vancouver's women were disappearing.

The one-per-week disappearance average for January slowed to only one in February 1997. Sharon Ward left the Downtown Eastside area sometime that month and never returned. No one has—yet—determined what happened to her.

It wasn't until March 1997 that another woman's disappearance would eventually be attributed to Robert Pickton.

Andrea Fay Borhaven, twenty-five, was believed to have disappeared in March 1997, but she was not reported missing, according to the police, until May 18, 1999, for reasons that were not made clear. A wild and tough young woman, she bounced back and forth between her mother and father, as well as between a few other relatives and an occasional stranger, frequently taking advantage of the goodwill shown to her by others. Born in Armstrong, British Columbia, a small town northeast of Port Coquitlam, but still in the southern part of the province, Andrea was often described as a troubled and unhappy little girl who often felt unloved.

She was diagnosed early in her childhood with attention deficit/hyperactivity disorder (ADHD), and was placed on medication for it at one point. She was smoking marijuana by the time she was thirteen, and was getting into trouble at school. Her mother made her a ward of the court system in an apparent act of desperation to try and get help for her daughter. Andrea was sent to a residential facility for children in another town. After barely two months in the facility, Andrea ran away and stayed with relatives for several months.

Although relatives described Andrea as an intelligent and loving teenager, she seemed to possess little ability to channel her impulses, often harboring feelings that would lead to uncontrollable outbursts, which only added to the growing number of problems she already had. As time went on, her feelings of worthlessness, irrelevance, and despair became worse. Even though she was always welcome to come home, and had the support of her family, she always had difficulty complying with the household's rules, according to her mother.

"You don't get into drugs," her mother would say. "You go back to school or you get a job."

Her family didn't know where she was staying much of the time, but she would occasionally show up unannounced with a boyfriend that few mothers and fathers would approve of for their daughter. During such visits she typically asked for money or a temporary place to stay, and family members usually complied. But things often went missing from the homes where she stayed, and family members noticed that Andrea would sell items that they had purchased for her as gifts so that she could obtain money for drugs.

"I asked her on occasion if that's what she wanted for herself, and she seemed to think that she would never end up there," addicted and on the streets, that is, said a relative. "But that's exactly where she ended up."

Shortly before she disappeared, Andrea's mother had

reason to believe that her daughter wanted to make another attempt at getting clean and off the streets.

"She was coming home," said her mother. "All her clothes were sent home on the bus. I have all of her clothes. And then I didn't hear from her."

Andrea did eventually get off the streets—and into a car that took her on a trip of unimaginable terror and horror—never to return.

3

Robert William Pickton was born on October 24, 1949, and raised on a small thirteen-acre farm in an area of New Westminster, British Columbia, where little besides nature existed. His father, Leonard, was born in London, England, in 1896, and immigrated to Canada in the early 1900s. Young Leonard eventually settled in southern British Columbia, where his father, William Pickton, purchased a parcel of land next to Essondale Mental Hospital—named after its founder, Dr. Esson Young—in 1905. William raised hogs with the help of a few hired hands, and later with the help of his son, Leonard. It wasn't a massive operation by anyone's standards—far from it. By the time it became Leonard Pickton's pig farm, after it had grown somewhat from its meager beginnings, the farm had anywhere from 150 to 200 swine on hand at any given time. It was enough to supply family and friends with enough meat to eat, and plenty left over to slaughter for meat sales to the public and a sufficient number to sell off at livestock auctions. There were a few milk cows on the farm as well by the time Leonard took over, perhaps eighteen to twenty, which family members, including Robert, when he became old enough, milked by hand. Since the farm was primarily a pig farm and not a dairy farm, the luxury of automatic milking machines was not feasible from either a practical sense or from a financial one during those early years. Although poor, Leonard Pickton always found a way to make ends meet and provided as many of life's necessities as possible for his family. Although life on the farm was often harsh, Leonard and his wife, Louise, always made sure that they had food on the table and a roof over their family's heads. Louise baked bread regularly, not out of fondness for baking but out of necessity. And they always ate pork—lots of it. Pork became one of Robert's favorite foods.

Louise typically made clothes for the children, and Robert, who grew up being called "Willie," frequently wore secondhand clothes. Willie never had the opportunity to wear new clothes until he was four or five years old. It was around Christmastime one year that Louise, having either earned or saved some extra money, went into town and bought Willie a new outfit for the holidays. She dressed him up in a nice shirt and pants, but the garments had been heavily starched and the newness of the clothes irritated his skin to the point of being painful. As a result, he took off all his clothes and hid in one of his secret hiding places on the farm. That was one of the few times that Willie had received store-bought, brand-new clothes as a child. He grew up wearing denim coveralls and knee-high gum boots.

Being the typical male of the period, and a late starter at fatherhood, Leonard left the duties of raising the children—Linda, Robert, and David, born in that order—to Louise. Linda, born two years before

Robert, didn't spend much time on the farm. She was fond of referring to Willie as "mama's boy," which Willie didn't much appreciate. Together with their brother, Dave, who was born two years after Robert, the Pickton children played regularly on the nearby grounds of the adjacent psychiatric hospital. An institution for the criminally insane, the edifice was called Colony Farm by the locals—so named after the government installed a farm there to supply food to the hospital.

By the time Linda had reached her early teenage years, she left home to live with relatives in Vancouver, where she also attended high school. Her brothers were left behind on the farm, where their mother barked out orders and handed out chores for the two boys to perform. Linda later went on to become successful in real estate, and mothered two children in a marriage that ultimately ended in failure. Nonetheless, she managed to all but leave the farm life behind and resided in an affluent area of Vancouver, away from it all, until their parents died. At that point she became involved in divvying up the estate, but she still had as little to do as possible with the farm operations.

Three generations of Picktons raised swine at the same Port Coquitlam location until the early 1960s, when the government forced the sale of their property, with payment for the land provided at the going rate so that the Lougheed Highway, also known as Highway 7, could be built. The forced sale necessitated the move to the new location on Dominion Road. The new land consisted of forty acres, much of it swampy, and a dilapidated, near-broken-down two-story farmhouse with unprepossessing white stucco siding. Robert "Willie" Pickton and his brother, David, spent their teenage years, right on up through adulthood, at this homestead. An old-style Dutch barn was eventually built on the site, along with a slaughterhouse and, later, a silver elongated structure built out of corrugated steel that had formerly been used as a plant nursery. Situated on approximately eleven acres—it had not been a part of the original Pickton farm—the building would eventually be purchased by the three siblings and become known as Piggy's Palace.

Neither of the boys did particularly well in school, especially Willie, and they had frequent scraps with other children, who made fun of them for the way they dressed, their hygiene, and the fact that they frequently carried with them the odor of pig shit. Both Willie and Dave often skipped school so that they could stay at home to help out on the farm. This way, their parents could avoid hiring some of the mental patients from the hospital, those deemed safe and not a threat to themselves or others. If the two brothers stayed home, their parents could also save money, leaving little motivation for either parent to enforce good school attendance. Willie nearly always welcomed the opportunity to stay at home because of his aversion toward going to school. Dave spent a lot of time during his later teenage years thinking about a business that he could run, and he eventually started a gravel and demolition enterprise, which would eventually become somewhat successful. Willie would sometimes help him out with it—when he wasn't busy slaughtering hogs and butchering women.

By then, Leonard and Louise had already passed on—Leonard died on New Year's Day, 1978, and Louise died the following year, on April Fools' Day, 1979. Leonard had left Louise an estate that was worth nearly $150,000, most of it in the form of real estate that the pig farm and its buildings were situated on. Although the pig farm had been valued at nearly twice that amount, Leonard had shared the ownership with his wife. He also left her three smaller parcels of land, one in Coquitlam and two others in northeastern British Columbia, with a combined value of slightly more than $42,000. Louise was also listed as beneficiary of two small insurance policies on Leonard's life, which totaled less than $5,000. While it wasn't a great deal of money, he at least hadn't left her penniless. With only a year and three months left of her own earthly existence, it wouldn't have mattered much anyway.

When Louise died, she left behind an estate comprised of what Leonard had left her and her own share of the pig farm, which totaled slightly more than $287,000. While Linda and Dave received their share of the estate almost immediately upon their mother's death, Louise had placed a provision in her will that required Willie's share to be held in a trust until he reached the age of forty—nearly ten years. The will's provision directed that the trust be managed by Linda and Dave during that time, with interest to be paid to Willie on his share at regular intervals. It was naturally a very sore point between Willie and his siblings, one that he greatly resented and argued about frequently with them. Nonetheless, there was nothing that he could do—except wait—about what he felt was his mother's treachery toward him. He never considered, even for an instant, that his mother may have been looking out for him, perhaps hoping that Willie might be more responsible with his life by the time he turned forty.

By early in the new millennium, after three parcels of land on and around the pig farm had mushroomed in value, and had been sold off through Linda's keen business sense and negotiations at Dave's urging, the area was promptly developed with condominium and apartment complexes, a park, a school, and a strip mall that even housed a Starbucks. It soon got to the point where it was difficult to tell which seemed more out of place—the new condominium development, the park, the school, or the pig farm, all only a stone's throw away from one another. Nonetheless, the area grew up fast. A subdivision named Heritage Meadows went up on Elbow Place, a street located north of the farm, and Carnoustie Golf Club was situated along the east perimeter of the farm. After the parcels had been sold off, only approximately sixteen acres of the original farm remained. The acreage was dotted with outbuildings that were little more than sheds, the original farmhouse, Willie's trailer and a slaughterhouse along the north perimeter, the Dutch barn, and Piggy's Palace—purchased in the mid 1990s by the siblings—was nearly a mile to the east of the farm on Burns Road. The area had literally grown up around what was left of the pig farm.

Since Linda, Willie, and Dave were all co-owners of Piggy's Palace, the three put their heads together and decided to set up a corporation. This had occurred in 1996, and they called the corporation the Good Times Society, and its nonprofit status was established to raise funding for worthwhile causes. After a kitchen and a bar had been installed on the premises, large parties, some accommodating as many as 1,700 to 1,800 people, were held there with liquor flowing and drugs being consumed while roasted pork, cooked outside on large spits, was served to the guests. Many of the attendees reportedly were Hells Angels and other bikers. Interestingly, the local Hells Angels clubhouse was located across the street from the main entrance to the Picktons' farm on Dominion Avenue, adjacent to a Home Depot parking lot.

The parties at the Good Times Society were numerous, and some events actually raised money for local charities and played host to local businesspeople and politicians. The police had been well aware of the parties, and some of the larger ones had been busted by the cops. For safety reasons local fire officials had ordered Willie and Dave to cease having parties at Piggy's Palace, but the two brothers basically ignored the injunction and held parties anyway. It wasn't until the Picktons failed to file financial statements for the Good Times Society that the local government of Port Coquitlam, in 2000, was able to have the society's non-profit status revoked and the corporation subsequently dissolved, thus permanently putting an end to the large parties at Piggy's Palace. The officials, of course, had no idea of what else had been occurring on the farm under Willie's design.

It was only a matter of time, of course, before each of the three Pickton siblings went their own ways. Linda, with her real estate career, had left the farm a long time ago; Dave, with his gravel and demolition business, remained; and Robert, whom nearly everyone referred to as "Willie," just as they had when he was a kid, stayed at home on the farm and did as little as possible. He spent much of his time walking around in the mud and the pig manure, wearing his "trademark" knee-high gum boots, which he used during the slaughtering operations. When he wasn't slaughtering pigs and generally loafing around, he tried to sell the junked cars that he had accumulated on the property, many of them purchased for scrap, and the vehicles that he had obtained from police department auctions, to anyone who would buy them or their parts. Most of those who knew him described him as a simple man, peculiarly quiet, who liked to sit around much of the time. He rarely spoke, unless spoken to. Depending on who was doing the talking, Willie was described as either a generous man with a big heart, or just downright creepy.

For example, a former truck driver who was engaged to be married to Heather Chinnock, one of the women on Vancouver's list of missing women, said that Heather, a known prostitute, had visited Pickton at his farm, on and off, for at least ten years, from 1991 until 2001. The truck driver's characterization of Willie didn't become publicly known, unfortunately, until after Willie was apprehended.

"Willie was quiet," said the truck driver. "He didn't like me, but he liked Heather. Heather went out there to party."

He said that there was always an abundance of drugs and alcohol at Pickton's place.

"She told me in so many words that she was there as a prostitute," the trucker said. "Heather loved animals and Willie was always promising her a job working on his farm."

But Heather, he said, had expressed her fear of Pickton, and that she often had nightmares after she came home from the farm.

"But then he'd call, and she'd be right back out there again."

According to the truck driver and others who knew him, Robert Pickton had become acquainted with Heather—and familiar with the area of Low Track, not to mention many of the other girls working there— when he made trips to a rendering plant, West Coast Reduction. The plant was located near the area where the working girls conducted business, and Pickton dropped off pig carcasses and associated waste materials, such as hog entrails, brains, nerve tissue, bones, and so forth, from his pig-farming operation. The carcasses and other waste material—and anything else that Willie may have conveniently thrown in for disposal—would eventually be turned into cosmetic products, such as soap, shampoo, perfume, lipstick, and other household items. Pickton had been coming to the rendering plant for the past twenty years or so, and many times after dropping off his load, he would cruise Low Track, which began roughly ten blocks away, looking for hookers. Pickton liked to hang out at the seediest of the seedy hotels in the Hastings and Main area, particularly the Roosevelt Hotel and the Astoria Hotel. As would eventually be seen by the Vancouver police, as well as by the RCMP, Willie had become quite well-known in the area and had girls out to his trailer on the farm on a somewhat regular basis. Some he picked up, and others called him and came out on their own, after having had previous encounters with him at the farm. Interestingly, it took what seemed an unreasonably long time for many of the girls to realize that many of their associates were not returning after meeting up with Willie.

By the time of the Good Times Society's demise, Dave had become a self-described entrepreneur who worked in his reasonably successful excavation and demolition business and at a landfill he also owned. Credited with being the brains of the family, according to some people who knew him and his sister's known business savvy, Dave pretty much left Willie to his own nocturnal and often unnatural activities. Unlike Willie, Dave had worked hard for most of his life, and Linda herself at least once declared that he was the mastermind behind subdividing the farm but left the business details of the sales to her. Divorced and the father of two grown children, it wasn't unusual for Dave to work eighteen-hour days, and then, in his off time, to party like there was no tomorrow. Dave liked bikers, and it was well-known that he liked to hang out with them. Some said that despite the shared ownership of the Good Times Society, he claimed that Piggy's Palace was actually his idea. It was known throughout the area that he had been proud of his "after-hours" club, where he had hosted so many large parties.

"We had eighteen hundred people at one of my parties," he once boasted. "And my parties were cleaner than any goddamn bar downtown."

Dave, often appearing grimy with grease and dirt, has also had his share of trouble with the law. In October 1967, when he was sixteen years old, and right after getting his driver's license, he was involved in a fatal accident in which he hit a neighbor boy who was walking along Dominion Avenue, according to Canadian investigative journalist Stevie Cameron. The boy was fourteen, and Dave had been driving his father's pickup truck when the accident occurred. Although details of the incident were sketchy, in part due to the fact that juvenile court files are sealed, the boy was found the next day in a slough following a search by neighbors, as well as the police. He had multiple injuries, but drowning had been the official cause of death, according to Cameron's account of the incident. Even though the boy's death had been ruled accidental, evidence surfaced that called into question whether Dave had left the scene of the accident—he had asked a mechanic to make repairs to the damage done to his father's pickup. When all was said and done, however, Dave was ordered not to drive for two years by a juvenile court.

In July 1992, Dave had another scrape with the law. He was convicted for sexually assaulting a female construction worker a year earlier at a site that he had been hired to excavate. He purportedly had cornered her inside a construction site trailer and told her that he was going to rape her, but he backed off when another construction worker showed up. After being found guilty, he was fined $1,000, placed on probation for thirty days, and was ordered not to have any further contact with the victim.

According to the victim, bikers would show up at her home prior to Dave's trial, and they would make subtle threats, as well as some that were not so subtle, which prompted her to move to another town. On one of the biker visits to her home, she was purportedly told that she would be encased in cement somewhere if she testified against Dave. She took their threats seriously, and feared that she would be harmed or killed if she remained in the area.

"You could smell him before you saw him," the victim told local reporters. *The Province,* among other newspapers, printed her story. *"He had no respect for women at all."*

Other women who knew Dave Pickton concurred with the sexual assault victim's assessment of him. He was described as being vulgar and bad-mannered when in the company of women, and he often used foul language when he was with women.

There are always two sides to every story, however, and many of the neighbors of the Pickton brothers had nothing but praise for the two brothers, as well as for their parties. One woman said that she had taken her ninety-year-old father to social gatherings at Piggy's Palace, and she described them as "excellent parties where local people used to go."

"Dave and Willie have been pretty good guys . . . a little rough around the edges," said another neighbor.

"I've known them for quite a few years and I've watched them do a lot of nice things for people. . . ."

As the Pickton siblings sold off the various parcels of their land, the locale in which the pig farm was situated became known as the Dominion Triangle and was touted as "Coquitlam's newest commercial area," as indeed it had become. On one side of the street were the townhomes that had quickly shot up, and in the same vicinity, but on the opposite side of the road, a new mall was installed that included Costco, Save-On-Foods, and other outlets. East of the mall there still existed a number of small farms where cornfields produced the fruit of the farmer's labor, and some where horses roamed within the confines of their fences, with much of the rest little more than marshy grassland. While the area sprang up around the Pickton farm, Robert and Dave went about their separate businesses and continued to party heartily, whenever they could.

People, however, would later say that Willie never took drugs and did not drink, despite his fondness for the parties held by him and his brother. Women—sex trade workers, as they had come to be known—from Vancouver's Downtown Eastside also continued to disappear.

4

By Willie's own account, in a tape-recorded "letter" to a woman known as Victoria, made on December 28, 1991, speaking rapidly and in nasal intonations that sounded somewhat similar to the late actor Wally Cox, Willie talked about the hardships of growing up on the pig farm. In speech that was sometimes erratic, Willie told a story that took him back to early childhood, when he was about three years old. In a voice that sounded neither threatening nor menacing, and which was laced with occasional chuckling, Willie seemed completely harmless as he joyfully recalled an incident that occurred while he was playing inside the cab of his father's old GM Maple Leaf truck and pigs were being loaded into the back. Jumping, bouncing around, and playing with the steering wheel, as any three-year-old would, Willie somehow shifted the truck into neutral, causing it to roll forward and down a hill. Frightened pigs began squealing and jumping from the back of the truck as Willie's father, Leonard, frantically chased the truck, pigs in tow, to try and stop it before any major damage was done. Despite Leonard's best efforts, however, the truck didn't come to a stop until it smashed into a telephone pole. The accident totaled the old truck, and Willie got "the hell" beaten out of him for the incident. But that was the way of life on the farm, he indicated, where punishment was doled out when it was due. In recalling the incident, it did not appear that Willie held any ill will toward his father for the beating, but he had simply accepted it as punishment that was deserved.

In recalling another incident, which occurred several years later, when he was about eleven or twelve, Willie's retelling of the story for Victoria's benefit seemed almost poignant at times. Willie had gone to a livestock auction and had purchased a calf, which he described as "beautiful," with a "little black-and-white face," that was barely three weeks old. He had paid $35 for it. Willie really loved the calf, and in his young mind, he had planned to keep it for the rest of his life. He looked after the calf each day, and fed it like he was supposed to do, rarely letting it out of his sight. But he had other chores to do, such as feeding the chickens and taking care of the pigs, and he couldn't keep the calf with him every waking minute, even though he would have liked to if it had been possible.

One day, approximately three weeks after he had purchased the calf, Willie went down to the barn to feed his new prized possession, but it wasn't there. He looked around the barn for it, and at first thought that perhaps it had somehow gotten out. The door, however, had been closed and locked, so he reasoned that it couldn't have gotten out on its own. After spending a few minutes looking for his calf outside, he walked over to the area that he called "the piggery," which was really nothing more than a slaughterhouse, where the pigs were butchered. He thought that the calf might have wandered over there. When he went inside, he got one of the first major shocks of his life. His calf was there, all right, hanging upside down, slaughtered, just like one of the pigs.

"They butchered my calf on me," Willie recalled.

He was furious, and couldn't believe that such a thing had happened to him. He refused to speak to anyone for several days, and "locked everybody out of my own mind. . . . Oh boy, was I mad."

His dad eventually paid him $40 for the calf, which was good money in those days, but it did little to placate him for what had happened to the calf that he had planned to keep for a long, long time. He was told that he could take the money and buy another calf, but Willie wanted no part of that—the calf was to have been with him for life. It was then that he realized that life held little, if any, permanence.

"We're only here for so long, and that's it," he said in the tape-recorded message to Victoria. "When your time is over, your time is over."

Although Willie couldn't remember the precise time frame, he recalled that his mother and father had met at the Aristocratic Restaurant, a "hamburger place, where they make hamburgers and breakfast, and this and that." They were married a short time later, in the early 1940s, he thought. In addition to the hard life that he described to Victoria, Willie told her how he and Dave frequently skipped school by "playing hooky," particularly how Dave would pretend to go to school but would return home and hide beneath his bed until school was dismissed for the day at 3:00 P.M.

During his youth Willie's mother had always pushed him to learn more about butchering farm animals, and wanted him to learn by watching their family friend, Bob Korac, during the slaughtering process.

"'Go see Bob, see how he's doing,'" Korac would

later recall Louise as having said as she urged Willie to take lessons from Korac. "'Because maybe you need it, like tomorrow, you know.'"

According to Korac, however, Willie just didn't seem to have much interest in slaughtering the farm animals, and would rather go fishing. He loved the farm animals, and talked more about feeding and nurturing them, as opposed to killing them. When he was away from the farm for any length of time, his first concern upon his return was always to feed the animals. When in another mood, however, Willie could go on seemingly endlessly about how he hated being stuck on the farm, and sometimes complained that it was the farm that had kept him from having dating opportunities with women. He explained to Victoria that he had hoped that "we'd be out of here long before this, but it's holding me all back." The truth of the matter was, after his parents died, Willie could have left the farm, permanently, any time that he so desired—but he always chose to stay.

Willie claimed that he never wanted to learn things by following in someone else's footsteps. Instead, he wanted to learn things on his own, through trial and error and learning from his own mistakes—including the butcher trade. Perhaps Willie held such strong feelings about learning things on his own because he had been dominated for much of his life by his mother and by his brother, Dave, and had become tired of doing the things that Dave told him to do. Perhaps he held such determination because he was shy, and often awkward when it came to socializing with others and felt that if he did things on his own—even if it turned out to be a mistake—he would build his self-confidence.

Perhaps the only time that Willie had become involved in a relationship with a woman that had the potential for any permanence was on a trip to the United States, where he had traveled to the Midwest, including Illinois and Michigan, in the mid-1970s. The woman, Connie Anderson, had been from Michigan, and although Willie claimed that he had fallen in love with her and that they had become engaged to be married, the relationship fell apart because she refused to move back to the farm in Port Coquitlam with him.

When Willie made the trip to the United States, he traveled by plane from Canada to Kansas City, Missouri. Much of the remainder of his six-week trip to the United States was spent riding the bus, from Kansas City to St. Louis, and on to Chicago.

"I was on a bus there, and I think I was the only guy that was on the bus," Willie said. "The rest was all girls. Holy geez, I was only twenty-four years old at the time. . . . I said, 'What's happening? Where's all the guys?' They said they're all in the army, uh, I was supposed to go to the army, too. The only thing is, my mother says, 'No. We gotta keep the . . . farm.' I gotta stay on the farm."

Not being very good with dates, Willie told Victoria that he thought that the year that he had made the trip to the United States had been 1974. However, he was reasonably certain that the month had been February. Cherry pies were being given away at many of the stores he had visited.

"Something about . . . somebody chopping a cherry tree down," he said. "They were giving all these cherry pies away . . . every store I went into. 'Here, take this with you.' 'What's this here, another pie? Holy geez, how come they're giving so many pies away?' And he said that this was on the house . . . something about somebody . . . I forgot who it was . . . somebody chopped a cherry tree down and it was . . . his birthday or something, or whatever. I can't quite remember."

Willie hadn't cared much for Chicago, and had told Victoria that it could be pretty rough and that caution was needed when going out at night. From Chicago, however, he had gone to Michigan, where he had met Connie. He claimed that he had met a lot of nice people along the way, and had even been offered a job as a model.

"Once I had a chance for me, believe it or not," Willie said. "Me, I'm just a plain old farm boy. . . . They want me for a model."

Willie said that he had explained that he was there on holiday, but he had become somewhat interested when he was offered $40 per hour and new clothes. He ultimately turned down the opportunity, however, because he said that he was on vacation and was there to learn more about what the United States was like. He also claimed that he had turned down the modeling job because he was unsure about what he might be getting himself into. In the end he returned to life on the farm and continued complaining about the long hours and the hard life that farm living entailed. He said that he would have liked to have started over, and at times he had wanted to sell his part of the farm. His goal, if he'd had his way, was to build a dream house, "with a nice high ceiling," and a swimming pool.

"I am going to start a whole new life, in a whole new place, start everything over," he said. "You'll never own a piece of land, the land owns you. This land has been here for many years before you've been here, and the land will be here many years after you're gone."

Willie talked about his work and the various jobs that he had held over the years, including that of a house framer and builder, truck driver, body shop repairman, and at recapping tires. He claimed that he had always wanted to work in a sawmill, but when positions opened up at the one where he wanted to work, he was always already employed somewhere else.

In addition to talking about some of the hardships and mishaps that he had experienced over the years on the farm, including how he had been "mauled by bulls" and "torn apart by wild boars," he spoke of having been on his own for a long time since the deaths of his parents. "Wanting out" of life on the farm and starting a new life seemed to be a common theme of Willie's desires. He mentioned the death of his father in passing, or so it seemed, by saying that Leonard had died of old age, at seventy-seven. He had much more to say about his mother's death from cancer, as if it had affected him more profoundly than his father's.

"Hard to believe," he said of his mother's death. "She was up and going, and going, and going. . . . You never keep her down. . . . Even almost . . . right to the end, we had to put her on a stretcher when she left here. She said, 'I want to have a look at this place one last time.' So we sat her up. . . . She had a look at the place . . . all over the place, and said, 'I will never see this place again.' And she's right, she never did . . . come back."

He said that she spent about two months in the hospital before succumbing to the cancer.

"That's life," he said. "I mean, life comes and life goes. You're here today, you're gone tomorrow."

Willie seemed intent on talking about life's experiences, particularly the deaths of friends and how new ones always came along after the old ones had died, but he seemed especially concerned about the dwindling numbers in his own family. As he was growing up, he said, he thought there had been eleven or so relatives on his father's side of the family still living in Canada, but at the time that he had made the tape for Victoria, he thought that perhaps only four relatives still existed, presumably including himself and his siblings.

"Accidents happen," he said. "All our family been logging all of our lives. . . . My dad's brother got killed on a bicycle on the last day of work from the mill. . . . He was retiring . . . and he was on his way back home, just—just—just retired," he stuttered. "He never drove, he always rode his bike."

In retrospect, Willie's discourse on death and dying, particularly his position about people being here one day and gone the next, gives one cause to wonder whether such an attitude had somehow overlapped into his reasoning, or perhaps justification, for all of the killings for which he would ultimately be so well-known. Perhaps such reasoning in Willie's mind had also played a part in relieving any of his guilt feelings—if he'd had any—over the atrocities that would be attributed to him.

Throughout much of Willie's tape-recorded letter, he rambled vocally about one subject and then another, with little transitioning between them. Though it seemed that he had mentioned nearly every aspect of his life, including butchering meat for neighbors to providing *lechon* for the area Filipinos to barbecue, he never mentioned going to the Downtown Eastside to pick up prostitutes to bring back with him to the farm. Perhaps he had not mentioned it because he had not yet begun the routine in 1991 of cavorting with hookers, or if he had already started his bizarre behavior, he apparently possessed enough judgment or foresight that it might not be prudent to mention it anywhere.

At one point Willie explained how he had put in

long hours as a meat cutter, going to school two days a week and working the other five days as a butcher in a position away from the farm. He claimed that he had worked as a meat cutter for six and a half years, and complained that if he had only stayed with it for another six months, he could have satisfied Canada's requirement of attaining the equivalent of a journeyman meat cutter and could have held a butcher's job anywhere in the country. However, he had thrown it "all out the door at six and a half years." His dream of starting over had apparently failed him again. Fed up with cutting meat, Willie decided to return to the farm to look after the pigs, cows, and horses once again, where he would eventually put some of his meat-cutting experience to use in a macabre and ghoulish sort of way—butchering women—instead of "starting over."

5

In street lingo used by some of the sex trade workers in Vancouver's Downtown Eastside, Robert Pickton was known as a bad date. That's how the prostitutes typically refer to a john who has gained a reputation of violence for a history of committing acts of cruelty, brutality, and bloodshed against them. It appeared that some of the women knew quite well what went on at Willie's farm, either through firsthand experience or through word of mouth from hookers who had managed to either escape or were let go before Willie reached his killing frenzy. At least one hooker would claim that the women she worked with knew him and had some knowledge about acts of violence that had occurred at Pickton's farm, but the details, naturally, were sketchy at best—as would be expected considering the lifestyles of Vancouver's streetwalkers. Some of the women, in their drunken and/or drugged stupors, likely numbed themselves with the alcohol and the heroin, hoping that they could forget about whatever it was that they knew. Others likely were afraid to talk about the goings-on out on Dominion Avenue. The girls who knew nothing about Willie Pickton were the ones who were in the most danger.

"When his car came around, they knew he was a bad date," said one of the women who obviously knew about Willie's unnatural desires.

Nonetheless, such knowledge never stopped many of the drug-addicted prostitutes from getting into Pickton's car, or truck, as the case may have been, on the days he visited the nearby rendering plant. Willie was free with his money and was known by the women for his generosity. An employee at a Downtown Eastside hotel said that Willie liked to talk to everyone.

"All the girls used to go after him because they knew that he would give them money," the hotel employee said. "They would run after him outside. It was sad, but they were very short of money down there."

There was his appearance to consider as a factor as well. An employee at West Coast Reduction, a rendering plant located a short distance from downtown and Low Track, where Willie always took animal parts for disposal, offered an opinion that Willie may have balanced his unkempt and dirty appearance by drawing street women close to him with the promise of money.

"He was such a dirty guy," employee Robert Bayers said. "He was just gross-looking actually. I kind of felt sorry for him. . . . Here he is, rolling these old barrels off the back of the truck, and he has got his bare hands. I mean, we work in the rendering industry, and it's, uh, you know, it's dead animals. It's not a very pretty thing to be working with, with your bare hands."

Regardless of *why* Willie was generous with his money, many of the women had come to know that they could get cash and drugs from Willie if they got into his car.

One such woman was twenty-four-year-old Sherry Leigh Irving, an attractive young woman whose life on the streets hadn't caught up with her yet. She and her parents had lived in Comox on Vancouver Island, and her father recalled how he and his family had lost her in 1991. He had been in the military then, and had been transferred to Ontario in eastern Canada. Sherry, nineteen years old at that time, had agreed that she would move there with them. They waited for her on moving day, but Sherry never showed up.

"I couldn't force her to come with me," her father said. "That's when I lost contact with my daughter. She was at the age when I couldn't force her to come with me. Right up until the day we moved and left here, she was coming to Ontario with us."

Sherry's father said that she took off after apparently changing her mind about making the move. She simply had decided that she didn't want to accompany her parents, and her father, being in the military, was unable to stay behind and begin looking for her. It was at that time, her family believed, that she began the downward spiral into a life of drugs and prostitution.

Sherry's family described her as an innocent adolescent who loved to attend family functions, camping, and outings sponsored by their church. By the time she had reached her late teens, however, Sherry had begun to associate with a rough, streetwise crowd. That was when the drug use began as well, and in time she began running away from home. Her father believed that she gave in to the influence of her so-called friends.

"It's the peer pressure," he said. "And you've got some kids who are very streetwise, and when you have young innocent adolescents who are new to that scene, they are very easily led. With the drug scene and everything else, there are adults who thrive off that."

At one point Sherry's family, with about eight other families in the Comox area, formed a support group that functioned as a vehicle, in part, to help keep track of their daughters, particularly those who had run away from home. Her father said that the group had been able to keep track of their daughters as long as they remained in the local area, but that it had become impossible by the time they left and moved away.

Another of Sherry's relatives described her as a decent person who seemed to struggle with her emotions during her teenage years, despite the fact that the family seemed close and enjoyed doing things together. It was her struggle with her emotions, the relative believed, that had led to her association with the wrong crowd.

"Generally, she was more of a happy person," the relative said. "A sort of a go-getter kind of person. She was into track and field. She had tons of friends. She was very popular. There were ups and downs all the time, but I think it was pretty normal. . . . She was the type of person who would phone her family all the time."

Then, all of a sudden, she just stopped calling.

Her family had always remained hopeful that Sherry would return to them. Her father hoped that she would enter a drug treatment program, straighten herself out, and perhaps return to school. At one point her father returned to British Columbia in an attempt to persuade her to begin a rehabilitation program, and had made arrangements for her to do so, but she just couldn't make that crucial first step.

"At the very end she was into hard drugs," her father said. "I was trying to help her out. . . . She'd just disappear on us."

In 1996, Sherry was convicted in the Vancouver suburbs of New Westminster and Burnaby of offenses related to prostitution, one of which was never resolved because she had disappeared. As a result, the charges were eventually thrown out.

One of Sherry's friends described her as a fun-loving, outgoing teenager with a beautiful smile. The friend expressed shock when she saw her mug shot years later.

"That mug shot of a tired-looking young woman, who had obviously had a hard time, completely shocked me because that was Sherry . . . my friend from long ago . . . who had a smile that would melt many. . . . Once vibrant and beautiful. Still beautiful."

"She was a very pleasant girl," her father said. "She was a very easygoing kind of child. Very pleasant to be with, to be around, always trying to help. It was just as she got a little bit older, she got in with the wrong crowd, and things that used to matter to her didn't matter so much. She just wanted to go her own way."

According to the police, Sherry was last seen in April 1997.

She was followed by the disappearance of Janet Henry, last seen in June 1997; Ruby Hardy, last seen in July 1997; Cindy Beck, last seen in September 1997.

It is interesting to note that one of the major differences between the case of Vancouver's missing women and that of the Seattle area's case of the Green River Killer was the fact that the bodies of the Green River Killer's victims had eventually begun to turn up. The people, particularly the women, in the communities where the Green River Killer's victims were being discovered were naturally frightened and demanded explanations and actions from the police. Gary Ridgway seemed to revel in the fear he was creating due to the bodies that he was leaving in the often remote outdoor areas, just waiting to be found. In essence, Ridgway had forced the hand of Washington's law enforcement community—which many people had perceived as indifferent, at first due to the fact that the victims were prostitutes and drug addicts—by leaving his victims' bodies outdoors, in the open, where he knew they would eventually be found. As time went on, many in the law enforcement community felt that he was mocking them, showing them that he could kill and remain undetected.

Conversely, it seemed certain that the police in Vancouver would have taken an interest in the missing women sooner if bodies had begun showing up there. Although the communities in Vancouver would become frightened, even horrified, later on, at the outset the fear had been contained mostly within the prostitution community and that of the families of the missing women. When all was said and done, everyone would realize that the situation in Vancouver was horrifying beyond anyone's wildest imagination. To put it bluntly, Robert Pickton's vile acts of inhumanity made Gary Ridgway look like a demented Boy Scout.

Pickton, however, wasn't necessarily perceived as the monster that he was—at least not until he had worked himself into a killing frenzy on a particular day or night. Instead, people sometimes characterized Willie Pickton as a farmer who had become frustrated with his life; others viewed him as a backward simpleton who had not completed school; few people viewed him as the vicious killer that the government portrayed him as later, when the elements of the case began to come together. Those who got to see Willie's violent, dark side rarely lived to talk about their experience.

Gina Houston, a woman in her mid-thirties when the case eventually broke and a close friend of Willie's, would later tell the authorities that Willie had once told her that he loved her. Houston, a former neighbor of Willie's, characterized him as gentle, kind, considerate, polite, and soft-spoken. Two of her children frequently referred to Willie as "Dad," and Houston was known as one of Willie's most unwavering allies.

6

According to the Vancouver Police Department (VPD), Marnie Lee Ann Frey was last seen in August 1997, although her photograph on the Joint Missing Women Task Force poster indicated that she disappeared in September 1997. Born on August 30, 1973, in Campbell River, British Columbia, a fishing village along the coast, Marnie was twenty-four at the time she went missing. Police say that she was reported missing on September 4, 1997.

As described by her father, Rick Frey, a commercial fisherman, Marnie was a generous young woman and had been so throughout much of her life. Often, when she came home, she would be missing articles of her clothing, items such as shoes, or perhaps a coat, and when her parents would ask her about the missing clothing, she would laughingly tell them that she loaned whatever was missing to a friend because her friend had needed it. Sometimes she would trade articles of her clothing with her friends for older, tattered garments. She was always concerned about helping out others who were in need, making it difficult for her parents to become angry at her for her efforts to help others who were less fortunate.

"She'd give the shirt off her back to anybody," said her stepmother, Lynn Frey, who had loved her as if she had been her own.

According to her family, Marnie attended a Christian school as a youth, but she went to a public high school in Campbell River. She loved animals as a child and on into adulthood, and she often took care of the chickens and rabbits that her family raised. She liked the outdoors, and she could be found outside in nearly any kind of weather. She particularly liked to play in or near the chicken coop, and she was known to build forts, where she would play with her cat, Tabi, and friends from the neighborhood. Sometimes her stepmother would find her reading a book, and Marnie would tell her that life was sometimes just very difficult to handle. When she was younger, she seemed easily inspired, and sometimes the simplest things, such as going hunting with her father, made her the happiest.

When she was eighteen, Marnie gave birth to a baby girl, and although she cared deeply for the child, she had difficulty raising the girl, in part because she had become involved with an Asian gang in Campbell River that had initiated her into the world of drugs. She eventually moved on to the streets of Vancouver, leaving her baby girl behind with her parents to raise. Despite being on the streets of the city, working as a prostitute to support her drug habit, where she went by the moniker of "KitKat"—just like the candy bar, her stepmother's favorite—she called home regularly, sometimes several times a day, just to check in to see how everyone was doing, especially her daughter.

The last time that her stepmother ever heard from her was on Marnie's twenty-fourth birthday, when she called home to ask for money. Instead of promising her money, her stepmother told her that she had a box of clothing, candy, cookies, homemade bread, and other items that she promised to send her. She asked Marnie to call her when she received the package, and Marnie promised that she would. However, the telephone call never came.

By the time that Marnie Frey had vanished, enough women had disappeared from the Downtown Eastside that people had begun to take notice, including the Vancouver Rape Relief and Women's Shelter. Even though women who would eventually be connected to this case in one manner or another had begun to disappear as early as the 1980s, and continued into the early 1990s, it was more commonly known that the majority of the women began disappearing during 1995 and thereafter. Newspapers also had begun suggesting that perhaps the numbers of missing women were higher than what the police had estimated, or were willing to admit. As the numbers of missing women continued to stack up, speculation that a serial killer was at work in the Downtown Eastside also increased—but fell on mostly deaf ears at the VPD.

In the autumn of 1997, shortly after Marnie disappeared, Marnie's stepmother, Lynn, accompanied by Lynn's sister, hit the streets of Low Track in search of the missing young woman, asking questions and carrying with them a photograph of her. It wasn't long before they began hearing about Willie Pickton's pig farm east of Vancouver, in Port Coquitlam.

"My sister and I were walking the beat, showing pictures of my daughter to the prostitutes," Lynn said, speaking to reporters with the Canadian Press (CP). She said that several of the women told her and her sister that many of the prostitutes from Low Track went there to get high. They described the pig farm as a very dirty place.

"It was four or five women we were talking to," she continued. "They were on the corner in a little group and they all knew about it. . . . They said you could go there anytime and party. Lots of noise, lots of alcohol. They said you just had to call and a woman would come to pick you up."

If the women on the street knew about the Pickton farm—while women were continuing to disappear—it was only reasonable to presume that the Vancouver police knew about the goings-on there as well. The woman that the girls could call to be picked up and driven to the farm also raised questions that needed answering. Who was she? What was her relationship to Pickton? Did Willie have a willing accomplice to help him carry out his murderous deeds? No one knew, of course, but it seemed reasonable that all of the chatter on the street about Pickton's farm, particularly with so many missing women on the ever-growing list, would have been picked up by the police and at least piqued their interest. Unfortunately, that hadn't been the case. To the families of the missing women, it seemed as if the police couldn't have cared less about what was happening in the city that they were hired to serve and protect.

Lynn Frey, however, had other ideas. After sifting through all the details that they had compiled from the women in Low Track, Lynn and her sister decided to drive out to Pickton's farm on Dominion Avenue late one evening. They had found the setting very unnerving, and Lynn would later tell the police about her experience that night.

"We just drove down this dark road and stared at the house," she said. "It was pitch-black. The dogs started barking and we thought, 'What are we doing here? This is crazy.'"

She said that night in 1997 hadn't been the only time that she had driven past the farm. There had been another occasion, and, like the first, she had been inexplicably disturbed by her venture. She had informed the police about it, urging them to check it out.

Lynn believed that they might have done so, but she wasn't certain about it. She said that she believed that two of the sex trade workers that she had spoken to had told the police about Pickton's farm, but she was careful to not be too condemning of the police action, or lack thereof. She understood how the police needed accurate, solid details before they could act appropriately, thereby giving them credit that may not have been deserved.

"I'm not knocking the street girls," she said. "But when you're high, all of the days blur together. . . . I think the police did investigate, but they can't listen to everything. And these women weren't known for their reliability."

The case of Wendy Lynn Eistetter was another example of how the police had known about the Pickton farm and how Willie had attempted to kill her. Wendy's mother believed that if Wendy hadn't been able to reach a knife with which to stab Pickton, she would be dead today. But the fact that she was a drug addict, and the fact that she had once stolen a police cruiser and had dragged the officer whose car she had taken, presented credibility issues for her with the prosecutor's office, which partly accounted for the reason that Willie had gotten off.

"The Crown reviewed the state of the evidence and

there was no likelihood of conviction," Geoffrey Gaul, a spokesperson with the prosecutor's office, had said.

Although 1997 had proven to be a significant year, as far as showing that the police had known about Willie Pickton and the pig farm—what with the talk on the streets, the Wendy Eistetter incident, the fact that two prostitutes had spoken to police about the farm, and Lynn Frey's urging that the goings-on at the farm be investigated—it would be several years before Willie's reign of terror was ended. In the meantime, women continued disappearing.

According to the list that was eventually compiled by the Joint Missing Women Task Force—still nearly four years away from being formed—Helen May Hallmark, thirty-one, was the next woman to disappear from Vancouver's East End and the crummy landscape of flophouses, sleazy bars, and dirty restaurants that made up so much of the area. Born June 24, 1966, in Vancouver, British Columbia, Helen was reported missing on September 23, 1998, according to the police, but she may have disappeared anytime between June 15, 1997, and the latter date. The Joint Missing Women Task Force poster lists her as last seen in October 1997, so it's anyone's best guess, based on witness accounts, of when she actually vanished. A relative recalled seeing Helen outside a New Westminster convenience store sometime within the aforementioned time frame, but did not stop to avoid being late for an appointment. It had been the last time anyone in her family had seen her.

Helen was the oldest of three children that her mother had with as many fathers, and according to a relative, there had been significant abuse at home, much of it directed toward Helen and her brother committed by one of their mother's spouses or live-in partners who was now deceased. According to one of her siblings, Helen had taken much of the abuse to protect her younger siblings from having to go through the same horrible experiences as she had been forced to endure. The purported abuse was one of the reasons that she had eventually decided to leave home, though her mother had described her as being a rebellious teenager who didn't want to be told what she could or couldn't do—particularly clubbing and partying with her peers. She had been placed in a group home at age thirteen, and later into a foster home, which is where her mother contended that her problems actually started. Nonetheless, regardless of the reasons that she took to the streets, Helen never forgot about her family, particularly her siblings.

"We all meant a lot to her," said one of her siblings. "She was actually a strong enough person, she forgave a lot of the things that she experienced growing up a lot easier than maybe some of us did."

Following two failed marriages and a number of boyfriends, Helen, at age nineteen, gave birth to a baby girl, whom she gave up for adoption when the girl was a year old. Much later that daughter's DNA would play a major role in an effort to identify her mother's remains. Helen's life on the streets consisted of little more than drugs, prostitution, and attempts being made to rescue her by those who loved her— efforts that ultimately always ended up with Helen going back to her pitiful life in Low Track. Her family finally realized that something was terribly wrong when she failed to come home for the Christmas holidays in 1997—she never missed spending Christmas with her family until that fateful year.

* * *

The cold and rainy month of November seemed to have passed without any known or reported disappearances of women from the Downtown Eastside. In fact, according to police, the next known disappearance did not occur until December 1997. That was when the police added forty-two-year-old Cynthia Feliks to the roster of missing women. The police were not certain when Cynthia actually disappeared; they backtracked a little and said that she might have disappeared in November, but they went with December because of sketchy reports indicating that she had been seen during that month. It was difficult to pinpoint an actual date because she had a history of disappearing, often showing up later in jail or at a relative's home, sometimes even at a hospital, but nearly always because of her ongoing drug problem.

One of the first clues that something was wrong was when her friends and associates, those who used drugs just like her, began calling her relatives' homes to speak with her. They were concerned because they had not seen her for some time, they said. When her family began making their usual inquiries, Cynthia was nowhere to be found. When family members reported her missing to the police, the cops took the same cavalier attitude that they had taken with family members of several of the other missing women and simply told them that she would show up sometime. They even told one of her siblings that they had seen her on Kingsway, one of the busy streets where hookers try to drum up business. However, the relative believed that the cops had either lied to her or had been mistaken about having seen Cynthia.

Cynthia Feliks was one of the working girls not originally from Canada. Born in Detroit, Michigan, she was the second of four children. Following their parents' failed marriage, the children lived with their father, a watchmaker, who moved them to Vancouver in 1960 after marrying a second time. Eight years later their father left his second wife, leaving the children with her, and went back to the United States. Because their father failed to provide financial assistance to their stepmother for their well-being, the children grew up having a tough time—along with the stepmother. But their stepmother did the best that she could under the circumstances, often holding down two jobs.

According to the stepmother, Cynthia became involved with drugs following a trip to Florida at age sixteen to visit her father, who is now deceased. Her stepmother claimed that Cynthia's father had coaxed her into smoking marijuana and drinking alcohol with him, and she alluded to the possibility that Cynthia's father had also sexually abused her during that trip. Soon after her return to Vancouver, Cynthia began skipping school and running away from home. She finally left home for good at age nineteen, got married, and had a child, a daughter. Unfortunately, her husband, who has since died, was also a drug abuser, and neither of them provided much of a life for their child. Although Cynthia had been very proud of her daughter, the child ended up being raised by relatives and living much of her youth in foster homes.

Cynthia Feliks became the thirty-ninth woman to disappear from Vancouver's Downtown Eastside, but she wouldn't be the last.

7

'Twas the night before Christmas and all through the streets, not a soul to be found except two little pigs and two working girls.
—Robert Pickton, after turning two small pigs loose in Low Track, Christmas Eve, 1997

After Dave Pickton moved to the other side of the farm, near Piggy's Palace off Burns Road, which was nearly a mile away from the main farmhouse, his brother, Willie, finally had the freedom to come and go as he pleased. Dave had escaped much of the stench of the pig-farming operation, and Willie could now do what he wanted without having to explain anything to Dave, or to anyone else. Dave had moved out of the main farmhouse soon after the sales of the parcels of land had gone through. A short time thereafter, he had constructed his after-hours social club. He, too, enjoyed the freedom that living away from his brother had given him, even if he was only a short distance down the road. When the wind was just right, however, he could sometimes still smell the pig shit, blood, and rotting carcasses that Willie had left unattended. Nevertheless, the separateness afforded each of the brothers the freedom that each had wanted, and needed, to do as they pleased. Willie, of course, liked to cavort with prostitutes, and Dave could continue his efforts at becoming closely aligned with bikers—particularly, some said, the Hells Angels. All the while Dave lived with a woman who seemed willing to put up with his love of partying.

A number of people who had known and worked with the Pickton family painted a picture of happier times that dated back to the 1970s, when there was not so much junk lying around on the farm and there were greener pastures in wide-open spaces. There were also horses on the farm at that time. One woman, Alison Gailling, was six years old when she first visited the farm in 1979, when her older sister, Vicky, began dating Dave Pickton. Now a high-school teacher in her mid-thirties, Gailling recalled a memory that was not so pleasant. She said that there was a large sludge pit on the farm, where dead pigs and other pig waste materials were discarded. On one occasion, she said, Willie took her into the farm-house's basement, which she described as dark and "scary," where he showed her how to make sausages using a meat grinder. Gailling's memories, of course, dated back to a time, presumably, before the horror that the Pickton farm would become famous for had begun.

As a young boy Willie Pickton did not want to watch the pigs while they were in the process of being slaughtered by other family members or hired hands. On butchering days, when the hired help would slaughter the pigs in the barn, Willie would go fishing or take part in other activities away from the area. Perhaps it had been the sound of the pigs "screaming" that had bothered him, or the sight of their blood had made him squeamish. Whatever it was, his interest in the pig slaughters just had not been there as a child. Those who knew him as a kid said that he did not become interested in slaughtering pigs until he was older, by which time Willie had begun doing most of the dirty work. By the time he was into his early twenties, he was not only slaughtering pigs, but he was killing and butchering other farm animals, such as goats, cows, and at least one horse, and apparently was enjoying it.

In 1974, when Robert was approaching his mid-twenties, a woman, Sandy Humeny, began dating his brother, Dave, and eventually moved into the farm-house. She described how she helped the elder Pick-tons, Leonard and Louise, and how Louise had seemed in charge of running things because Leonard's mind had begun failing at that time. Sandy explained that so-cially the Picktons kept very much to themselves and did not participate in many local social events despite the opportunities available to them. One of the few social events that she remembered them taking part in was entering several of their horses in a May Day parade. By this time Dave had obtained his first large truck and had begun hauling topsoil for extra money, while Willie continued to work on the farm. By the end of the decade, after both parents had died, Dave took over the various aspects of the business and delegated most of the work to his brother and hired hands.

Sandy's sister, Ingrid Fehlauer, recalled watching Robert slaughter a variety of animals when she would visit the farm, and she said that she had returned there as an adult and had visited Robert Pickton several times a week for a six-year period in the 1990s. She said that she had never seen anything unusual on the farm, such as prostitutes or anyone using drugs, during some of those visits. She described Robert Pickton as a "good friend." She did say that the trailer he lived in was unkempt and dirty, and on one occasion she had seen "lots of blood" in the trailer, but she had not known its source.

The Pickton farm during those days, and especially later in the 1990s, was very busy with visitors coming and going at a rapid pace. At one point it was common for two hundred cars per day to visit the farm, with activity occurring from 6:00 A.M. to 2:00 A.M. seven days a week, according to Bill Malone, a friend and employee of Dave Pickton's. Security eventually became an issue when things began disappearing. Many times people dropped by just to use the phone because they knew that one was available; some people came onto the property looking for Willie; others, according to rumors, used the Pickton address to receive their welfare checks and other items. In fact, there was so much mail arriving at that address that there often was not sufficient room inside the mailbox, forcing the mail carriers to leave large amounts of mail alongside it on the ground.

"There were so many people coming onto the property, we did not have control over what was happening," Malone said, who was often there because of his employment with Dave. "There was a continual stream of people going in, once they knew they could use the phone even when there was no one there. . . . There were people I did not recognize. Even if I said Willie wasn't around, they would still proceed and say they would wait for him."

Even the warning sign PIT BULL WITH AIDS did little to keep people out.

The parties at Piggy's Palace were another matter altogether. They were frequent and raucous, with drug-addicted female prostitutes showing up in large numbers because they knew that they could find drugs there. Occasionally a male hooker would arrive in drag. There were also people there, like Willie, who would pay the guests for sex or trade drugs for sexual favors. It was a forbidding place, but those in attendance at the parties would not realize just how grim it was until much later—or unless they became a victim who had not been allowed to leave.

"The farm was the dregs of the earth," said one sex trade worker from Low Track who knew it well. "It was a hellhole. You can say to someone, 'Don't go,' but if they're an addict, the addiction overcomes the senses. The police had known about the Pickton farm for some time, but nothing changed."

Despite the police awareness of the goings-on at the Pickton farm, the only thing that occurred were more parties, many of which were bigger and louder than the ones that had occurred in the early days of Piggy's Palace. Little did anyone know of the sinister backdrop that the parties helped to safeguard, and they kept coming for the drinking, drugs, food, dancing, and loud music that emanated from the Palace's exceptional sound system.

Bill Malone, Dave's friend, claimed that the sound system in Piggy's Palace had been his idea and that its installation had been under his supervision. He said that the system was as good as or better than those in many of Vancouver's nightclubs. As far as the parties were concerned, Malone said that the kitchen had been equipped to serve as many as five hundred guests. Buffets were a favorite at Piggy's Palace, and in addition to the roasted pigs that Willie always provided, turkey was frequently on the menu.

Tanya Carr was another person who provided details about life on the farm. Tanya lived down the street from the farm as a young girl in the late 1970s, but she visited it frequently and eventually became close to Willie in what she described as "an uncle-niece relationship." Pickton allowed her to stable a horse at the farm and, as he seemed with many people, was genuinely happy to have been able to help her, even in such a small way. In 1994, when Tanya was twenty-one and Willie was forty-five, she moved in with him and they lived in an old recreational vehicle parked on the farm. She, too, described the farm as a busy place, but said that much of the traffic had consisted of customers doing business with Dave's topsoil and demolition businesses, P&B Salvage, or those who stopped by to buy pigs, which Willie would happily butcher for them. However, by 1997, Tanya was no longer spending much time on the farm and had begun to build a life on her own. While she had appreciated Willie's kindness and generosity, something had signaled her that it was time to move on.

When intelligence had been handed out, Willie, by his own admission, was not the sharpest tool in the shed. A simple man, Robert Pickton possessed poor verbal skills and had an IQ of 86, which is at the low end of the average scale, where approximately two-thirds of the population fell. He failed the second grade, and

school administrators placed him in special classes
that educators at the time thought might help get him
through school. However, his educational abilities
seemed to top out in the fifth grade, even though
records show that he was in school until the ninth
grade. As an adult Willie's vocabulary appeared minimal at best, and he frequently did not understand the
punch lines of jokes that others would tell him. However, he seemed to excel during bidding at pig auctions,
and his skills as a mechanic seemed very good, according to those who knew him. In addition to butchering,
he was very adept at rebuilding internal combustion en-
gines, small or large. Nonetheless, those who knew him
considered him a simple, unsophisticated pig farmer
who could never get to first base with a woman unless
he paid her for sex. Even then, he often ended up mas-
turbating himself to achieve orgasm.

Pickton, whom people often described as a work-
aholic, was in reality a dirty little man with personal hygiene that would make most people cross the street to
avoid passing in close proximity to him. Always repairing
and fixing up used cars and trucks, some of which he obtained from auctions held by the Vancouver Police Department, was one of his sidelines to earn extra money;
the other way, of course, was butchering pigs for other
people, for which he charged a fee. Although he wore
his gum boots nearly everywhere he went, he never wore
gloves in his work. Echoing the comments of a coworker
at West Coast Reduction, an employee there said that
Robert Pickton could not have cared less about engaging in sanitary conditions when he dropped off discarded pig carcasses and associated parts, sometimes
called offal, at the rendering plant in Vancouver.

"It's just that he was handling these old dirty
barrels with his bare hands," said the employee at the

rendering plant. "He was such a dirty guy. I almost felt sorry for him."

One of the biggest questions that would be on many people's minds as the case unfolded was whether Willie possessed a psychopathic personality or not. On the surface he did not appear to be psychopathic. He seemed to enjoy helping other people, whether by giving a person a place to stay for a while, providing them with food, giving them a job, or simply giving away money to people he liked and whom he believed to be in need. (The typical psychopath, or sociopath, doesn't care about others, is focused on himself and his own personal gratification, and has little, if any, conscience.) There were people who knew Willie that described him as a caring, generous person who would give anyone in need the shirt off his back. Nonetheless, as would be pointed out later on, not all serial killers are sociopaths; yet, Willie, as a kid, would often hide inside the carcasses of hogs that had had their entrails removed so that his mother and others could not find him. While that act in and of itself would not necessarily distinguish Willie as a psychopath, it was a behavior that most people would not ever consider engaging in.

Growing up had not been easy for Willie. He worked hard on the farm, driven by a domineering mother who forced him to take baths instead of showers; he would not even take a bath until forced to do so. He performed poorly in school before dropping out shortly after starting high school. Not only had he not liked going to school, he reportedly had been picked on regularly by the other kids, which, some said, weighed heavily in his decision to not finish his basic education.

Girls had had nothing to do with him until later in life, when he learned that he could pay women for sex.

The problems that had led to Willie becoming a vicious sex killer had not begun in early adulthood, but rather had started early in his life. Even though he purportedly had been close to his mother, Willie had suffered much during childhood from having been forced to work long hours, which had kept him from being able to enjoy many of the activities that most children engage in. He also resented his mother after her death for the manner in which he perceived she had treated him in her will. It seemed like he had faced humiliation frequently while growing up and even into adulthood. Rejected by girls and made fun of by boys, Willie grew up unable to fit in anywhere. Even his brother's biker friends did not seem to like him. Since he did not drink or take drugs, Willie attempted, it seemed, to fill the voids in his life with sex in the form of fantasy and masturbation, and later with murder. On one occasion he purchased a plastic blow-up doll, presumably from a Vancouver sex shop for his brother's birthday, but he purportedly kept it for his own use.

For reasons that were never entirely clear, Willie decided to end the year 1997 on a somewhat high note. While trolling the streets of Low Track on Christmas Eve, perhaps thinking that it would be funny, Willie released into the streets two pigs that he had brought with him from the farm. On the surface, based on the accounts of those who witnessed the incident, he seemed to think that it was a hilarious, even mischievous thing to do. However, perhaps in a sinister sort of way, he may have reasoned that the levity of his actions would make it easier to connect with some of the working girls that evening.

8

As 1998 rolled around, there were many people, both inside as well as outside the Vancouver Police Department, who were very much aware of the terrible things that were happening to the women who lived in the single-room-occupancy (SRO) hotels located in Low Track, as well as those who resided in shelters, and those who had no place at all in which to sleep. For decades the area had played host to the less fortunate, including single mothers, the mentally ill, the elderly, handicapped persons, and, of course, drug addicts and prostitutes. Women there would sell themselves for a fix of heroin, a rock of crack cocaine, a pack of cigarettes, or a bottle of booze. There was even a significant child population there, boys and girls—as young as ten or eleven—who had run away from home and who were forced to begin selling themselves in an area known as "kiddie stroll" in order to survive.

Statistics show that approximately 80 percent of the adult prostitutes living and working in Low Track began selling their bodies for sex when they were only children. Life there does become a vicious cycle for most, many of whom do not survive it, in part because of drug overdoses, HIV infections—the highest rate of HIV infection in North America—other sexually transmitted diseases, including hepatitis C, which, if gone untreated, causes rapid liver deterioration, among other things, and, of course, murder.

"To live in this area," an SRO resident once said, "you have to know you aren't going to walk out the front door of your hotel and find a bed of roses."

During the late 1990s, the average income of the people who lived in the area of Main and Hastings was barely over $700 per month, even less for those on disability or on welfare. Seething with misery, the Downtown Eastside made a fertile hunting ground for those seeking to prey upon the less fortunate, knowing that just about anyone who lived there would do anything for a few dollars. Upon retrospect, there was little doubt in anyone's mind that something could have been done about the missing women long before anything actually was done—if only enough people, aside from the missing women's friends and family, had cared.

Some people would blame the culture of Canadian society, which had long held deep-seated disdain for those at the bottom of the human food chain, such as the drug-addicted, alcoholic sex trade workers, many of whom were aboriginal women. By 1998, however, many of the activists whose mission was to look out for the perceived "dregs of society," as well as the friends and families of the missing women, continued to mount pressure toward the police to do something instead of handing out excuses.

"The police kept saying that the women had probably gone to live in another town, and that their lifestyles had made them so chaotic, they would forget to call home," said a relative of one of the missing women, who asked for anonymity. "They must have thought we were stupid."

John Lowman, a criminologist from Simon Fraser University in Vancouver, was among those who wondered why it had taken the police nearly twenty years to accept the fact that there was a serious, ongoing problem in Vancouver's Downtown Eastside.

"These women are the most stigmatized group in society other than pedophiles," Lowman said. "And sometimes I think more so. They are not as important to society as other women. . . . Some press reports on the case give the impression that for drug-addicted prostitutes, rape and murder are just occupational hazards."

"Our justice system does not respond well to women who are black and criminalized," said Suzanne Jay, of the Vancouver Rape Relief and Women's Shelter. "Prostitutes are seen as worth less than other women. They fall low on police priority."

In Jay's opinion it was such beliefs held by the police, including racist and sexist attitudes so ingrained into the police culture, that held back the start of the investigation into the missing women for so many years.

Few people familiar with the case would argue that the investigation into Vancouver's missing women needlessly got off to a poor start. Had it not been for the urging of one man, Kim Rossmo, a geographic profiler and detective, the start of the investigation may have taken much longer. Rossmo, a twenty-two-year police veteran, had worked for several years in the Low Track beat and had believed for some time that the disappearances were the work of a serial killer. His beliefs, at first, were dismissed by his peers and his superiors in the police force, despite the fact that he had continued his education and had become an expert in the area of geographic profiling. He had even developed a software program to help investigators identify the location of where such a serial killer might reside.

"Crimes tend to occur at those locations where suitable victims or targets are found by offenders as they move throughout their activity spaces," Rossmo said.

By focusing his attention on the area where the greatest number of prostitutes were disappearing, Rossmo concluded that the disappearances were occurring in far too many numbers within the same geographic area, in too brief a time span, making it illogical to think that the disappearances were not the work of the same person. Nonetheless, despite his best efforts, Rossmo's colleagues in the department chose to either think illogically or, more likely, to live in denial that a serial killer was at work. They dismissed his theories without looking into them.

"They had great difficulty in accepting the fact that the only explanation that could account for this evidence was a serial murderer," Rossmo said. "They failed to see the fire beneath the smoke, and acted too little, too late."

Not only had Rossmo's colleagues not accepted, much less acted upon, his theory, but he had, in fact, been fired in 2000 for his views, after being mired in controversy for years. His superiors just hadn't been able to see it, and, according to Rossmo, who had been forty years old in 1995 when he had been promoted to the position of detective-inspector, his colleagues feared that they would not be able to handle a serial murder investigation of such magnitude. Rossmo, who had earned a doctorate in the area of criminology at Simon Fraser University in nearby Burnaby, was known as the first police officer in all of Canada to earn a doctorate degree. Furthermore, he had used his expertise in geographic profiling, along with the computer program that he had designed, to help identify prime suspects who committed serial crimes of nearly any type—arson, rape, or murder—by narrowing down the geographic area in which the perpetrator appeared to be the most comfortable carrying out his crimes. After entering all of the different variables of a particular series of crimes into the computer program, Rossmo was often able to identify a suspect based on the proximity of where the crimes occurred and where a suspect resided.

His colleagues feared how Rossmo's expertise and theories might make them look. Even if it was the truth, no one on the force wanted to appear inept, or as if they didn't care—at least not publicly. By being vocal about his belief that a serial killer was at work in Vancouver, Rossmo inadvertently threatened to expose exactly what his superiors wanted to keep hidden.

After word got out about Rossmo's advanced degree and his geographic-profiling program, he received an offer from the RCMP for the position of inspector, a position in which he would be allowed to set up a geographic-profiling unit. A short time later, when Ray Canuel, Vancouver's police chief at that time, was told about Rossmo's offer from the RCMP, Canuel promoted him to detective-inspector and asked him to set up a geographic-profiling unit within the Vancouver Police Department. Because the program worked so well, the department won a number of awards and received international acclaim for their successes. Despite the program's success rate, Rossmo wasn't allowed to use it officially in the cases of Vancouver's missing women after suggesting that he believed their disappearances were tied to a serial killer. Because of what Rossmo would eventually refer to as the "old boys' network," he was snubbed by many of his colleagues who resented his success. He was later dismissed after being given the choice of being demoted to constable and returning to his old Low Track beat.

Even with the attempted murder of Wendy Lynn Eistetter, who had managed to get away from Robert Pickton's evil clutches and report what had happened to her to the police, and in spite of Rossmo showing them in black and white what he believed was occurring, the police still felt that they needed more, much more, to convince them that women were disappearing because of the actions of a serial killer. Furthermore, few people within the VPD could believe that the gaunt, balding pig farmer with dishwater blond hair was capable of such dreadful things. In the meantime women continued disappearing from the Downtown Eastside, one by one.

9

The year 1998 proved to be a very busy one for Robert Pickton. No fewer than nine women vanished from the streets of Vancouver's Downtown Eastside that year, and there may have been more—women who did not make the official list because they might not have been reported missing or somehow had otherwise been overlooked by the police. Those sex trade workers whose disappearances did get noticed and were eventually added to the list of missing women: Kerry Lynn Koski, thirty-nine, last seen on January 7; Inga Monique Hall, forty-six, last seen on February 26; Tania Petersen, twenty-eight, believed last seen sometime in February; Sarah Jean de Vries, twenty-nine, last seen on April 12; Sheila Catherine Egan, twenty, last seen sometime in July; Julie Louise Young, thirty-one, last seen sometime in October; Angela Rebecca Jardine, twenty-eight, last seen on November 10; Marcella Helen Creison, twenty, and Michelle Gurney, nineteen, both last seen in December.

The desk clerks at many of the Downtown Eastside's seedy hotels were in an ideal position to see many of the hard-up, desperate drug-addicted prostitutes on an almost daily basis, and the police eventually learned that they were among the first to notice when the women began disappearing. Many of the women stayed at the run-down hotels, and the first clue to the hotel clerks that something was amiss was when the women would just up and leave without giving any notice or checking out, leaving what few possessions they owned behind in their rooms.

One of the desk clerks, Helene Major, who worked at the Roosevelt Hotel at Main and Hastings, would eventually tell authorities how she noticed the women disappearing "one by one," and how she never knew where they had gone. Major became personally acquainted with some of the women who disappeared, and knew Willie Pickton as well. Pickton, she said, would sometimes show up at the hotel to visit a friend, Dinah Taylor, a thirtysomething woman who, at least at that time, had cocaine and heroin problems. Taylor lived at the Roosevelt and had also lived on Pickton's farm for eighteen months at the height of the disappearances.

"He was friendly. He used to talk to everybody," Major said about Pickton. "He never stayed very long. He picked Dinah up, or picked someone else up."

The police would eventually suspect Dinah Taylor of arranging terminal visits between Willie Pickton and several of the women who worked and lived in the Downtown Eastside, but they would never be able to prove it. Nonetheless, they never had any problem connecting Pickton with Taylor and the eastside hotels. Many of the working girls frequently waved at Pickton as he drove through the area, either on his way to or on his way from the nearby rendering facility.

The Astoria Hotel, located several blocks east of the Roosevelt, was another Willie Pickton hangout. While not quite as seedy or notorious as the Roosevelt, the

Astoria had a bar situated on the ground floor that Willie would frequent and where he would have a few drinks, nearly always alone. Those who worked there did not particularly like him, and a bartender there told Seattle weekly newspaper *The Stranger* that Pickton was a "faker."

"He was a wannabe, you know," the bartender said. "He wanted to be a biker, a Hells Angel, a mean leather guy. Nevertheless, everyone knew he was a weasel, a wannabe. I mean, you can't imagine hanging out with a guy like that without something bad happening."

The scenario involving Willie seemed simple enough. He would go to the Downtown Eastside on any given day or night, and pick up women who needed money, either through prearrangement with an accomplice or on his own, and then drive his particular victim due east on Hastings on a nearly direct route to his farm almost twenty miles away in Port Coquitlam. It seemed astonishing that the police had not picked up on his routine early on, particularly after the assistance and suggestions offered by Kim Rossmo, who had become more vocal by 1999. By year's end, however, five more women had disappeared: Jacquelene McDonell, twenty-three, vanished in January 1999; Brenda Wolfe, thirty-two, the following month; Georgina Papin, thirty-four, in March; Wendy Crawford, forty-three, and Jennifer Furminger, twenty-eight, both disappeared in December 1999.

Although she would have difficulty remembering the precise date, Robert Pickton's longtime friend, Lynn Ellingsen, twenty-nine, at the time, had what she would likely remember as the most terrifying experience of her life, in March 1999, around the time that

Georgina Papin disappeared. Although she would remain quiet for years about what she had seen one night on Pickton's farm out of fear for her own life, Ellingsen would eventually come forward with a story that rivaled anything that Hollywood could dream up and put on celluloid in the form of a horror movie.

Ellingsen had met Pickton through Pickton's friend Gina Houston. The two women had met at a Vancouver halfway house, where Ellingsen had been staying temporarily while breaking away from an abusive relationship. Later, on the night in question, Ellingsen had been residing on Pickton's farm for about two months, doing odd jobs for him to help with her upkeep, after Willie had offered her the work. The work included cleaning up Willie's trailer, and sometimes driving a truck for him. That night, which she believed was March 20, 1999, but admittedly was not absolutely certain about the date, she and Willie decided to drive to the Downtown Eastside in search of a hooker for Willie. She would later tell the authorities that she had remembered that particular date because the police had stopped Willie that evening and had given him a sobriety test. They picked up a prostitute, whom Ellingsen would identify as Georgina Papin, and went back to the farm.

They smoked crack cocaine that evening, both en route to the farm and after their arrival there. At one point Willie took Papin into one room of his trailer, while Ellingsen went into another. She continued getting high by herself, and eventually she fell asleep. Sometime later, however, Ellingsen, awakened by a loud noise, looked out the window and saw a light on in the nearby barn, where, she knew, Willie slaughtered pigs. Somewhat shaky and curious, she went outside to investigate.

As she walked toward the barn, following the light source, Ellingsen felt ill—either from the excessive drug use that night or the sickening odor that hung in the night air, which grew stronger as she reached the barn. She cautiously pushed open the barn door a bit when, suddenly and without warning, Willie Pickton, covered in blood, reached out and grabbed her, pulling her inside the barn. He pulled Ellingsen over to a table and forced her to look at the dead woman, naked and hanging from a hook. The woman, Georgina Papin, was just hanging there, covered in blood. Willie had placed her on a hook in the same manner that he always hung up the pigs that he was going to slaughter. The victim's feet, whose toenails were painted red, were at Ellingsen's eye level. On a "shiny table" next to the hanging body, Ellingsen saw long black hair lying there, Georgina Papin's hair, and a lot of blood. She also saw two bloody knives. It looked to her like Willie had skinned Papin, and was preparing to butcher her like an animal.

Willie told Ellingsen that if she told anyone anything about what she had seen that night, the same thing would happen to her. Vowing to keep her mouth shut, Willie called a taxi for her and sent Ellingsen out to buy additional drugs. Fearing for her own life, she stayed with a friend and did not return to the farm. She also never uttered a word about what she had seen that night, until nearly three years later.

By April 1999, it seemed that the powers-that-be in Vancouver had begun to listen to the pleas for action from the missing women's relatives because the Vancouver police board posted a $100,000 reward that month for information leading to an arrest and conviction of the person or persons responsible for whatever happened to the missing women. It was a move supported by Mayor Philip Owen, chairperson of the police board. Until that time, however, Owen had been adamant that there was not any evidence that a serial killer was at work, and he stated that he would not be responsible for financing "a location service" for hookers. Contact with family members of some of the missing women apparently helped bring about the mayor's change of heart.

"This is developing into a very major issue," Owen said to *The Province* reporter Bob Stall. *"Everybody's jumping on to it and getting connected. I think it's worth having a very close look at it because the press are pointing that out and the public are wanting it, and certainly the families are wanting a little more attention and a little more seriousness."*

Owen pointed out that the reward offer needed to be very clearly worded before going public with it.

"We have to make sure we don't have a big reward out there for a missing person's issue," Owen said. *"We don't want a person in Vancouver saying, 'My sister Carol is now in Portland. Send me a hundred thousand bucks.' So then you think of making it a reward for information on a homicide of some kind, or some kind of serial activity. . . . Do we want to go on the assumption that they've all been brutally murdered? Families could say, 'You've already written off my daughter? What if she's badly wounded somewhere? What if she's kidnapped somewhere? Or a hostage somewhere? What if somebody's got her locked up in a cabin somewhere? You've concluded that she's dead. I don't want to conclude that.'"*

The mayor even expressed concern that the reward offer, if worded poorly, might elicit one or more murders that had not yet occurred. He cited a case in Belgium to make his point.

"I have a horror of something like those girls in Belgium who were locked up for almost a year in a basement," he said. "And because we put this one-hundred-thousand-dollar reward out, he murders them and then two months later, he says, 'I found these bodies.' Maybe I'm getting out of line. Maybe my imagination is running ahead, trying to think of all the parameters of it, but it's my job to think of all sides."

He said that his goal, at that point, was to encourage anyone with information about the case to come forward with it, hopefully with evidence to back it up.

"But we've got to craft it so that it solves the issue and gives us the evidence we need and doesn't cause some kind of negative situation."

Rossmo, along with retired police inspector Doug MacKay-Dunn, spoke out about the tragedy of the missing women, which had been encouraged, in part, by the inaction of the police department over the past several years. While stressing that stranger-to-stranger crime is among the most difficult type of crime to solve, Rossmo said that if his profiling system of geographic profiling had been used sooner, it could have helped trim some of the information overload experienced by the Vancouver police.

"Police forces have limited resources and these cases take extraordinary resources, so they have to come from somewhere and usually that involves politics, a political decision," Rossmo said later in hindsight.

Deborah Jardine, mother of missing woman Angela Jardine, told the *Vancouver Sun* that her daughter—as well as many other women—might have been spared a horrible fate, had the police, sooner rather than later, issued a public warning that a serial killer was at work.

"I think it might have made a difference," Deborah

Jardine said. "The women would have taken extra precautions, including my daughter."

Deborah was among those who believed that officials within the Vancouver Police Department should have listened to Rossmo's warnings and taken action. Deborah believed that the police should have taken her daughter's disappearance, as well as the disappearances of all the other missing women, more seriously.

"I was told that it wasn't a serial killer, that she just disappeared and started a new life somewhere," Deborah Jardine said. "I've said all along it was a serial killer or killers."

There were those, of course, who publicly disagreed that a serial killer was operating in the Downtown Eastside area, including Detective Scott Driemel, VPD media liaison officer. When asked if the department had purposely disregarded Rossmo's warnings, Driemel told the Canadian Press that there was no firm evidence that a serial killer was at work in the area, citing the fact that no bodies had been found yet. He added, however, that such a possibility was not being ruled out.

Groups that provide assistance to those in need in the Downtown Eastside area did not agree that the police had been remiss in their handling of the disappearances. Judy McGuire, chairperson of the Women's Information Safe House, defended the police work on the case.

"There was a unit set up and a number of officers worked incredibly diligently," McGuire said. "The police obviously took (the disappearances) very seriously and acted on . . . a lot of fronts."

The fact that sexual predators operated regularly in

the area was "common knowledge," McGuire said. She added that the police did as much as possible to increase the sex trade workers' knowledge of that fact.

"A lot of officers were getting the word out that women were going missing," she said. "That sexual predators were out there. Whether they should have issued a particular notice, I don't know."

By Tuesday, July 27, 1999, John Walsh and the crew of the popular crime-fighting television show *America's Most Wanted* had arrived in Vancouver at the request of the police, and at the continued behest of families of the missing women, to film a show that would air the following Saturday evening, July 31, 1999. Outspoken Walsh made it clear from the get-go that he believed it was obvious that the missing women were the work of a serial killer. Although it was not what the police had wanted to hear, they nonetheless went along with Walsh's assessment.

"Anybody can put two and two together," Walsh said. "When there are thirty women missing and no bodies have been found, and they're all of the same type of background, that always smacks of a serial killer. . . . By putting the millions of eyes of American viewers and Canadian viewers of this case, there might be a chief of police or a coroner who has a Jane Doe or unidentified body or a similar case they can link together."

Constable Anne Drennan, while neither confirming nor denying the possibility that a serial killer was plucking women off Vancouver's streets, continued to downplay the likelihood that a serial killer was at work. She insisted that it would be inappropriate to reveal police thoughts, theories, and strategies regarding an ongoing investigation.

"We're following many different avenues of investigation," Drennan said. "Some initiated by our department and some we've learned through speaking to other departments that have been through similar circumstances with multiple murders, multiple missing [persons]."

Walsh, on the other hand, said that Vancouver police may have been concerned about unduly alarming the public about what they thought was occurring.

"Law enforcement tries not to scare the public or talk about details they can't really confirm," Walsh said. "Hopefully, Saturday night we will be able to end some of the mystery surrounding the disappearances of these thirty-one women."

It was the hope of everyone concerned that the *America's Most Wanted* episode would generate solid leads that would help solve the mystery of the missing women, or at the very least would prompt any of the women who had left Vancouver for other destinations to contact their families or the police about their whereabouts. Although the show did generate telephone calls, little came out of it to help move the case forward.

If one person within the media could be credited with helping to light a fire under the Vancouver Police Department and to jump-start the case to get it moving forward, it would be *Vancouver Sun* reporter Lindsay Kines. Kines began covering the story for the newspaper in 1998, and has been credited as the first reporter to delve headfirst into the case. Kines, who developed sources within the department who revealed slipshod work and incompetence among the ranks of investigators, pressured the police through his stories and repeated questioning of officials. It was, in part, because of Kines's work and that of his colleagues, which included reporters Lori Culbert and Kim Bolan, that the Vancouver Police Department began stepping up their efforts in 1999, and would continue and intensify over the next few years.

"Once we became aware that clearly there was something wrong here, we kicked in additional resources," Drennan said.

"Although the police don't have any evidence of foul play, there is a gut instinct that all of us have," chimed in British Columbia attorney general (AG) Ujjal Dosanjh.

Rossmo, meanwhile, angry over his perceived ineptitude of his colleagues at the Vancouver Police Department and his termination from his $120,000-per-year job, began putting together a civil lawsuit against his former employer. In the meantime, as the twentieth century came to a close and the twenty-first century began, women continued disappearing, without a trace, from the Downtown Eastside.

10

Despite all of the fear and paranoia generated and fueled mostly through conspiracy theorists, Y2K passed with nary a significant event anywhere in the world. Many people stocked up on supplies and rations for what they believed was going to be an "end of times" event, only to find out later that they should have saved their money for the hard times that would hit much later in the first decade of the new century. Except for the colossal celebrations pertaining to ringing in the new century that was going on in major cities around the world, it was mostly business as usual.

It was, as well, business as usual in the case of Vancouver's missing women. There had not been any takers of the standing $100,000 reward, and the police were not any closer to identifying Willie Pickton as the perpetrator who was taking many of the women away from their misery on the streets of the Downtown Eastside to one final, likely drawn-out bout of unimaginable pain and suffering. The police would eventually learn that there were plenty of people who had information about what was going on at the Pickton farm, but none of them were coming forward with it.

The year 2000 only saw four new names added to the list of missing women: Tiffany Drew, twenty-seven, was last seen in March 2000, according to the Joint Missing Women Task Force poster. However, others said that she was last seen in December 1999. Strangely, and unlike in prior years, seven months passed before the next woman, Dawn Crey, forty-three, went missing. Crey disappeared in November 2000. Sharon Abraham, thirty-five, and Debra Jones, forty-three, both disappeared in December.

As numerous detectives and police officers went about their business of investigating the cases of the missing women that had been assigned to them, a somewhat clearer picture of Robert Pickton and his pig farm began to emerge, thanks in no small part to a man named Bill Hiscox. Why it had taken so long to begin deriving a conclusion remained a mystery. Many on the outside looking in surmised that the problem was caused by too little focus and lack of communication because of the sheer numbers of missing women being investigated by officers who failed to see the forest for the trees. Nonetheless, Hiscox, thirty-seven, had been there and had seen and heard things on the farm that had disturbed him, and he had reported his concerns to the police. Either his concerns had initially fallen on deaf ears, or his information had failed to reach the appropriate investigators in a timely manner. Hiscox, however, had become a part of the story.

Hiscox apparently began using drugs and alcohol after the death of his wife in 1996, but a caring relative, who also happened to be close to Robert Pickton, came to his rescue and had helped find him a job at P&B Salvage, located in the community of Surrey and owned by the Pickton brothers, in 1998. Surrey was due south of Port Coquitlam, near Mud Bay, and was not far from the Pickton farm. Because Sandra Humeny, Dave Pickton's former common-law partner and mother of two of his children, handled the business's accounting operations on the farm, employees of P&B Salvage were required to go to the farm to pick up their paychecks. It was a routine that Hiscox had quickly come to dislike.

Hiscox had told the police as early as 1998 that the Pickton farm was a "creepy-looking place," made even more so by a nasty-looking and ferocious six-hundred-pound wild boar that Willie and his brother used to help guard the property.

"I never saw a pig like that, which would chase you and bite at you," Hiscox told the cops. "It was running out with the dogs around the property."

Hiscox had become concerned about what he had observed on the farm and at Piggy's Palace after reading the numerous newspaper reports about Vancouver's missing prostitutes, not to mention what he had heard from others. He had been particularly alarmed by the drunken parties at Piggy's Palace, which had included amusement and diversion by numerous women from the Downtown Eastside. Hiscox said that Willie drove a converted bus around town, and that the bus had dark-tinted windows that made it impossible to see inside.

"It was Willie's pride and joy," Hiscox said. "He wouldn't part with it for anything. He used it a lot."

Hiscox described Willie as a "pretty quiet guy" who was difficult to engage in conversation.

"I don't think he had much use for men," Hiscox said. "Willie is a very strange person to talk to. He is, like, antisocial. He was very quiet to us. That's why I found him sort of strange."

Although Hiscox had already decided that Willie was a "strange character," he was certain of it when he heard about the stabbing incident involving Willie and Wendy Lynn Eistetter that had occurred a year before he began his employment with the Picktons. He told the police about purses and female identification cards that had been seen inside Willie's trailer, information that he had apparently learned from a woman he identified as Lisa.

"A good friend of mine told me lots of things," Hiscox said. "She had her suspicions as well."

The female constable that he had spoken to, however, informed him that there was little, if anything, that the police could do regarding evidence that Hiscox had not personally seen.

"She said they couldn't really do anything, they can't just go in there based on assumptions," Hiscox said. "The constable wanted to talk to Lisa, but Lisa did not want to get involved with the police or anything."

Hiscox refused to give up, however, and went to the police several times with his information, even if it was hearsay. He told the police that Willie frequented the Downtown Eastside, often driving his "magic bus," as Willie sometimes referred to it, looking for girls. The police recorded his statements, and an investigator eventually went with him to the pig farm, to no avail. The detective promised to push his superiors, "all the way to the top," to follow up on Hiscox's information. Despite the promises and good intentions of those who had tried to get involved and intervene, little, if anything, was done at that time.

Even though the police had received several reports about the events going on at the Pickton farm from a number of people besides Hiscox, the case seemed to remain in a near-constant indeterminate state. Although women continued to vanish in 2000, at a rate that was perceived as less than in prior years, it was no secret that many of the missing women were not being placed on the official missing list for one reason or another. Some of the women eventually turned up alive, some turned up dead from drug overdoses, and still others were classified using vague characteristics. One thing was certain, however—whoever was responsible for causing the women to disappear from Low Track was still brazenly at work, almost challenging the police to catch him. It seemed, however, by that time all that the police would have had to do was place some of their own people, undercover, on the streets of the Downtown Eastside, to simply keep an eye out for Willie Pickton and his magic bus.

11

As the year 2000 ended and 2001 began, much was happening with regard to the case that would come to be known as "The Pig Farm Murders.". It just was not happening with regard to the police making much headway toward solving the mystery of the missing women. Instead, most of the activity—much of which the police had not learned about yet—was occurring on Pickton's farm after Willie picked up women off the streets of Low Track, using the promise of drugs and money as lures to get them inside of Willie's vehicle— truck, bus, or whatever he was driving on any given day or night.

The six-person RCMP/VPD Joint Missing Women Task Force was formed in 2001. The idea for a task force had germinated at a police meeting of the two agencies on November 23, 2000, *after* a senior member of the RCMP had sent out an e-mail to higher-ups suggesting that the Mounties should help Vancouver with their stalled investigation. The joint task force would be code-named "Project Evenhanded."

Following several weeks of meetings and negotiations over who would lead the new task force, veteran

RCMP inspector Don Adam won the post. Adam knew from the outset that his job would be difficult and that the task force work would be complicated, in part because the police did not have any known crimes scenes to work yet, and the responsibility of showing that the missing women had not simply moved to another location—but had, in actuality, likely met with foul play—would be theirs.

By the time the task force got down to business, the official number of missing women stood at sixty. Compounding the difficulty of their work was the need to sift through a large group of possible suspects, primarily men who were known to police for having had committed acts of violence against prostitutes. RCMP sergeant Margaret Kingsbury, a senior member of the task force, caught that assignment, among others, and immediately began reviewing hundreds of files that involved such potential suspects, as well as the victims who had reported crimes of violence committed against them.

"There might be more women missing out there that we didn't have knowledge of," Kingsbury said in reference to the daunting task she oversaw.

Another problem investigators faced, according to Adam, was that Vancouver police investigators had at one point attempted to link three unsolved murders of sex trade workers near Mission, a small community southeast of Vancouver and Port Coquitlam, situated along the Lougheed Highway, to the cases of the Downtown Eastside missing women. In addition to the bodies found in the Mission case, DNA of an unidentified suspect had also been recovered. Because bodies of the missing Vancouver women had not yet begun to turn up, Adam did not believe the Mission case was connected to Vancouver's. He realized, however, that the possibility of such a connection required investigating, if for no other reason than to rule it out. Adam nonetheless acknowledged early in the task force's work, as women continued to vanish from the Downtown Eastside, that a serial killer was at work.

"Unless they (the missing women) could be found, the evidence was that there was an ongoing serial killer active," Adam said.

The fact that Vancouver police investigators told the task force that women had ceased disappearing from Low Track in 1999 created another problem. During that period Vancouver police had mistakenly believed that the killer, if one existed, had moved out of the area or was in jail somewhere. Because of such ineptitude the task force, once formed, would have to allocate at least some of their focus by going over Vancouver's older files. Other major problems that had affected Vancouver's ability to properly investigate the case was the fact that a DNA data bank for missing persons did not exist in British Columbia. That made it impossible for the police to check the DNA of the missing women against the corpses of unidentified women held at the morgue at any given time.

During the years that Vancouver police handled the missing persons cases in question, they collected more than 1,300 tips and stored many of them in an archaic computer system that did little, if anything, to help the investigators working on the numerous cases. By the time the task force received the computer files, they merely served to waste their time requiring them to sort them into a paper filing system until they could devise something that worked more efficiently. They eventually settled on making use of a computer program utilized by investigators of the September 2, 1998, Swiss Air flight 111 tragedy that occurred in Nova Scotia.

Although it helped them, it didn't stop the women from disappearing.

At one point Adam, realizing that no one on his team had any experience in trying to track down a serial murderer, decided to take the task force on a field trip of sorts to Seattle and Spokane, Washington, to confer with investigators in those cities. Both cities had experienced their own problems with serial killers—Seattle with their Green River Killer, fifty-two-year-old Gary Leon Ridgway, who was still a few months away from being caught, and Spokane's Robert Lee Yates, fifty, father of five, decorated military helicopter pilot and National Guardsman, had been convicted the previous year of killing thirteen prostitutes in and around the eastern Washington city. Vancouver's Joint Missing Women Task Force hoped to benefit by talking with the experienced serial killer manhunters, since both killers had chosen prostitutes as their prey. It was the first of several such meetings that would take place between the task force members so that they could compare notes with their counterparts south of the border. It also would not be the only time that Gary Ridgway's name came up in relation to *their* case—soon after the Green River Killer murders stopped in Washington State, but long before Ridgway's capture, women in Vancouver began disappearing. Ridgway, at one point, would tell the sentencing judge that "I killed so many women I have a hard time keeping them straight." The task force would also make another trip to Seattle to interview Ridgway.

One of the major points that Adam and his team learned by conferring with the detectives in Seattle and Spokane was that serial killers were very adept at staying ahead of the police. They typically watched news reports and read newspaper articles to find out as much as they could about what was happening in the investigation. In cases where bodies were turning up, a serial killer was typically committing his next murder, often before his prior victim's body had been found. In cases like that of the Green River Killer and the Yates case in Spokane, the investigators always had a crime scene to work. The crime scenes didn't always become available immediately, and in many instances it would take months before a body was discovered and detectives had a crime scene to work. Of course, in the case of the Vancouver task force, they had yet to get a crime scene related to the missing women.

So if a serial killer was at work in Vancouver, Adam kept asking himself, why hadn't any bodies turned up yet?

Although Adam and his team had not experienced any immediate results from their meetings with the investigators in Washington State, they had learned a lot that had the potential to be very useful to them later on. They learned a lot about forensics, DNA, and processing crime scenes, and by mid-2001 additional officers were added to the task force. In an effort to become more proactive in their efforts to not only identify but to locate a suspect, the task force put together a team that would spend more time on the streets and act as a go-between that would communicate more effectively with not only the prostitutes working the streets but with the agencies that existed to provide assistance to the women. Although it was an effort that had been started later rather than sooner, it was everyone's hope that it would pay off and bring them closer to ending the madness.

* * *

Over the course of 2001, eight more women disappeared from Vancouver's seediest streets and were eventually placed on the official list of missing women: Yvonne Boen, thirty-three, and Patricia Johnson, twenty-five, both last seen in March 2001; Heather Bottomley, twenty-four, and Heather Chinnock, thirty, last seen in April 2001; Andrea Joesbury, twenty-two, last seen in June 2001; Sereena Abotsway, twenty-nine, last seen in August 2001; Dianne Rock, thirty-four, last seen in October 2001; Mona Wilson, twenty-six, last seen in November 2001.

It should be noted that the dates used herein are the dates that the women were last seen as recorded by the police, and that the actual dates that they were officially reported missing were often later. The dates that their names were added to the official list of missing women also came later as the task force went about its business of sorting through the names of many more missing women than those that would ultimately make the official list. Some of the women who had not made the official list turned up alive in other locations, while others had died from drug overdoses and some from disease, and part of the task force's job was to eliminate those names that it deemed not applicable to the case. When all was said and done, the task force had come up with sixty-five names that it placed on the official list. Later, after the case broke, it would add another, a Jane Doe.

12

On Monday, June 25, 2001, while the Joint Missing Women Task Force went about its business of trying to determine why so many prostitutes had mysteriously disappeared without a trace, Kim Rossmo testified in a civil lawsuit that he brought against the Vancouver police board and Deputy Chief John Unger for wrongful dismissal, stating that it was his opinion that a task force should have been formed much sooner. At the time of his lawsuit, Rossmo had moved to the United States to become director of research for the Police Foundation in Washington, D.C. He claimed that ten senior police officers had resented his promotion from constable to detective-inspector, and had acted disapprovingly and contemptuously toward him during the five years that he had held that position. Rossmo particularly blamed Inspector Fred Biddlecombe, who was then in charge of the department's major crime unit, for much of the negativity that had been displayed toward him.

Biddlecombe, Rossmo said, had literally thrown a temper tantrum when Rossmo advised him in 1998 that the police should consider the possibility that a serial killer was responsible for the missing women and recommended that the public be told that such a possibility existed. Instead, Biddlecombe went before the public and denied that a serial killer was operating in the Downtown Eastside. A report about the situation that Rossmo had created and submitted to his superiors on May 27, 1999, had been virtually ignored. The report, which he had submitted to Deputy Chief Constable Brian McGuinness, Fred Biddlecombe, and Inspector Chris Beach, downplayed the likelihood that the police would ever be able to locate more than two of the missing women alive, contrary to the image that the department was trying to convey to an eager public that wanted answers.

In his report Rossmo outlined three possibilities regarding what may have resulted in the disappearances of so many women: 1) They had fallen prey to separate killers. 2) Each had been murdered by a serial killer. 3) They had fallen prey to multiple serial killers. Rossmo said that because serial murders are relatively rare, it seemed unlikely that more than one such killer was at work in Vancouver. He also said that because none of the women's bodies had been found yet, the first scenario was also unlikely. His choice was that a single serial killer was picking up the women, killing them, and possibly cluster dumping their bodies at a still-to-be-determined location.

"Similarities in victimology and the short time period and specific neighborhood involved all suggest the single serial murderer hypothesis is the most likely explanation for the majority of these incidents," Rossmo said. "The single predator theory includes partner or team killers—approximately twenty-five percent of serial murder cases involve more than one offender."

According to Rossmo, it was not unusual for a serial

killer who did not want to be identified to hide his victims' remains in one location or area. Using several different dumping sites would naturally increase the odds of being discovered.

"When a body is found in a cluster dump site," Rossmo said, "several others can often be located within a range of fifty meters or less. Considering Vancouver's surrounding geography, potential burial sites are most likely to be in wilderness areas or, less likely, on the offender's residence or property."

In testimony given at the civil lawsuit trial, Rossmo said that his opinions about the possibility of a serial killer had gone virtually unheeded despite the afore-mentioned report. He blamed an "old boys' network" for controlling the senior ranks of the police depart-ment and holding back earlier inquiries into Vancou-ver's problem.

"If we believe, with any degree of probability, that we have a predator responsible for twenty to thirty deaths in a short period of time, do you think our re-sponse was adequate?" Rossmo asked during the civil trial. "I thought it was the wrong approach. We did not put together a task force anywhere near what a real serial murder investigation would involve."

Instead of being consulted on cases by the major crime unit and the sex offenses unit, after setting up his geographic-profiling department, he was instructed to assist in cases out of the area, as well as on interna-tional cases. When his contract was not renewed and he was offered a "highly undesirable" position of going back to work as a constable, an offer that he felt was an insult and unreasonable, he left the department two years short of being eligible to retire with a pension. Rossmo ultimately lost his case against Unger and the police board.

* * *

At one point later on, Rossmo and Inspector Doug MacKay-Dunn, retired, called for an investigation into the handling of the missing-women cases by Vancouver police. Their goal, Rossmo said, was to prevent such shoddy police work in the future.

"This is unprecedented," Rossmo said of the missing women investigation. "This wasn't investigated in an optimal fashion, and an inquiry would help determine what went wrong and why. Most of these problems are systemic and it could help lead to improvements in policing. . . ."

Vancouver mayor Philip Owen and senior members of the police department countered the call for an investigation into how the case was being handled by saying that there was nothing wrong with the manner in which the police conducted the case. The mayor and police officials also argued that the timing for such an inquiry was inappropriate because the investigation was ongoing.

"I'm not sure that the victims and their families would agree with the mayor's assessment," Rossmo said, adding that the suggested delay was "clearly a stalling tactic."

"Right now, they're saying they want the investigation to be over," Rossmo added. "Well, then they're going to say they want the court case to be over (before starting an inquiry), then they're going to say they want the appeals to be over, and then we'll be ten years down the road. If things aren't working well, we want to fix them now, not in a decade."

The case of Vancouver's missing women was not the first time that Kim Rossmo's colleagues and superiors had chosen to ignore his theories. In 1994, the remains of three murdered aboriginal women were found in Saskatoon, Saskatchewan, two provinces east of British Columbia. After examining the three sets of remains, Rossmo suggested that a serial killer had murdered the women. Despite the fact that the police in Saskatchewan had been keeping convicted rapist John Martin Crawford under surveillance, Rossmo's theory was disregarded. Crawford, however, was eventually arrested and charged with murdering the three native women, in 1992, two years before their remains had been found, and was convicted of the charges in 1996.

Kim Rossmo today works as a research professor for the Center for Geospatial Intelligence and Investigation at Texas State University in San Marcos, Texas. The center primarily studies ways to improve response to crime and homeland security issues, and provides specialized training for law enforcement agencies, as well as the military and intelligence communities. He has also written and published a book on the subject of his expertise called *Geographic Profiling*.

Meanwhile, by November 2001, the task force investigating the missing women stated that it had catalogued approximately one hundred possible suspects that its investigators deemed a "high priority." A month earlier their list of potential suspects had exceeded six hundred, but through the process of categorizing those of highest priority, the task force had been able to shrink the list significantly, thus making it more manageable. They were aided in their effort by using case management software, Specialized Investigative Unit Support System (SIUSS). Investigators would enter each piece of evidentiary information into the complicated program, which would then analyze the new information by checking it against thousands of other records as it looked for a common denominator. The hope that everyone using the system had, of course, was that it would return the name of potential suspects that detectives could scrutinize further.

Following the arrest of Green River Killer suspect Gary Leon Ridgway on Friday, November 30, 2001, as he left the Renton, Washington, factory where he worked, witnesses began coming forward during the month of December, and later, to report that they had seen Ridgway in the Downtown Eastside area on several occasions during the time frame in which women had been disappearing. After seeing his photo on television and in newspapers, Vancouver prostitutes began saying that they recognized him, according to Vancouver detective Jim McKnight.

"There is some indication that he was in British Columbia," McKnight told reporters from a Seattle television station. "I can't be too specific, because I don't know for sure yet."

Ridgway's neighbors told police and reporters after his arrest that he and his wife frequently traveled to British Columbia in their motor home. Because of the reported sightings of Ridgway in Vancouver in the area where prostitutes had been disappearing since about the time that the Green River murders ended, the Vancouver task force naturally wanted to speak to him. After all, he had been charged with murdering several Seattle-area prostitutes over several years and was suspected of murdering many more, making him a high-priority suspect in the eyes of the Vancouver Joint Missing Women Task Force. Canadian investigators made another trip to Seattle in December 2001 to talk to Ridgway and members of the Green River task force, but any information they received was kept secret. Ridgway would, however, soon be ruled out as a major suspect in the Vancouver probe, but detectives would continue looking at him as somehow possibly being involved after rumors surfaced about him being seen at Piggy's Palace. Two years later, Ridgway would plead guilty to murdering forty-eight Seattle-area prostitutes, even though he had made claims that he had killed seventy-one.

13

RCMP constable Nathan Wells joined the Mounties in 2000, and he was assigned to the Coquitlam street enforcement unit. His job as a rookie was to develop and nurture informants who had knowledge of the district's drug traffickers. Although he had heard about the work that Inspector Don Adam's task force was doing regarding the missing women, he had not concerned himself with Adam's investigation—until he met Dwayne Scott Chubb, a thirtysomething heroin addict, a year later in the autumn of 2001. A longtime employee of the Picktons', Chubb had worked intermittently for the two brothers, sometimes for the dump truck business and at other times for the topsoil business, from 1993 to 2001.

In April 2000, following an assault outside a Coquitlam bar, Chubb sustained a head injury that required 160 stitches and, according to Chubb, had inadvertently led to his heroin problem. When his physician stopped prescribing morphine for his pain, he turned to heroin for the next few months. Afterward, he entered a methadone program for heroin addicts. During the period that he began talking to Wells,

Chubb sometimes worked as a bagman of sorts for area drug dealers in which he picked up money for them.

When they first began talking, Chubb had reportedly provided Wells with some information about drugs initially. However, during subsequent cop-informant meetings that occurred in early 2002, Chubb took Wells down a different path. During a meeting on Friday, February 1, 2002, Chubb told Wells about firearms and ammunition that he had seen on Robert Pickton's farm, dating from a year or two earlier. One of the firearms was illegal, a MAC-10 fully automatic handgun; some of them were illegally stored in Robert Pickton's trailer, contrary to Canadian firearms laws, which required them to be kept under lock and key. The new information was enough to cause Wells to do a computer search on Robert Pickton. After checking out Pickton, Wells considered whether he might be in over his head.

The computer search involving Pickton turned up a note attached to the electronic file advising anyone interested in Robert Pickton to speak to the Vancouver police. Since the note had been vague, Wells continued putting together information for the search warrant for firearms for which he would soon be applying through the court system. Before he could make much progress, however, a staff sergeant on Monday, February 4, 2002, advised Wells to contact the Joint Missing Women Task Force before proceeding any further.

Wells did contact the task force, but was initially told little aside from the fact that the task force knew about Pickton. After being made aware of Wells's inquiry, Staff Sergeant Wayne Clary, the task force's second-in-charge, informed Sergeant John Cater that he could speak with Wells if he so desired. Cater did, in fact, call Wells back, and suggested ways of how they might help each other during the search. There seemed to be little information at this point to suggest that the task force believed that anything significant pertaining to their case would turn up, and task force members seemed to be participating in the effort with a matter-of-fact attitude.

Arrangements were made to get Wells the search warrant for firearms at Robert Pickton's farm, and the plans to execute the search warrant were coordinated with the task force with Cater's help. It was agreed that Cater and another member of the task force would observe the search, but they would do so only from a vantage point that was not on the property itself. Their purpose, according to Wells, was to remain nearby with a police radio in the event that Wells's search turned up anything that might pertain to the task force investigation. Based on the information contained in Wells's search warrant, the police would be looking for a MAC-10 fully automatic handgun, a .38-caliber handgun, and a .44-caliber handgun on Pickton's farm.

On Tuesday evening, February 5, 2002, at a few minutes before eight-thirty, Wells and three other Mounties, each dressed in plain clothing, slowly made their way from their vehicles parked inconspicuously a short distance away toward Robert Pickton's residence, the run-down white trailer located on the north side of the farm. It was dark, cold, and damp as the police officers, walking through thick mud and carrying a battering ram, saw headlights in the distance and soon heard the sound of a vehicle approaching. It was headed toward the trailer. They stopped for a few moments, then proceeded after they heard the vehicle's door close, followed moments later by the opening and closing of the trailer's front door. Aware of the risk that the purported firearms inside the trailer posed, now that someone was there, the Mounties nonetheless gave the signal to proceed as planned.

Wells and the other three officers walked up onto the low deck, battering ram in hand, while another group of Mounties, which had arrived separately, remained nearby as sentries. It wasn't until the police cruiser, with its lights flashing and its ear-piercing siren sped down the muddy drive—the agreed-upon signal to assault the trailer—that Wells and his team shouted out from their positions on the deck, "Police! We are serving a search warrant!" Moments later the cops used the battering ram to break open the front door at about the same time that Pickton was headed toward another door to see what was happening.

Corporal Howard Lew was the first to confront Robert Pickton, who was standing off to Lew's left. He shouted, "Police! Get down!" Pickton immediately dropped to the floor, apparently noticing that Lew's gun was drawn and pointed at him. Lew carefully approached Pickton, ordering him to keep his hands where he could see them. With Pickton facedown on the floor, Lew handcuffed him with his hands behind him, brought him to his feet, and, moments later, placed him in the waiting police cruiser outside. The arrest went off without a hitch, quickly and without incident or resistance, and within a short time Pickton was driven off his farm and taken to the police station.

The interior of the filthy trailer consisted of six rooms, and each of the Mounties who had gone inside was assigned a section of it to search. Although Corporal James Petrovich had been instructed to search one of the bedrooms, he had heard that one of the guns might have been placed in the laundry room. Unable to control his curiosity, Petrovich checked out the laundry room first. He was not disappointed in his decision. He discovered, on a shelf situated above the trailer's heater, a .22-caliber Smith & Wesson revolver. When he retrieved it, he saw, much to his shock and surprise, that it had a dildo attached to its barrel. When he examined it further, he noted that it had five live rounds of ammunition and one spent casing in its cylinder.

Over the next ninety minutes or so, Mounties searching Pickton's bedroom discovered several sex toys, including fur-lined handcuffs. Inside the headboard compartments of his bed, they found items of jewelry and a purse, and in another area they discovered a notebook containing the name of one of the women that the task force had placed on their list of missing women.

When Lew searched Pickton's cluttered office, with its untidiness, he noted that it was more orderly than other areas of the trailer. Phone books lay atop his desk, and many papers were strewn about the desktop as well. Directly behind the desk a cuckoo clock hung on the wall, right above a large corkboard that had items mostly related to the farm and the businesses neatly pinned to it, filling it to capacity. There were also a number of boxes stacked on the floor at one end of the room, and bags of clothing lay piled on the floor.

On the wall directly to the right of the desk, assuming that one were sitting or standing behind it, hung the head of what appeared to be a light-colored stallion. The head, which hung on the wall right above a watercooler, was well-preserved, complete with bridle, and appeared to have been stuffed and mounted by a professional taxidermist—or at least by someone who knew exactly what they were doing. An award ribbon of some type also hung from the right side of the horse's head. The horse's head appeared to be staring toward the desk, and appeared to the casual onlooker to be more of a macabre oddity than anything else. No one knew yet that the head belonged to Pickton's prized 1,400-pound horse, Spring Golden, which he had nicknamed "Goldie." The horse, they would learn, had to be put down after it had been kicked and injured by another horse.

At one point while going through the clutter in Pickton's office, Lew found an asthma inhaler inside a silver sports bag lying on the floor. It had been prescribed to Sereena Abotsway. Although the name on it did not mean anything to him, Lew nonetheless called it in to Cater, sitting in a car on the outside perimeter of the farm. Cater, recognizing Abotsway's name as one of the missing women, dutifully called his boss, Staff Sergeant Wayne Clary, and described the inhaler—along with the date that it had been prescribed, July 19, 2001, which was merely a few weeks before she disappeared in August of that year. The inhaler was a major find, an important piece of evidence, and both Cater and Clary recognized it as such. A few minutes after calling in the discovery, Clary ordered that the firearms search be called off immediately. Aside from leaving guards posted around the outside of the farm's property line, everyone was ordered to leave. Clary instructed Cater to tell Wells that he was not to deal with Pickton from that point forward. Wells was ordered not to speak to Pickton, and not to obtain his fingerprints.

Clary hurriedly scheduled a task force meeting for the next morning, and Wells was left with the distinct impression that his investigation was being formally turned over to Inspector Don Adam, who would then proceed in an entirely different manner after the task force obtained its own search warrant for the Pickton farm.

Part 2

Down on Robert Pickton's Farm

14

Robert Pickton spent the night and half of the next day in jail because of the evening raid on his farm by the RCMP. He was released from custody, however, at 1:30 P.M., Wednesday, February 6, 2002, after making bail. He went back to the farm and was soon confronted with yet another search warrant being served on him, this time by the Joint Missing Women Task Force. Although Pickton and his brother were allowed to feed some of the animals located in a barn near Dave Pickton's residence, but were otherwise not permitted to go onto the north end of the property, Robert Pickton seemed to take everything in stride. If he had been bothered by the RCMP news media announcement the next day, February 7, 2002, proclaiming that the task force had made a major break in the case, it did not show at that time. He did not even seem particularly bothered when the police sealed off his farm and set up a mobile command post near the old Dutch barn, which was near his own trailer. According to RCMP staff sergeant Mike Coyle, Pickton was told that he would be arrested for obstruction of justice if he did not comply and stay away from the farm's north side.

"I can tell you a search is being conducted on that property, and the search is being executed by the (Joint) Missing Women Task Force," declared Constable Catherine Galliford, spokesperson for the task force, at a hastily called news conference to inform the public of their break in the case. Galliford also indicated that Pickton was being investigated as a suspect in at least some of the cases of the missing prostitutes. The public was also informed about the earlier firearms search and that Pickton had been charged with three firearms violations, and that he had been released from jail.

An undercover police officer had been placed in the cell where Pickton had been kept overnight, but he had said little—certainly nothing that could have incriminated him in the deaths of any of the missing women. Following his release from jail, the RCMP's special surveillance unit tapped Pickton's telephone lines and tracked his movements, to no avail.

It was all big news, the type that the citizens of Vancouver had been waiting to hear for a long time. Many of the missing women's relatives were accepting the news as progress that was being made in the case, the type that should have been made long before now. While no one who had a missing loved one that was involved in the case was pleased by any of it, many felt a sense of relief now that the case seemed to be moving forward. They, likewise, experienced a sense of anxiousness and dread at what might turn up during the investigation. No one, after all, could possibly fully prepare himself or herself to receive news that a loved one had been murdered.

Although the press had effectively surrounded the Port Coquitlam property, they were not allowed inside the boundaries set up by the task force. No one on the task force, after getting a break of this magnitude, wanted to risk losing or contaminating any potential evidence during their processing of the pig farm, and as such followed the book completely. None of the investigators, at this point, had any idea what they would find, nor did they have a clue how long their search of the farm would take.

The views of Robert Pickton's farm that were being shown by the press showed a property that appeared to be dilapidated and, like many things in Pickton's life, was in a state of chaos and disorder. The photos being shown in newspapers and on television depicted trash that had been strewn here and there, and there were many broken-down vehicles of different types, as well as old appliances littering the muddy landscape. A NO TRESPASSING sign hung on one of the large metal gates, and another signed warned trespassers that the property was patrolled by a pit bull with AIDS. There was no mention of the purported 600-pound wild boar that ran on the property with the dogs, nor had anyone really hoped to encounter it, if it truly existed. Large groups of curious onlookers gathered outside the farm's perimeter throughout the day, and police mapped out the farm and took photographs from the air. They also brought two dogs trained in detecting corpses to the farm, and as part of their preparations to work during the evening hours, they set up generators and bright lighting systems to assist them at night.

When asked by the media how the task force would proceed with the search of Pickton's farm, Inspector Don Adam said: "This isn't TV. You don't go to a farm like this and start rushing around as if you're on some Easter-egg hunt looking for a hot piece of evidence."

No one at that point, not even Adam, envisioned that the search effort would last for twenty months, and ultimately would become the largest crime scene investigation in Canada's history. It would also become that country's most expensive criminal investigation.

At one point that day, February 7, searchers found a syringe with a hypodermic needle attached to it hidden in Robert Pickton's office. Filled with a blue liquid, it had been concealed inside Pickton's stereo console. That same day, when word began circulating about the unusual discovery, rookie Wells's informant, Scott Chubb, shed more light on the situation by recalling a conversation that he'd had with Willie Pickton sometime in the summer of 2000. He and Pickton, Chubb said, had been working on the farm, pulling nails from boards, when Chubb asked Pickton why Lynn Ellingsen no longer lived with Pickton inside his trailer.

"He said . . . that . . . she was stealing from him and that she was costing him a lot of money," Chubb told one of the RCMP officers.

Pickton's inference, it was believed, was that he was being blackmailed for something by Ellingsen, and at one point he had offered Chubb $1,000 to "speak" to her about the money that he claimed she was costing him. Of course, for that kind of money, Chubb understood that Pickton expected something more out of him than having Chubb merely talk to her— Pickton had taken the conversation to the next level by conversing with Chubb about a way that someone might be killed.

"'If you wanted to get rid of someone,'" Chubb said, paraphrasing Pickton, "'you could take a syringe of windshield wiper fluid or radiator fluid, and inject that person and kill them.'"

According to Chubb, Pickton had said that a "junkie" has track marks, and a new injection mark would likely go unnoticed because the cops and the medical examiner (ME) would conclude that the person had died from a drug overdose and likely would not look any further for a cause of death. Chubb believed that Pickton had Lynn Ellingsen in mind as a candidate for such an injection at the time the conversation occurred. Chubb said that he did not want to have any part in such a deadly scheme, however, and he denied being involved in killing anyone or disposing of bodies.

Early in the search effort for evidence at Robert Pickton's farm, the task force brought in RCMP sergeant Tim Sleigh, a crime scene investigation expert, to assist with the overwhelming task that was getting under way. Nearly seven years earlier, Sleigh had been involved in the search for evidence near Mission, British Columbia, where a neatly bisected skull had been found near the Lougheed Highway. Since Sleigh was just getting started with the work at Pickton's farm, he did not know, yet, that the skull found near Mission would eventually be a Jane Doe added to the task force list of missing women and tied to his current work. Never in his wildest dreams did he know to what extent his knowledge and experience would help in this case, nor did he know that his earlier investigation at Mission would be linked to the present case at Pickton's farm. Based on chilling discoveries that would be made at the farm, however, he would know soon enough.

After a few days to become familiarized with the farm and the overwhelming task that lay ahead, Sleigh, and many others, helped decide how the property would be searched for evidence. In addition to searching the interiors of all the buildings on the farm, the property was laid out or divided into 216 separate grids, each of which consisted of twenty square meters, and each was staked off and tagged. Each of the grids would eventually be processed in a manner that would include excavating the land until virgin ground or soil was hit. The nearly four hundred thousand cubic meters of soil would be examined by anthropology and archaeology students using soil-extracting machinery and conveyor belts to move the dirt to large sifting screens or devices where they would look for evidence, such as body parts, teeth, bones, bone fragments, hair, or any item that could be linked to a human.

Over the next twenty months, the task force would grow from a staff of thirty employees to 270. Even though they had experts of various types on their own staff, the task force would come to rely on the assistance of many outside experts as well, professionals such as an entomologist, a botanist, several pathologists, anthropologists, a radiologist, an anatomist, and a forensic odontologist. It would become an investigation unlike any that had ever been undertaken in North America.

As investigators canvassed the farm in preparation for the work that lay ahead, they observed sights that many would regard as chilling, such as the meat hook that dangled from a chain attached to the ceiling in the slaughterhouse, with the stainless-steel table next to it, and rotting pig carcasses left on the floor to decompose, creating a stench that was at times nearly unbearable. There were also knives and electric tools strewn about, some of which had either blood or rust on them. When they found cassette tapes by Cat Stevens, The Band, Creedence Clearwater Revival, and others, the cops knew that Willie apparently liked to listen to classic rock while he worked. Three chest freezers sat eerily in an adjacent pigpen area of the slaughterhouse, as if beckoning the investigators to look inside, challenging them to find the mother lode.

As much as Robert "Willie" Pickton was perceived by those who knew him as being loving and caring toward his barnyard animals, crime scene investigators made some horrific discoveries during the early days of the search. One pig's litter had died, and a pit bull dog was ravaging the dead piglets. Vancouver police constable Daryl Hetherington, who had been on the force for twenty-six years, found a group of pigs lying together trying to stay warm. One of them had a foot that was decaying, and none of them had any food or water. Hetherington brought food for them from her home, and gave them water. Many of the pigs ended up being destroyed, and the ones that were healthy enough to survive were removed and taken to another location, where they would be given proper care.

Although the crime scene investigators wore protective suits, gloves, and footwear in an effort to prevent evidence from becoming contaminated by their presence, they did not wear masks or breathing gear at first—not until some of the searchers began getting sick and health department employees came in and recommended that masks be worn.

As the police converged on Robert "Willie" Pickton's farm, working into the night and returning day after day for nearly two years, the plans that Willie made in the early 1990s, and began talking about to those who would listen of someday building a dream house with six bedrooms, a spiral staircase, and high-vaulted ceilings—his escape from life on the farm—disappeared, right along with the veil of mystery of what had happened to many of Vancouver's missing women. Although the police and the public did not know it yet, Willie had turned his vision of building a dream house into that of a charnel house, right there on the farm from which he had hoped to someday escape.

15

Robert Pickton has been described as "a man about farm." Neither suave nor debonair, he was in actuality a filthy little man who could not give a hoot about personal hygiene. Although certainly not a sociable type, Willie was once characterized by a neighbor as a "good-natured little bastard" who rarely spoke, unless spoken to first. The "little old pig farmer," as he sometimes referred to himself, walked somewhat hunched over, with his head slightly bent downward, and his oily, stringy hair, which had become sparse on top, served to accentuate his angular, bony face, rendering him quite unattractive. Willie clearly lost out when the gods handed out handsomeness and intelligence. Although he often did not get the punch line whenever someone told him a joke, and had difficulty keeping himself attuned when having conversations with workers on the farm, no one could definitively characterize him as being of lower intelligence. While his IQ of 86 did not make him the smartest tool in the shed, his level of intelligence was considerably higher than that of someone who was considered mentally retarded. His IQ was higher than 18.6 percent of the people his age that had been tested. While he was clearly lacking in the intelligence department, there was never any question that he knew right from wrong.

As task force officers and those who assisted them continued erecting fences around Robert Pickton's farm and put up a tent next to their mobile command post, relatives of many of the missing women began stopping by the farm. Even though they were not allowed behind the police barriers, many of them just wanted to see for themselves that something was finally being done regarding the missing women. It had taken a long time for the police to get to this point, and seeing was believing for many of those who had been skeptical of the police for so many years.

By February 8, 2002, several people also began voicing their thoughts about the investigation. Among them was Wayne Leng, a man who ran a missing-women Web site and started a grassroots effort to find prostitute Sarah de Vries. He spoke out about a man who called him in 1998 after he had set up a hotline for callers to provide tips about the missing women. The man, whom Leng identified as "Bill," had called in and said that Sarah was dead. Based on the information delivered by Leng, it seemed that Bill was most likely Bill Hiscox.

"This man, who couldn't give me any more identity than Bill, told me a prostitute he knew had been taken to a big pig farm at Port Coquitlam, where she had been badly assaulted," Leng told the Canadian media. "What's more, the prostitute had told Bill she had seen numerous items of women's clothing and pieces of women's identification all over the place. . . . We were all concerned because it didn't seem anybody wanted to take this guy seriously. We never heard whether they actually did searches of Willie's place or whatever . . . but we knew he had lots of land and he was fairly well-off, it seems."

Leng said that he had received other tips as well, and the tipsters had mentioned a pig farmer named Willie. Leng said that he had reported all of the information that he had received to the Vancouver police, but he never heard back from them and was left wondering why they did not follow up on the leads he had provided.

Leng said that posters that he had placed around the city of Sarah deVries had instigated a series of unsettling calls to his pager, which was the type that recorded short twenty-second messages. In one of the messages, a man's voice said: "Drop the case. Stop looking. Get off the case." In another, the same man said: "Sarah's dead."

"He said that he was with a man who killed her," Leng said. "And another time he said he killed her. . . . He also said, 'There's going to be a prostitute killed every Friday night.'"

These messages, like the ones from Bill Hiscox, had been reported years ago to the police. Because the messages had come from a pager, they were untraceable and little could be done with such scant information.

Leng said that the current search was overpowering him with feelings of both "dread and hope," and that although he wanted to know what had happened to deVries, he was fearful that he would learn that she died horribly.

"What are they going to find?" Leng asked. "How did these women die? Was it horrible? It probably was. . . . It's so hard when you don't know."

Although Willie had not shown much emotion or reaction at first about what was taking place at his farm, the next day, February 9, 2002, his lawyer, Peter Ritchie, announced that Willie was "shocked" and "flabbergasted" that he was being looked at as a person of interest by the Joint Missing Women Task Force. Ritchie, who represented Pickton in the case involving the stabbing of Wendy Eistetter, represented all three of the Pickton siblings in their varied business interests. He spoke on behalf of all of them.

"I've spoken to the sister and two brothers," Ritchie said. "They spoke to me yesterday. . . . The family is shocked by this and is trying to assist police."

Ritchie said that the family was ready and willing to offer the police the use of their farm equipment to assist them in their search. They were concerned, he said, about "underground digging, because there are wires and gas lines and various soils stored in a certain way."

Three days later, on Tuesday, February 12, 2002, Pickton family friend Gina Houston, thirty-four, a drug user and cancer patient, came out and spoke to the media on behalf of the family, according to information published on Crimezzz.net. Houston characterized Willie as a "nice, caring man" who enjoyed helping single mothers. She said that he would not hurt a soul, and that he had befriended many prostitutes because "he kind of feels sorry for them." She said that he was known to give them money to help them out.

Houston said that Willie would often give a prostitute $20 or more to purchase things like cigarettes, tampons, condoms, knowing that they would take the money and use it to buy drugs. The ones that he liked, she said, he would rather give them a few dollars if it kept them from working to support their drug addictions. According to Houston, the police had decided to focus on Willie Pickton regarding the missing women because of a drug addict who was known for making false accusations against the pig farmer.

"She's got a great personality, but as soon as she gets a little heroin or a little coke, and she can't get no more drugs, she goes right off," Houston said.

Houston described how she had been taken to the serious crimes unit because of accusations the woman had made. Describing the woman as a crackhead, Houston said that if Willie did not give the woman money for drugs, she would purportedly call up the police and tell them that Willie was slaughtering hookers and burying them on the farm.

"This chick watched him slaughter a few pigs, and she went and phoned, and she described in detail how he slaughters and skins them and cuts them," Houston said. "So she phones the police up and tells them that she watched him and I doing that there one night, and it was just a pig. She said it was one of the missing hookers from the Downtown Eastside."

Houston also mentioned the 1997 Wendy Eistetter incident involving Robert Pickton, indicating that Pickton had stabbed the woman in self-defense. In her opinion, Pickton had gotten a raw deal, even though prosecutors had dropped the charges against him.

"They dropped the charges against him," she said, "because all of the stab wounds on him were in the back. He defended himself and ended up stabbing her."

Also by February 12, 2002, the task force, without saying why, had expanded its scope to include the rendering plant near the Downtown Eastside, where they had learned that Pickton had taken pig remains for disposal for more than two decades. Also without saying why, the task force asked relatives of some of the missing women to provide DNA samples.

"There are forensic experts, major crime investigators, family consultation experts, and a variety of other subject experts adding their own knowledge to this case," Detective Scott Driemel said. "Investigations of this magnitude are a complex and often shadowy web of interconnected issues and bits of information. As we discover yet another link in the web, it can change the nature of what we already know. Hopefully, we will soon see the full picture."

According to Driemel, the task force has been inundated with telephone calls since installing a special phone line for tips. More than four hundred calls were logged during the first few days of the phone line going live, which made it impossible for the police to provide immediate responses.

"The joint task force has assigned three dedicated staff to review the tips, index them according to subject matter and other details, and pass the information on to investigators," Driemel added in a media message directed at the public. "They are asking the public to be patient. Every call is taken seriously . . . but it would be fair to not expect a call back right away. Please, if you do call and leave a tip, let it go for a little while before calling again, because we're getting the lines plugged by repeat callers."

Driemel said that some of the tips had provided significant information, and task force investigators had updated some family members of the missing women.

"Some family members have told us that they would rather not hear every specific detail about what's going on," he said. "Others feel some knowledge about our search may help their grieving process."

At one point a psychologist, Richard Dopson, who

had counseled a number of underage prostitutes who worked the Downtown Eastside came out and publicly talked about the investigation and the families of missing women who had been visiting the farm, watching the work that was going on from a distance. He said that family members were being drawn to the site in the hope that some form of closure was close at hand. Many relatives of the missing women had made a memorial of sorts outside the fence, placing flowers and photographs of loved ones on makeshift shelves in front of yellow police crime-scene tape.

"Here's a place that they can go to, feel sad, talk it out, and tell their stories," Dopson said. "There's never been a place for them to do that. . . . They're exposing themselves now. . . . If it turns out all for naught, this could be devastating."

Even though the cops were keeping their cards facedown, it did not take a rocket scientist to figure out the direction in which they were moving.

16

Vancouver residents continued closely watching the Robert Pickton pig farm investigation as it unfolded. Investigators had focused much of their attention on Pickton's filthy trailer as they searched for evidence. RCMP sergeant Margaret Kingsbury had been assigned to go over the trailer with a fine-tooth-comb, and she had worked inside it nearly every day since the task force had taken over the farm, searching for any shred of evidence that might support one or more murder charges against Pickton.

By February 14, 2002, Kingsbury and other investigators had removed several DNA samples from the trailer, and had begun asking women who had been to Pickton's trailer to come forward and provide DNA samples to help the investigators in their effort to differentiate or eliminate people whose DNA did not match up with that which had so far been found. Police were still publicly saying that Pickton was only a person of interest in the case of the missing women, and they avoided media questions about whether Willie's trailer was used for parties, which were held on the farm, and whether prostitutes had been brought there regularly.

In the meantime, Kingsbury and others found numerous items of a feminine nature in nearly every room of Robert Pickton's trailer. They removed a woman's purse, a black boot, and makeup inside a closet; there was also a plastic storage tub with a variety of women's makeup inside it as well. They also found inside the closet a woman's black shirt, a woman's leather jacket, and two tubes of lipstick. Perfume, a hairbrush, and a mishmash of other items were removed from his nightstand and adjacent areas of his bedroom, and a black jacket was taken from the foot area of his bed. Although the investigators did not know to whom all of the female items being found inside Pickton's trailer belonged, each discovery was nearly as chilling as the last, considering the fact that they had earlier found an asthma inhaler that had been prescribed to Sereena Abotsway.

They also removed a pillowcase from Pickton's laundry room, hoping that it would be a good source for DNA. When they more thoroughly went through his office, where Abotsway's inhaler had been found inside the silver sports bag, they found women's running shoes, black high heels, and two hypodermic syringes.

At one point during the first two weeks of searching, detectives began going through garbage outside Pickton's trailer. It was not long before they found three more asthma inhalers prescribed to Sereena Abotsway, dated July 16, 2001. They would later discover that those inhalers, and the one found inside Pickton's office that was dated July 19, 2001, were the last four inhalers that had been prescribed to her—she disappeared a short time later. According to one of the officers, the name on the label for all four inhalers was Sereena Abotsway.

Nearby a group of investigators began going through

Pickton's old motor home. As filthy as his trailer, if not more so, the motor home was cluttered with empty bottles, and cigarette butts were all over the place. It was musty inside, as several articles of clothing and other items had begun to mildew. Officers observed blood smudges on the bathroom door, on a kitchen countertop and the cupboard above it, and on the refrigerator. There was a trail of blood spots that led to the front seat area, where blood evidence was present on the console between the two seats. It appeared that someone who was badly bleeding had been dragged out of the motor home.

The blood spots, it seemed at this juncture, had originated from a mattress inside the motor home. The mattress was heavily stained with blood. When they flipped it over, they found what appeared to be a bloody handprint on the other side. An expert on blood spatter said that he believed "bloodletting" had occurred there. Everyone agreed that there was certainly no shortage of DNA evidence anywhere on the farm—the challenge would be matching it to a victim.

After finding the asthma inhalers that had belonged to Sereena Abotsway, as well as all of the blood evidence, the syringe filled with a blue liquid, the dildo on the end of a handgun, among other things, the task force took their case to prosecutors and asked that Pickton be charged with murder. The Crown, however, told the task force it needed additional evidence before charges could be brought against Pickton. They hoped that DNA evidence would be their ticket.

It turned out that their hope was soon realized as the effort of DNA collection from relatives of the missing women paid off. By Friday, February 22, 2002, crime lab analysts had determined that the DNA of Sereena Abotsway and Mona Wilson were found on Pickton's farm. The black shirt found in Pickton's bedroom closet was also linked to Abotsway. Mona Wilson's DNA was found inside the motor home, and on the tip of the dildo that was attached to the loaded .22-caliber revolver found inside Pickton's trailer. Wilson's blood was not present on the mattress that contained the bloodstains, nor did it contain DNA that could be linked to anyone.

Nonetheless, the task force went back to the Crown with their new findings and again asked that Pickton be charged with murder. This time the Crown agreed, and later that same day Pickton was located at a demolition site in Steveston, part of the Vancouver suburb of Richmond, where he was arrested and brought to the Surrey RCMP substation and jail. He was placed inside a cell with an undercover police officer, who pretended to be his cellmate. The next day Robert Pickton was charged with two counts of first-degree murder in the deaths of Sereena Abotsway and Mona Wilson. Abotsway and Wilson were two of the last three women to disappear in Vancouver in 2001, at least insofar as this investigation was concerned.

RCMP constable Cate Galliford said that as the investigation progressed, additional people may face charges.

"We do have hundreds of potential suspects," Galliford said at a news conference announcing Pickton's arrest. "As the investigation unfolds and we continue to follow up on tips, we may start focusing on other potential suspects."

While Galliford had kept her statement short and to the point, the talk of additional potential suspects created an additional aura of mystery surrounding the already bizarre case. It was unclear whether she was just blowing smoke, or whether her remarks had been made as an effort to smoke possible witnesses out of the woodwork, people who knew things but had been afraid to talk. But now, it seemed possible that such people might begin coming forward with information out of fear of being charged with crimes right alongside Pickton. Only time would tell.

17

Robert Pickton settled quietly into his ten-by-ten cinder block cell at 3:57 P.M. on February 22, 2002, after being led into it by an RCMP officer. The walls were beige, and two single bunks were joined together, each against separate walls, and formed an L-shape. They were hard and uncomfortable, making the otherwise austere cell even more unpleasant. A toilet was situated against a third wall. When Pickton was placed in the cell, a man was lying on the right bunk. Dirty and unkempt, Pickton took the bunk on the left, unaware that the man across from him was an undercover officer, who had been placed there to gather information. Pickton, dressed in a dark-colored jogging suit, looked somewhat surprised when his cellmate jumped up from his bunk and yelled at the officer who had placed Pickton in the cell with him.

"Hey! Where's my f***ing lawyer?" yelled the cellmate. "I pay my f***ing lawyer!"

The police officer told him that his lawyer was on his way to see him, but he did not know precisely when he would arrive.

"F***ing yeah! I don't f***ing share cells here," exclaimed the cellmate. "What's going on?"

Pickton, who had been seated on the edge where his bunk connected with his cellmate's, got up during the commotion and walked to the toilet, where he urinated.

"F***ing bastards," his cellmate said as Pickton finished his business at the commode. "I'm f***ing waitin' for my lawyer to call."

"So, what are you in here for?" Pickton asked.

"Hey?"

"What are you in here for?" Pickton repeated, rubbing one of his dirty hands against his untrimmed facial hair.

"Well, for my health," the cellmate responded flippantly. "Yeah, it's f***ing bullshit."

"What's your charges?" Pickton persisted.

"F*** me. It's f***ing warrants from back east."

As he was explaining to Pickton that the warrants were from six months earlier, a jail officer brought Pickton a thin mattress and a blanket. Pickton laid it out on his bunk, and then made a makeshift pillow out of his blanket. When the guard left, Pickton began speaking to his cellmate again.

"That happens," Pickton said of the warrants. "F***. I can't believe this here."

"What's up?" the cellmate asked.

Pickton explained how he had been arrested upon leaving a demolition site.

"Why they want to f***ing throw you in jail for driving?" said the cellmate. "Not where I come from."

"Oh yeah, I know," Pickton said. "They said they got attempted murder, I got murder charges against me. Two murder charges."

"You?"

"Well, f*** me," Pickton said. "F***ing a working

kinda guy. I've been working all the time, f***. Anyways, they're trying, and I don't know what's goin' on," Pickton said.

He lay down on his bunk and covered his face with one of his arms.

"They got to f***ing prove it, too," his cellmate responded.

"No, they don't have to prove anything. They don't have to prove nothing," Pickton said.

Pickton's cellmate told him that the authorities could not keep him in jail if they did not have anything on him. They needed evidence to hold him for very long.

"They can set you up. They can set you up. They can set you up," Pickton repeatedly said.

"You think?"

"F***ing right. These are cops, and dirty at that," Pickton said.

"Can't trust a cop, man, believe that," his cellmate offered.

"They got me up for murder one, two counts," Pickton said. "And I know nothing about it," Pickton said.

"I wouldn't worry about it then."

Pickton laughed at his cellmate's suggestion.

"Easy to say," Pickton said. "Easy to say."

"Hey, f***ing relax."

Pickton told his cellmate that he did not do what he was being charged with, and his cellmate advised him not to worry about it then. He predicted that Pickton would be out of jail before he knew it.

"Maybe, maybe," Pickton responded. "Maybe never, either."

"Won't you get a good lawyer?"

"Yeah, but that's not the answer," Pickton said.

"No?"

"Lawyers can only do so much," Pickton continued. "The news media and everything else on my back."

"F***ing news media don't give a shit about you," his cellmate said.

"I know that. That's what I says, they might be on my back, like yesterday," Pickton said.

"Why the f*** would they be on your back? Am I f***ing sharing my f***ing bunk here with a celebrity?"

"Yeah, I'm on top of the world," Pickton said sarcastically. "I'm just a plain old pig farmer," Pickton said.

"Pig farmer," repeated the cellmate. "So you're that f***ing guy that . . . Ah, yeah, sure you are. F***ing pig farmer."

"You must have heard about me from the paper," Pickton said. "Everybody knows about me, right?"

"I heard something about . . . a place called . . . ," the cellmate trailed off, feigning that he could not recall the location.

"Port Coquitlam," Pickton offered matter-of-factly.

"F***, is that it?" the cellmate asked. "*F*** . . .* you're a celebrity, man."

Pickton, who was by now lying faceup on his bunk, laughed at his cellmate's characterization of him.

"I could f***ing cry," Pickton responded. "You know what? I was supposed to be there (on the farm) till age forty. I'm fifty now, and I'm buried."

"Age of forty. What's that?" his cellmate asked, attempting to elicit information.

Pickton repeated what he had said about being fifty years old, and being buried. In reality he was fifty-three, and his plans had been to be free of the farm by age forty. He said that it was the farm that had buried him.

"Maybe they got f***ing nothing," his cellmate said.

"I'm just too big—me up so high," Pickton said as he sat up in his bunk. "I'll fall like a ton of lead."

After a few moments of silence, Pickton laughed.

"I'm a legend already," Pickton pondered aloud.

"Yeah, you're a f***ing pig farmer," his cellmate said. "That's all I am."

After a few moments had passed, Pickton told his cellmate that his hometown was now being referred to as "Pork Coquitlam" because of him, an obvious reference to the fact that people were saying that he had fed humans to his pigs. His comments had brought laughter from his cellmate.

"I heard of mad cow disease—I heard this, I heard that," Pickton said. "Now you . . . now you got f***ing pigs eating people."

"That's funny," his cellmate said, laughing.

A short time later, Pickton told his cellmate that there were too many cops at his farm.

"Yeah . . . they can't even find their ass with both hands, they're so f***ing stupid," his cellmate said. "Look at O.J., remember that f***ing trial?"

"O.J. Simpson?"

"There you go. F***, there's a f***ing great example for you. Where's he today?"

"I don't know whatever happened to him," Pickton said quietly. "Is he okay?"

"He's a f***ing . . . free man," the cellmate said. "Like I say, cops can screw things up so bad."

"F***ing pig farm," Pickton said, reflecting on his situation as he lay on his back and stared at the ceiling. "Over a f***ing gun. Now I'm up for murder. Murder, on two counts."

Pickton and his cellmate each lay in silence in their bunks for what must have been several minutes. The silence was broken at 4:30 P.M. when an officer came into the cell and told Pickton that his lawyer was there to see him.

"Follow me and we'll put you in a private room," the RCMP officer said.

Pickton did not return to his cell until 5:21 P.M. He lay on his bunk and said nothing until dinner arrived. The evening meal consisted of a bowl of brown beans, two pieces of bread, and a cup of coffee. Not being a coffee drinker, Pickton gave his cup to his cellmate. He told the cellmate that he did not drink coffee or alcohol, smoke, or use drugs.

"Come on now, nobody's that f***ing straight," his cellmate said.

"I'm a workin' boy," he responded, sounding as if he were beginning to feel sorry for himself. "And here I got charged for murder."

Although he complained to his cellmate that his food tasted "shitty," Pickton, sitting cross-legged on his bunk, nonetheless ate it until it was finished. At one point during the meal, Pickton told his cellmate that he had been charged with attempted murder in 1997.

"Really," said his roommate, sounding interested. "What the f*** did you do for that?"

"The problems is I got knifed," Pickton said, referring to the Wendy Eistetter incident without mentioning any names. "I got thirty-four hundred dollars on me, and the bitch wanted my money. I got slashed from here, my chest, across my throat, through my tongue, right through my bottom jaw," he said, motioning to the various body locations with his hands. "Took the whole top of my tongue right off."

"No shit!"

"And across the back," Pickton added. "And I got an attempted murder charge and went down to the police station. You see my testimony . . . was true. Hers wasn't."

He explained that the case had not gone to court.

"I don't f***ing understand how did you get charged if she f***ing stuck you," his cellmate said.

Having taken off his shoes, Pickton answered that he guessed he had been charged because he was a male. "Now I got a murder charge, two murder charges."

"What the f***. Well, you beat the one, you know what I'm saying?"

"But I haven't been in jail," Pickton said.

"You'll f***ing walk," the cellmate said. "Kinda like Teflon man. You can't make that stuff stick to you."

Pickton explained that his brother had advised him not to go near the work site because the cops would know where to find him. But he had not listened, and had gone there anyway.

"You should have f***ing flew, man, jump on a plane," his cellmate said. "F***. I'm sure someone would f***ing throw you a few bucks to go—"

"Oh, I got no problem there," Pickton said. "Money, everything else."

"You got money? F***! You could have just f***ing bought a plane ticket."

Pickton acknowledged that he could have left the area, but he admitted that he would not have known what to do.

"Yeah, but you gotta f***ing cover your own ass, I'm telling you," his cellmate said.

"That's what my brother said to me," Pickton said.

"Well, it sounds like your brother's a pretty smart guy, been around awhile."

"Yeah."

"He knows how business is done," the cellmate said.

"He warned me," Pickton responded, feeling sorry for himself again. "Now the farm buries you. . . . I worked hard. . . . No, I'm screwed, tattooed and nailed to the cross, and now I'm a mass murderer."

"Hey?"

"Now they're coming after me, f***ing pig man, because they says pigs . . . ate people now," Pickton said.

"Since when?" the cellmate asked.

After some silence Pickton changed the subject somewhat and began explaining to his cellmate how he did not have a computer and that he had never been on the Internet. He indicated that he was not prepared "for the modern stuff," and indicated that he was concerned about the past but wanted things to be "the way it used to be." He said that his crime was being "stupid" and not being "up with the times."

After lamenting his current problems a bit more, Pickton, lying on his bunk and staring at the ceiling, asked if the light was ever turned off. The conversation eventually turned toward the camera in the ceiling, which Pickton apparently had not noticed.

"There's a f***ing camera," his cellmate said.

"Is that a camera?" Pickton asked as he stared at the ceiling.

"Oh f***, yeah," his cellmate responded. "F***in gotta watch us somehow. You think those lazy guards are gonna get off their fat asses and walk around all the time?"

"So that's a camera," Pickton said.

"You sound surprised," his cellmate said, laughing at Pickton's apparent naiveté.

"I didn't know that."

"No?"

"I thought it was an ornament," Pickton said.

"Come on, you're f***ing with me."

"Nope."

"They always have these in f***ing cells," his cellmate said. "They get a camera here with a plastic thing over it—like a clear plastic, you know?"

Pickton stood up and walked beneath the camera so that he could see it more clearly. He stared at it for several seconds, much like a child would do when examining something that he was not familiar with.

"I'm be God-darned," he said. "I had a good life."

"So times were good?" his cellmate asked.

Pickton seemed like he was in deep thought for a few moments.

"Those street people are wasting their lives away," Pickton finally said. "They throw their whole life away . . . doing nothing."

"F***ing stealing from you and me is what they're doing," his cellmate said, "so they can f***ing stick a needle in their arm. F***ing trash, that's all it is. I've worked hard."

"I've worked hard all my life," Pickton chimed.

"You don't get to where you are, from sitting on your ass f***ing living off the street," his cellmate added.

"That's right—very, very true," Pickton agreed. "And here I'm in jail for murder, murder one."

"Yeah."

Part 3

Interrogation

18

Shortly after Robert Pickton's first night in jail on murder charges, RCMP staff sergeant Bill Fordy interviewed Vancouver's prime suspect in the disappearances and murders of that city's missing women. The interview occurred on Saturday, February 23, 2002, at the RCMP detachment offices in Surrey, located just outside Vancouver. The dialogue that follows consists of Fordy's first interview with Pickton, much of which would be presented at Pickton's trial nearly five years later. All in all, Pickton would be grilled for more than eleven hours. Fordy would hand off the interrogation at one point to Constable Dana Lillies, and at another point to Inspector Don Adam, who, at that time, was head of the Joint Missing Women Task Force.

The interview room was small. Its furnishings consisted of a simple black desk chair, which had been placed in one corner of the room, next to two plants. A small desk was situated next to the chair, and on top of it sat a small television and a bottle of water. A video camera had been placed in the room on a tripod, its lens directed toward the chair between the two plants. Fordy was seated in a second chair that faced the other one from across the desk, his back to the door, when Pickton entered the room. He sat in the designated chair across from Fordy, with his hands clasped across his stomach, and stared at the police officer. Pickton looked like hell, his hair stringy and greasy. Fordy stood up and introduced himself, offered Pickton a glass of juice, and told the suspect that he could call him by his first name, Bill. Then he asked Pickton if he could call him Rob. Pickton nodded his approval but said nothing at first.

"Everything I say to you is recorded—that's for your protection and mine—a couple of things I wanted to make sure you understand," Fordy began. "Rob, I'm not going to be mean or yell at you or get physical. I'm going to treat you with the respect you deserve, and I'm going to treat you with dignity—because if I was in that chair, that's how I'd want to be treated. And no one else is going to hurt you, or get physical with you, I promise you that. I am a police officer and I have a job to do. You were arrested yesterday for murder, for a couple of murders."

Fordy confirmed with Pickton that he had been arrested at the demolition work site, and charged with two murders.

"That's what they say, yup," Pickton responded.

Fordy explained that charges had been laid against Pickton, and that detectives had done a thorough job, so far, in the investigation. As Fordy explained that Pickton had been arrested for two murders, he also explained that detectives were investigating the disappearances of at least fifty sex trade workers. The comment brought forth a laugh from Pickton.

"Okay . . . I see you laughing there. Let me clarify something, okay?" Fordy asked. "You haven't been charged with fifty murders."

"I guess not," Pickton replied, again laughing.

Fordy told Pickton that there was evidence to support the charges, and confirmed with Pickton that he understood.

"All right," Fordy said. "Based on the way the investigation is going, and the way that the evidence is coming in, you're also suspected of being involved in the disappearance and murders of the other girls."

Pickton laughed again and looked away from his questioner.

"When you're under investigation, I have to tell you that . . . you're being investigated for 'em," Fordy said. "I didn't say you've been charged with those murders. I know that yesterday you consulted with your lawyer—last night, I guess."

"Uh-huh."

"Your conversations with your lawyer are privileged—you don't have to tell me anything that was said," Fordy stated. "I can't imagine how you feel. You've probably got a ton of questions. Lawyer gave you some advice."

"No kidding," Pickton responded. After a short pause he said: "The advice from my lawyer is don't talk to the police."

Fordy told Pickton that he wasn't there to bad-mouth his lawyer, and insisted that it was his job to obtain the truth during the interview and the investigation. Obviously, he was hopeful that Pickton would tell him what had been going on for the past several years with regard to the missing women and Pickton's role in their disappearances. He reiterated that Pickton had been charged with two murders, and wanted to make certain that Pickton understood the seriousness of the investigation, as well as the charges that had been leveled against him so far. Fordy again told Pickton that, based on the investigation and the manner in which the evidence was being uncovered, he was suspected of being involved in the disappearances and murders of the other girls. Fordy's statement merely brought forth another laugh from the pig farmer.

"I know that might seem humorous," Fordy stated matter-of-factly. "There's just one thing that I want you to know. In Canada, there are some things we have to do by law. . . . You don't have to talk to me."

"Right."

"Because the law considers me a person of authority," Fordy continued. "This is a criminal matter. It's very, very serious. As a police officer, I can get subpoenaed to court. . . . I've been in court in different provinces, different towns, and I can give evidence on what's gone on between you and I."

"I don't have anything to hide."

"Anything you say to me can be given as evidence. But you don't have to talk to me. You're being investigated for up to fifty murders. In your own words, can you describe to me what that means?"

"What that means to me," Pickton said, "is it's hogwash. That's all I can really tell you. I can't say much. I don't know nothing about this. It could be a setup. I've got nothing to say, because I know nothing. You're here to ask me questions—I'm just a workingman. That's what I am. . . . It's a little far-fetched, isn't it?"

"Well, we're gonna talk about that later, Rob," Fordy said. "What I'm gonna do is go through . . . a lot of this investigation. As you can imagine, Rob, this investigation is huge, it's massive."

Pickton laughed again.

Fordy then told him that he was as well-known as the pope, but Pickton did not respond immediately. When he did speak, he told Fordy that he'd been set up, and that he had done nothing wrong. When Fordy asked him why he thought he was there, interviewing him, Pickton sat quietly for several seconds.

"I'm mind baffling," he finally responded. "And I'm just a working guy . . . just a plain working guy, that's all I am. . . . It's a little far-fetched, isn't it? Well, I'm just a pig man, that's all I got to say," he added, chuckling.

Fordy told Pickton that he was not joking when he told him that he was as big as the pope, which brought forth a few more snickers from the murder suspect.

"What's the worst thing that ever happened to you?" Fordy asked.

"Being stabbed, I guess, back in '97. I'm a bad dude. Name of the game, I guess. . . . I'm screwed. Nailed to the cross," Pickton said.

"If I said, describe yourself, how would you do that?"

"We're the same guys . . . same show, same shoes, just different sizes in suits. We're actually the same."

"That's on the outside," Fordy said. "Tell me about you on the inside, Rob. What kind of person are you on the inside?"

"We eat the same food, use the same toilet, same washroom, drink the same water, everything else," Pickton said. "I have pigs. Pigs are brought up for meat. That's what animals are for."

"Um-hmm."

"I'm a bad dude," Pickton said.

"Um-hmm, yeah," Fordy said.

"But that's life, life goes on," Pickton said. "We're only here today, we're not here tomorrow, we're not here forever."

"You sound a lot like me," Fordy said. "I have a line that I say to a lot of my friends—life is not a rehearsal."

"Yeah," Pickton agreed. "Another thing is, if I could turn time around, change a few things, whatever I did wrong—but I don't think I ever did anything wrong— I wouldn't change my life very much."

"My mom died of cancer." Fordy had just thrown the statement out there, apparently in an effort to elicit comments from Pickton about his own mother. He knew that Pickton had been described as having been close to his mother. The tactic seemed to work.

"My mother did, too," Pickton responded.

"Really? How long ago?" Fordy had decided to stay with the mother approach.

"1979. April first. It was a spreading cancer."

"How old were you?"

Pickton responded that he didn't know. Staying on the subject of Pickton's mother, Fordy asked him her name.

"Louise."

"How did you two get along when you were a child?"

"Two peas in a pod."

"Close?

"*Yesssssssssssssssss,*" Pickton said, dragging out the response in a long breath that sounded like steam escaping from a kettle of boiling water. "Yeah."

"Do you miss your mom?" Fordy asked.

"Well, do you?" Pickton shot back without answering the question.

"I do, yeah."

"Well, yeah," Pickton finally answered.

Fordy then talked about himself for a while, and told Pickton that he had been a hard worker and that he had taken care of his brothers, his sister, and himself. He credited his mother for his strong family values, and afterward asked Pickton, who did he respect most in the world?

"Who do I respect most in the world? My mother."

Responding to Fordy's questions, Pickton said that

he liked his mother because she was a strong woman—she had a strong mind and a strong heart, he said. He added that she was a hardworking woman. Pickton explained that he was taking care of his mother when she died, and that it had taken four months for her to die.

"Were you with her when she died?" Fordy asked.

"I don't know where I was."

Pickton said that his father had died on January 1, 1978, from old age. He had gotten along well with him as a child.

"Old age is a good way to die, isn't it?" Fordy asked.

"Yeah."

"How do you want to die?"

"I don't know. Old age, probably."

"Like your dad."

"Yeah . . . there's a reason for everything."

"Why do you think you're here today?" Fordy asked.

"I don't know. . . . Life is not a rehearsal." Pickton laughed again.

"What's the best thing that ever happened to you?"

"Don't know," Pickton said. "Work. I went on holiday once. Kansas City, Missouri. I had a return ticket and cashed it in there. It was in 1974. . . . I had a chance to work for forty bucks an hour. Said, no, I'm here on holiday. I was twenty-four at the time. I went to Chicago. Chicago's a dirty town. A lot of blacks, not that I'm prejudiced or anything. You had to be careful at night. There was no gas."

He explained the difficulty of the gas situation, as best he could. His visit to the United States had occurred during the Arab oil embargo of 1973 and 1974, when OPEC nations, as well as Syria and Egypt, refused to ship oil to nations that had supported Israel in its ongoing Yom Kippur War, also known as the Ramadan

War and the October War, a conflict Israel had with Syria, Egypt, and Iraq.

"Get just two or three dollars of gas," Pickton said. "The gas wars were on. I was gone six and a half weeks. Got engaged. But she couldn't leave her job, and I couldn't leave mine. I had to get back to the farm. She's probably married off now . . . kids. . . . It was a long time ago. Yup, she's probably married off. But I had to get back to the farm. That's life."

The remembrance of his trip seemed to set off a flow of information. Pickton went on to describe how he and his former fiancée, Connie, had become pen pals. After discussing his fiancée for a bit longer, Pickton and Fordy somehow got onto the subject of food.

"I don't eat vegetables," Pickton said.

"Just meat?"

"Yup."

"What's your favorite meat?"

"Pork."

Pickton and Fordy both laughed at Pickton's response. After they stopped laughing, Fordy turned the subject of the conversation back to Pickton's trip to the United States.

"How long were you down in the U.S.?"

"Five weeks."

"When did you get engaged?"

"I got engaged right away. She was tall. Five-eleven, blond, one hundred forty pounds, nice body, nice eyes."

"You guys were together for five weeks and then she couldn't come up?"

"Her parents wouldn't let her come up," Pickton explained. "She was supposed to come and never did. . . . She worked there. I had to run the farm. . . . Well, shit happens."

"What did the two of you do when you were there?"

"It was Pontiac, Michigan. We'd go here and there. Out. We weren't into the bar scene."

"Did you tell your mom about Connie?"

"Yeah, it was all right, it was cool. She was supportive of the relationship."

"What about your dad?"

"Dad was always on the go, keeping the farm going."

"What did he think about Connie?"

"Whatever. I never really talked to Dad."

"Do you have a picture of your mom?"

"No, I don't have any."

"Do you look like her?"

Pickton shook his head, gesturing that he did not. He said that his sister, Linda, looked more like their mother.

"Tell me about Linda."

"Not much to say. She went to a Catholic school and grew up. That's about it. We were never close. She liked the high life. To go out, go here, go there, she likes school, university, everything. Myself, I have no problem with it. It's good, but some people didn't make it through school. Some people can't."

"I wish I'd gone on to university," Fordy added. "What did she take?"

"Law, I think. Lawyer or a Realtor."

"Making tons of money, I bet."

"That's her own prerogative."

"What did she do on the farm?"

"Nothing. . . . She's just herself. That's what she wants, so no big deal. I got no problem with that."

They talked about Pickton's brother, Dave, for a while, and Pickton agreed that he enjoyed his brother's company.

"Who's your best friend?" Fordy asked at one point.

"Girlfriend? Boyfriend? I have lots of friends . . .

everybody. I don't hold nothing back from nobody. If they're in a jam, I help 'em out. Anything got stolen, stolen stuff off me, I'd go right back and help 'em out again. Maybe someday they'll help me. Even if they gonna steal from me."

"What goes around comes around."

"You got it."

Pickton said that one of the most important qualities that he looks for in a friend is that of honesty.

"What do you like in your friends?" Fordy questioned.

"It doesn't matter. . . . I don't knock anybody down."

"That's a good quality to have."

"Thank you. Because someday you expect the same in return. Even if they steal from you," Pickton responded.

They continued small talk for some time about stealing and why people steal from each other, but Pickton reiterated that he has always been able to overlook such a flaw in people.

"If you haven't got money out there, if you don't have money to buy it, you don't need it," Pickton said. "But otherwise that, like I says, we all wake up in the morning, go to sleep at night . . . always in the same bed. . . . Someday you don't wake up . . . but the sun still comes up."

"It doesn't come up on you, that's the only difference," Fordy offered.

"No, not necessarily," Pickton countered. "It still comes up if I'm ten feet under. It's still gonna come up . . . it's still gonna come up. My mom's gonna shine."

"Now, you said to me the worst thing that ever happened to you was getting stabbed," Fordy said, obviously trying to change the subject.

"Yeah, that wasn't the worse thing."

"What was the worst thing?"

"Tore apart by two pigs."

"Tell me about that."

"It was '75. I was trying to breed a sow. She was in heat. I got the boar in there to breed it. The boar didn't want any part of it. I brought another boar in. They started fighting. Just about killed each other. Then they turned on me. Ripped me up. I went down to the hospital. Was in July 1975. Went to the hospital. Got to get sewn up. They got me half sewed up and asked me what happened. I said I was mauled by wild boars. They took the stitches apart and said we can't do anything for you. Said go home, rest. I said I can't, I got to farm. I had to use my hands to push my knee down to activate the break on the tractor. I had people coming in to look after the animals. I couldn't get off the tractor—my leg all swolled up. It was so hot. I took my clothes off. Pus was running down my leg. I stayed on the tractor. Got burnt. Heat from the wound. Heat from the tractor. Heat from the sky. It hurt just to cough. Another time . . . I got mauled by a big Angus bull. Summer 1978. That was a scary feeling one time there. See the grass coming off the ground right in front of your feet. But those are the good old days. I got scars. I couldn't work for three to four days that time. I was all black-and-blue. I got crushed under my truck once. I was working on a hubcap. Thought I had it on safety—guess I didn't. Come down and crushed my hard hat. I barely got out."

"Tell me about your horse," Fordy said. He seemed to be focusing his line of inquiry on things that mattered to Pickton, and at times appeared to be attempting to arouse the murder suspect's emotions.

"I bought her in . . . 1977. I killed it December 21, 1981. First day of winter. Reason? It had hurt itself."

Pickton went on to explain that a horse, an

eight-hundred-pound mare that belonged to another person, had kicked his horse, a 1,400-pound stallion, in the back leg, and that it would have cost $5,000 to get it the veterinary attention it needed to mend its leg, but it would have been a gamble. He explained that he couldn't actually kill the horse himself, but instead had a veterinarian destroy it.

"You can't baby it," he added. "If it twists its leg the wrong way, it's broken again. December 21, 1981, five thirty-five P.M. I tried to get another horse—nothing."

"What was its name?"

"Goldie."

"Fourteen-hundred-pound stallion," Fordy said. "I bet you never dreamt it could get hurt by those little things."

"Eight-hundred-pound fillies. But again, it was an accident. The best go first."

19

"How did you get into pig farming?" Fordy asked as the interview with Robert Pickton continued. "Your dad?"

"Yeah, many years ago," Pickton responded. "Many years ago. 1957 to 1958. Opened the first butcher shop. Twenty-four twenty-six Pitt River Road. That's where the house came from."

He explained that his mother had been pregnant with his brother, Dave, when his family had opened their first butcher shop. He said that his father's uncle Clifford lived with them at the time. He explained that he was close to Clifford, who had been hit by a drunk driver when Pickton was a little older, but he wasn't sure about his age at the accident's time. He indicated that as a result of the accident involving his uncle, he didn't drink alcohol.

"I got drunk once," Pickton clarified. "I was twenty-four years old. On my birthday. Maybe twenty-three. I had seven screwdrivers. I said I wanted orange juice. I said that's pretty strong orange juice. I wanted to drive and they said you've had seven drinks. I said orange juice. They said orange juice and vodka. I felt a bit light-headed. When I was four, my mother said, 'Do you want to smoke? Be a man.' She gave me a cigar. She made me smoke a cigar. That's the last . . . I ever had."

"Who taught you to butcher pigs?" Fordy asked.

Pickton described a family friend, and said that he, Pickton, had been thirteen when he first learned how to slaughter and butcher a pig. Following a long pause, he began talking about the calf that he had purchased at an auction, at about the same time.

"I got a calf," he continued. "I said I'm keeping this calf for the rest of my life. I slept with that calf. I was twelve or thirteen. Then I came home from school and the calf was gone. 'Where's my calf? Where's my calf?' Dad says maybe it went for a walk around back. No way. They kill animals down there. No way. I told him (the calf) not to go down there. They butcher animals down there. I looked all over, everywhere else. Maybe it did go down there. Maybe I'll go around back. I'll sneak around, to the butchering. Anyway, my calf was there. I couldn't talk to anybody for four days. They said you can have another one. 'No, I want that one.' That's when I realized, we're not here forever. We're here for a time. We're here for a time . . . that hurt. But life goes on."

"Everything happens for a reason," Fordy offered.

"Yeah, everything happens for a reason."

"Are you hungry?" Fordy asked. It must have been close to lunchtime.

"Doesn't matter."

"What would you like?"

"I don't eat anything fancy."

"I'm allergic to chicken, believe it or not," Fordy said. "Do you want a sub? I could get us subs?"

"I don't eat no lettuce, no mayo, no celery, nothing. . . . How'd I get into butchering pigs?" Pickton went back to Fordy's question about butchering.

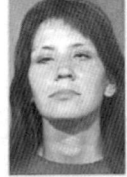

Georgina Papin
Victim

Marnie Frey
Victim

Mona Wilson
Victim

Andrea Joesbury
Victim

Sereena Abotsway
Victim

Peter Ritchie
Lead defence lawyer

Michael Petrie
Crown prosecutor

Robert Pickton
Accused

Justice James Williams
Trial judge

Brenda Wolfe
Victim

Robert Pickton Trial

Robert "Willie" Pickton was charged with first-degree murder in the deaths of Georgina Papin, Marnie Frey, Mona Wilson, Andrea Joesbury, Sereena Abotsway, and Brenda Wolfe. *(AP Images)*

A poster showing forty-eight missing women is put on display outside the courthouse during the trial of accused serial killer Robert Pickton.
(Newscom/Reuters Photo Archive)

Downtown east side Vancouver, Canada, where fifty women, mostly prostitutes, have vanished over the past twenty years. *(Newscom)*

A resident of Downtown East Vancouver, who said he is a drug dealer and a friend of one of the women Robert "Willie" Pickton allegedly killed, shows a photographer his crack pipe in an alleyway near Main and East Hastings streets, an area he referred to as "Pain and Wastings." *(Newscom)*

Mission, British Columbia marshland area being cleared and searched by crews on July 20, 2003 in the vicinity where a "Jane Doe" skull, neatly sawed in half, was found years earlier. *(AP Images)*

Aerial view of the Pickton pig farm taken by police during their investigation in 2002. *(AP Images)*

Pig farmer Robert William Pickton inside a barn on his pig farm in Port Coquitlam, Canada. *(Newscom)*

Robert Pickton was initially charged with two counts of first-degree murder in the case of 50 women who disappeared from Vancouver's downtown east side. *(Newscom)*

Excavators (background) unearth soil as a security officer (front) walks near the entrance of Pickton's farm, located 35 kilometers (22 miles) east of Vancouver. *(Newscom)*

Partial view of the site of the infamous pig farm where police alleged that Robert Pickton had murdered many women. The surface dirt was searched for human remains and other evidence, and the new homes in the background (built before Pickton was accused) might cover additional human remains. *(Newscom)*

Another partial view of Pickton's farm. *(Newscom)*

Firemen examine a barn on Pickton's farm. *(Newscom)*

Newly constructed condominium project (background) on land that was once part of Pickton's farm. *(Newscom)*

Royal Canadian Mounted Police (RCMP) investigators work with a drilling crew and heavy machinery while searching for human remains and other evidence on Pickton's farm. *(Newscom)*

RCMP investigators dig and sift soil for clues. *(Newscom)*

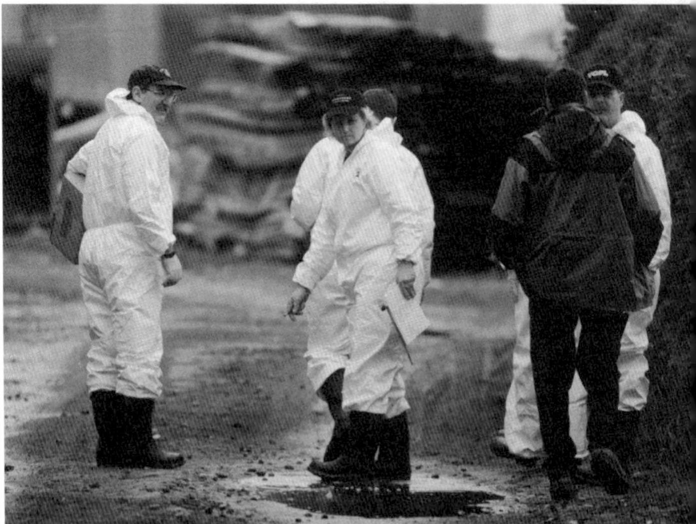

RCMP investigators walking through the Pickton property as they prepare to search Piggy's Palace. *(Newscom)*

A woman's purse, bagged as potential evidence by RCMP investigators on February 7, 2002, as found on Pickton's farm. *(Newscom)*

An RCMP forensic team officer retrieves a shoe out of a water-filled ditch on Pickton's property, also on February 7, 2002. *(Newscom)*

Another RCMP officer bags the shoe as possible evidence.
(Newscom)

On December 4, 2002, a police investigator carries a bag containing human remains to a refrigerated trailer stationed at Pickton's pig farm.
(Newscom)

Cards, candles, photographs, and flowers are left at a memorial outside Pickton's farm for the more than fifty missing women. *(Newscom)*

RCMP officer, Cst. Cate Galliford, is interviewed on February 7, 2002 by news media from Canada and the U.S. for information relating to the pig farm investigation. *(Newscom)*

Defense lawyer Peter Richie seen on January 30, 2006 in front of British Columbia Supreme Court in New Westminster on the first day in the pre-trial of his client, Robert Pickton. *(Newscom)*

Crown prosecutor Mike Petrie talks to reporters during a break between the reading of impact statements by the relatives of victims of serial killer Robert Pickton and the sentencing of Pickton by Justice James Williams. *(Newscom)*

Royal Canadian Mounted Police Staff-Sgt. Bill Fordy arrives for the trial of accused serial killer Robert Pickton in New Westminster, British Columbia, February 1, 2007. (Newscom/Reuters Photo Archive)

Royal Canadian Mounted Police Insp. Don Adam arrives at the courthouse for the trial of accused serial killer Robert Pickton in New Westminster, British Columbia, January 30, 2007. (Newscom/Reuters Photo Archive)

Royal Canadian Mounted Police Cpl. Dana Lillies was one of three officers who questioned Pickton after he was arrested in February 2002. *(AP Images)*

Karin Joesbury (left) cries outside the courthouse in New Westminster, British Columbia on December 9, 2007, after the guilty verdict for accused serial killer Robert Pickton. Remains of Joesbury's daughter Andrea were found on the Pickton farm. *(Newscom/Reuters Photo Archive)*

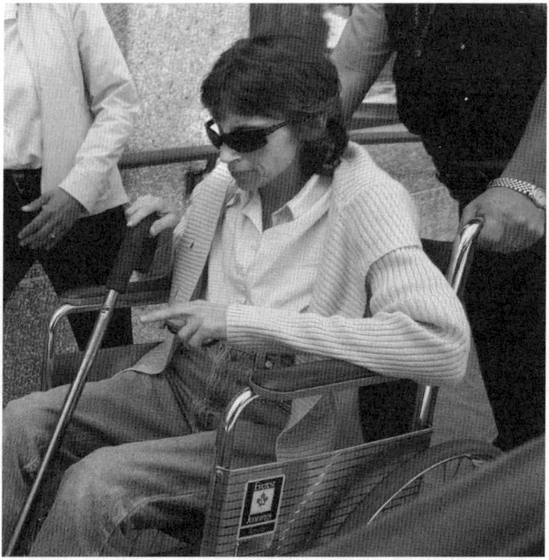

Gina Houston, a friend of accused serial killer Robert Pickton, arrives for a second day of testimony in Pickton's trial in New Westminster, British Columbia on May 30, 2007. Houston said Pickton discussed committing suicide during a conversation with her. *(Newscom/Reuters Photo Archive)*

Crown witness Lynn Ellingsen leaves BC Supreme Court in New Westminster, British Columbia on June 25, 2007. Ellingsen, who knew accused serial killer Robert Pickton, was arrested in February 2002 after police raided Pickton's farm. *(Newscom/Reuters Photo Archive)*

This courtroom illustration shows accused serial killer Robert Pickton as seen in his jail cell on video during court proceedings on February 6, 2007. *(Newscom)*

Courtroom drawing shows Robert Pickton during a preliminary hearing.
(Newscom)

"Just did. Did thirty-four head in a day. December twenty-third, right through to December twenty-fourth. I think it was in 1977. Thirty-four in a day."

"How'd you learn to do that? Somebody must have taught you. . . . What's the fastest you ever done?"

"Nothing fast about it. The problem is, you got to do it. Got to do it right, gotta make it respectable because people are going to eat it. . . . Has to be a clean job because this is for the public."

"I wasn't raised on a farm," Fordy said. "How do you do it? How do you kill them?"

"You got to make sure the pot has the right temperature water. That's half the battle. . . . If you don't have the temperature, don't do anything. You put the pig in there till the hair comes off, hair loosens up. That's about it."

"They still alive when you put them in the water?"

"No, you use a handgun. They're big boars. One hundred eighty pounds."

"What is it you enjoy about pig farming?"

"Nothing. Make money. I want to get out. Everyone else is asking, 'Do this one for me' or 'Do that one for me.' It's all favors."

"How many have you killed? Ten thousand? Five thousand?"

"Yeah, five thousand, ten thousand."

"More than ten [thousand] you think?"

"Possible."

"Who's the best butcher you've ever seen?"

"I don't know what you're referring to. . . . Everybody's got their own special ways of doing things. I don't know who is better than the next. Lots of people out there doing it."

"Killing animals. That's what they're for, right?"

"Well . . . I guess so. I guess so."

"How do you feel about sitting in here talking to me?"

"All right. . . ."

"I don't have to tell you how big an investigation this is," Fordy said.

"I don't know about that."

"This is a massive investigation," Fordy explained. "Huge. In my time with the RCMP, I've never seen unlimited people and money like this one. After it broke last week, some of the best cops in the province were brought in. I don't know if you know how many people are out there. They've brought in forensic experts, forensic anthropologists. They're going through that site and finding all sorts of bones, I guess. They're able to look at it and say this is from one thing, this is from another. They might even have forensic entomologists, which [is] a person who studies different types of bugs. They've brought in experts in blood spatter—people trained by the FBI experts to analyze the bloodstains and patterns and how they work, experts in DNA."

Fordy took a few moments to explain about DNA, and how it could help solve homicide investigations.

"I don't know about that," Pickton said. "I'm just a pig farmer."

"I'll help you with questions because I'm here to help you and me understand where you are," Fordy said. He continued with additional details of what the investigation entailed, and descriptions of the various experts assisting with it.

"As you know, there are people all over your property," Fordy said. "They'll be there a year."

"A year!" Pickton obviously had difficulty believing Fordy's statement.

"Oh yeah . . . what they gotta do . . . they're going to go through the dirt, go down twenty-five feet. That's why it's going to take so long."

"What are they looking for?"

"They're looking for evidence. I'll tell you, some of the people, friends of yours—one of the things police are doing is talking to people who are your associates, talking to them about what's going on."

"What is going on?"

"You're going to be charged and convicted of two murders. The investigation is huge—and is going to identify all the other ones you were involved with. I'm not saying you killed all fifty of those girls. Maybe you killed more, maybe less. You're the only person who knows. They're talking to people who were your associates for the past fifteen years. . . . So if I said I have your DNA on this marker, how would you explain it?"

"I'd have touched it."

"Yeah, what else?"

"I don't know."

"Would it have been possible for your DNA to be in this room yesterday?"

"Possible."

"How?"

"Anything can be set up. Or put in."

"If you've never been in this room, your DNA can't be here. You have to agree."

"It could have been set up."

"All right, in the absence of being set up, yes?"

"Yes."

"There's more than one side to a story."

"Yes, there's always two sides, and maybe more," Pickton agreed.

"Think back to the incident with the girl that stabbed you. When she went to police, there were two sides. Your story, and hers. I don't care what you said to anybody else about the other girls."

Fordy paused the dialogue between himself and

Pickton for a few moments while he brought in a large white poster board with all of the missing women's photos on it. He took it near where Pickton was seated and displayed it in such a manner that Pickton could easily see it. There were photographs of forty-eight women on the poster at this juncture in the investigation—more women's photos would be added later. The names identifying the women in the photos were not on the poster.

"I want to walk through them," Fordy continued. "Tell me which girls that you remember have ever been out to your place. Let's just walk through them. Number one? Has she ever been to your place?"

Pickton looked at the photos, which were numbered, as Fordy asked him to carefully examine each one.

"I don't know. There are so many people coming in and out of my place. I don't know."

"Okay, what about number two?" Fordy asked.

Pickton shook his head, indicating that he had not, and provided the same response for the third photo.

"Number four, remember her? She's got a lazy eye. Has she ever been to your place?"

"Her lazy eye," Pickton said, shaking his head no. "I don't know what you're talking about."

"She's got a lazy eye," Fordy said. "See her eye? Do you remember her? If she'd ever been to your place, would you remember her because of her eye? Probably, eh?"

"I wouldn't," Pickton said.

"Okay, number six?"

"She's pretty, that's all I gotta say."

On and on it went as they went down through the list, one photo at a time. Pickton complained that there were a lot of people on the poster to remember seeing, and Fordy suggested that he only tell him about the women on the poster that he had taken to his farm.

At one point he motioned with his foot toward number fourteen.

"I think I see her around some whores," Pickton said.

"Where did you see her?"

Pickton stammered a bit, and said some things that were incomprehensible before suggesting that the woman in the photo was a blonde.

"You know, there's so many people that look like her," Pickton said.

"Yeah, well, that's interesting that you remember her, though," Fordy said.

"Maybe I seen her around in Vancouver, if I'm right."

"Has she ever been to your place?"

"No."

The procedure continued, with Pickton saying no to each photo, indicating that he had not seen the women nor did he know them, until they got to number twenty-three.

"What is she?" Pickton asked. "She's a dark girl, isn't she?"

Fordy said that she sometimes looked black, and at other times Spanish. Pickton agreed that she looked Spanish.

"Has she ever been to your place?" Fordy asked. "I believe her name is Sarah. Remember her being there?"

Pickton shook his head no.

When he got to number twenty-six, he paused for a moment and then spoke.

"Twenty-six looks like . . . Lynn, but that's—"

"Lynn who?" Fordy interrupted.

"The one that was in my place," Pickton responded.

"Wish it was her?" Fordy asked, laughing.

They both obviously had been referring to Lynn

Ellingsen, the woman who claimed to have seen Pickton skinning a woman hanging from a meat hook years earlier and had kept quiet about it out of fear for her life. However, unknown to Pickton, she had told what she knew after learning of Pickton's arrest.

"Hmm?" Pickton was laughing again.

"Do you wish it was her?"

"No, it looks something like her," Pickton said. "I'm bad for remembering faces . . . but I remember dates real clear. But . . . there's so many millions of people out there, they look so much alike. . . ."

As they continued going down the rows of photos on the poster, Pickton suddenly asked which of the women he had been charged with murdering.

"If you don't mind my asking," Pickton added.

"No, I don't mind at all," Fordy said, pointing to Mona Wilson's photograph.

"That one?" Pickton asked. "Who the hell is she?"

"We're gonna talk about her," Fordy said as he went on to the next photo, and the next, and so forth. By the time he got to number forty-eight, Pickton again denied knowing her and denied that she had ever been to his farm. He began yawning as well, as if he had become bored with the process.

"Okay, you've just had a chance to look at all those pictures, right?" Fordy said. "Can you give me some sort of explanation as to why any of these women could have been at your place? Why another witness might say they know for sure they were at your place?"

"No way, no *waaay*," Pickton responded.

"Are you one hundred percent on that?"

"Yup."

"So you're telling me none of these women have ever been to your place? Do you want me to leave you alone for a while so you can rack your memory?"

"I don't know any of them."

"Have you ever had sex with any of these girls?"

Pickton sat quietly for several moments, as if he were contemplating the question. "Did I? Not that I'm aware of," he finally responded.

"Have they been . . . in your car then—that you were alone with them?" Fordy persisted.

"I don't have a car."

"Your truck then, your vehicle of transportation."

"No."

"Hundred percent on that?" Fordy prodded.

"Yup."

"Never been to your house, you've never had sex with them?"

"No. I had sex with a redhead. She's not there. I haven't seen her for a while. What's her name . . . Roxanne."

"She's a prostitute?"

"She's a working girl," Pickton replied.

"Is she the only working girl you been with?"

"No. I've had a couple. Don't know their names. I had Roxanne at my place."

"When?"

"*Hmmmmm* . . . a year ago?" Pickton responded.

"Who introduced you?"

"I met her. Nice person. Real nice person."

"What do you mean you had sex with her?"

"She was at my place. She went back and forth on the bus," Pickton stated.

"What do you call sex?"

"She was a nice, nice person. Nice everything. I don't know where she is now."

"Maybe we got to put her on the poster. Should we?" Fordy posed.

"She was at my place. I don't know."

"What do you call your penis—your dick? Your cock?"

Fordy began using a rougher approach, using talk of sex and Pickton's male anatomy, apparently hoping to shock Pickton so that he might slip up and make a statement that he might not otherwise open up about.

"I don't know."

"What did you do? . . . Put your dick in her?"

"I don't know what you're referring to."

"When you say sex, what do you mean? Some people mean the guy on top, some mean the girl on top," Fordy pressed.

"She [Roxanne] gave me head."

"After she gave you head, what happened?"

"Nothing. She was nice. She tried phoning me, back three months ago. She went to Abbotsford. I heard she moved back to Vancouver."

"Who's your girlfriend now?"

"Nancy. We never had sex."

"Who was the last girl you were with?"

"Roxanne."

"She gave you head eight to ten months ago and you haven't had sex since?"

"No, she had to go have an operation for a dislocated back. She wanted me to dance. I don't dance."

"What's your favorite way of having sex?"

"It doesn't matter. I'm not fussy."

"You haven't had sex in how long?"

"About a year."

"Funny, on studies of people who've been identified as killing lots of people, something happened to them as a child. When you look back . . . tell me about the first sexual relationship you had with a girl."

"Not much to say. I wasn't interested. Can't remember."

"The first time with a prostitute—tell me about that?"

"I never had sex with Connie, either," he said, referring to the girl he had met in Michigan. "She was the first girl I went out with."

"Who was the first prostitute?"

"I think it was Lynn. The one that knifed me. Probably the first time. I just wanted to go home and go to bed, but I had thirty-four hundred dollars on me."

Pickton was either confused about who had knifed him, or he was deliberately stressing his purported difficulty remembering people.

"The first time with a prostitute was Lynn, and then Roxanne," Fordy confirmed.

"Roxanne. She's a nice person."

"Do you think she's dead?"

"I don't know! I hope not. She's a nice person. I hope not. She phoned me about three months ago."

"So you're telling me, none of those girls has been to your place, and you never had sex with them?"

"No, but it doesn't mean much."

"It means a lot. We've got the best cops here. . . ."

Fordy trailed off as a woman entered the interrogation room with lunch.

20

As the interrogation continued in the small RCMP interview room in Surrey, Sergeant Bill Fordy continued with his probe of Pickton's life and tried to draw out what Pickton may have known about the missing women. Among the additional details he elicited from the suspected serial killer's background through his questioning was the fact that Pickton had held a contract with the Vancouver Police Department for purchasing unclaimed cars that had been impounded by the police.

"I buy cars from the Vancouver police," Pickton stated. "I have a contract there. Buy more than seventy a year. Had the contract almost four years. Just buy the old ones for salvage—there and other auctions. Strip the motor out and sell the motor. I found six hundred bucks in one. It wasn't mine. I couldn't take it. I took the money back to the owner. I don't steal from nobody. People steal from me—left, right, and center. People knife me in the back. I'm just trying to help people. I try to help people.

"In one car," he continued, "there was a single-bladed ax that had blood all over it. It came out of a 1989 Chevy

Astro. The backseat was folded together. There was blood all over the backseats, everywhere else. But life goes on. When I pick up anything, I take it back to VPD, they say we don't want anything back. Nothing. I go through about a hundred-fifty vehicles a year. I don't have time to worry about one needle or anything else."

"You said 'need all'?" Fordy asked, trying to clarify what Pickton had said.

"Needles," Pickton repeated.

"*Oh*, needles."

"I look through glove boxes, trunks—you won't believe what you find. It's outrageous. Outrageous. Bras, tops, blouses, clothes," Pickton said.

Pickton's comments about the women's items that he claimed he found in the vehicles he purchased could have been his way of deceptively attempting to show how so many women's garments and other items had come into his possession—or it could have been the truth. Fordy had no way of knowing yet just how much was truth and how much was bullshit—but he did know that Mona Wilson's DNA had turned up in bloodstains found on a garment in Pickton's closet.

"When you find that stuff, do you try to sell it?" Fordy asked.

"No, no time. I bring two, three, four a day in. I don't take anything out. If I see something valuable, I do. Tools, things like that, I put it aside."

"I can understand, with that quantity coming in. So you said you find bras, clothes?"

"Everything's there. People live in their cars. . . . A woman was supposed to come back and do laundry, take her clothes. They were all on the bed. She never came back. I don't know what happened to her. She was staying in a van behind the Cobalt (hotel). Another person was staying behind the Georgia Viaduct."

"What's her name?"

"I don't know. They all look alike, and so many come and go."

"You'd remember if you killed them—"

"I don't remember them!" Pickton exclaimed. "I don't. I don't! I'm telling you the honest truth. I'm telling you that. I don't know anything about it. I don't, I don't!"

At one point the interview turned toward the inhaler found inside Pickton's trailer, which he denied knowing anything about. He also confirmed that a girl named Sarah had stayed over at his place one night.

"I gave her a hundred-dollar bill," Pickton said. "And I never had sex with her. I have a black bag that came from her, a big, long bag. I got people coming in and out of my place, you wouldn't believe. Even after hours. If you don't believe me, you can talk to Nancy. She was staying there."

Pickton again referred to a woman named Lynn, and told Fordy that he had called paramedics for her on one occasion when she overdosed on drugs while staying at his place.

"Do I look like a murderer?" Pickton asked. "Innocent people get set up. People will set anybody up. I'm not trying to get away with anything. I'm telling you the honest truth. Take me the way I am. I'm myself. I'm sorry about living. I'm sorry for the way I am. There's quite a few people knew about my gun. I never kept any secrets. I kept open-minded."

"Tell me about your .22," Fordy prodded, now that Pickton had opened the door about the gun.

"I shouldn't be talking," Pickton said. "My lawyer's not here. I really shouldn't be. But I don't keep secrets. I've told everybody about everything. I sometimes use my .22—oh, I shouldn't be talking—on big boars. They have big heads, very solid, very heavy, very big bones. Sometimes it takes four, five shots to bring it down. I put plastic over the top of the gun to quiet it down. I shouldn't be talking about that.

"Take me any way you want," he continued. "I remember dates, faces—I don't remember any of these people. I'm charged, you can do whatever you want to do with me, but that doesn't make me a murderer. I was a plain little farm boy. I'm just myself. If I had to do the whole thing over again, I don't know if I'd change very much."

Pickton was near tears by this point, and his voice had dropped to almost a whisper.

"I'm sorry," he said. "I'm sorry for living. I'm tired. I'm sorry."

"I understand your need to lie to me, because you're scared," Fordy said. "In your gut you don't know what is going to happen. All you know right now is, you're just a big media celebrity. You're bigger than the pope—you're bigger than Princess Diana, than f***ing bin Laden. You're on the front page of every paper."

News of being in the newspaper seemed to bring Pickton back to life, but Fordy could not tell at that point whether Pickton was pleased or bothered over his sudden celebrity status and infamy.

"The paper?" he asked. "I'm in the paper today?"

"This is it," Fordy replied. "You are done. There is irrefutable DNA evidence you're responsible."

"You mean I'm in the paper today!"

"There's a map for each of us, a reason," Fordy said. "Your father was a hard worker, your mum was a hard worker. Your sister did what she did to you."

"She didn't do anything to me. She went to school."

"We'll look back and wonder why things happened. Why did my mom die? Why didn't Connie come up and marry me, when all I wanted was her to be [by] my side?"

"Not necessarily," Pickton said defiantly.

"That's what you wanted."

"Not necessarily. I miss her. I miss my mom."

"If your mum were still alive, you probably wouldn't be in this chair right now," Fordy suggested. "If you could go back, you'd change things."

"I wouldn't change much."

"That tells me you have a good side. You are who you are."

"I'm in the paper today?" Pickton asked again.

"Yes, you are. Do you know why? Because you're done. It's done. It's all over. All the things you need to build a house are in place."

"I don't think any of those girls have been to my place."

"I'd rather you don't tell me that," Fordy said. "No lies. I'd rather you not talk to me. I told you about the blood splatter people. They've been at your place. They're getting evidence from everywhere. They're spending a million a month digging. This is the biggest crime-scene investigation in Canadian history. They've done DNA, had people come look at blood spatter. If it was one isolated thing, it wouldn't matter—but this is a freight train, and it's only been going for two weeks.

"The only thing that matters now is what kind of person is Robert Pickton," Fordy continued. "I think you're a good person. If you were like Clifford Olson [a Canadian serial killer] that would be a different matter, my friend."

Fordy paused for a few moments and retrieved some photos from file folders that he had brought with him to the interrogation room. He explained DNA to Pickton again, and how it can be used as evidence.

"When you and I shake hands, your DNA is on my hands, mine is on yours," Fordy said. "Jack Nelles—

he's the blood spatter expert—he's in your motor home. He's done a forensic examination. What we've done is look at the mattress."

He showed Pickton a photo of the bloody mattress.

"See anything there?"

"No," Pickton said. "Drawings?"

"Looks like a dog," Fordy said. "What it is, is bloodstains. Lots of blood. It's bloodletting. We talked earlier about special lighting. This is the same mattress under a different light."

Fordy pointed out the blood spots and smears that had been identified as Mona Wilson's.

"What's that got to do with me?" Pickton asked as he leaned toward the photo for a closer look.

"Her blood is all over your place," Fordy said as he flipped through the photos. "Cupboards. This is where she was killed, rendered unconscious. See where it drags along out of the place—same thing there. This is a crime scene investigator's dream come true. The table, the counter, this is the part I want to show you."

"That doesn't mean I did it," Pickton protested.

"I'm going to show you how you're going to be convicted," Fordy stated. "It's normal to hold on to the lie, hoping it's going to pull you out. It's not. There's DNA all over the place—floor, walls. It's analyzed to come back to Mona."

"I don't know her."

"That's her shoes. She had her shoes on when you killed her. You put her shoes in the closet because they had blood on them."

"What! No—no."

"Your DNA. Her DNA's there. Now you're wondering how does her DNA tie to me. She died at my place," Fordy suggested.

"Possible, okay."

"But you're thinking, 'Bill, how are you going to prove it to [convict] me?' Experts say you're a logical thinker, Rob. And they say once I show you, you're going to accept responsibility. That's what the experts say."

"So my picture's all over the front page! Shit! I never did anything."

"Stop it! I don't want to hear lies. If your mother, whom you love and respect, were here now, she'd want you to stand up and be a solid, good person. You're probably scared inside."

"But I didn't do anything!"

"You're wondering how to get out of this."

"I didn't do anything! I don't know her!"

"It's okay to be scared," Fordy continued. "This is a scary, scary time. Because there's some cops who think you're a crazy, sick, demented wacko. Some cops think these girls are out there selling their bodies, have no self-respect, jamming needles into their arms—heroin, coke, whatever—they're the master of their own destinies. I've been in cases where girls steal from each other, breaking into houses, stealing from hardworking people—there are different camps in this building. There are camps that see you as some sick, demented man—some weirdo. I hope that's not the case. You're probably wondering, 'What are my friends going to think of me? Are they still going to be my friends? Are they going to abandon me? I'll go away to jail forever, and be alone. I can't work anymore. I can't go back to my farm. Why is this happening to me?'"

"Why?" Pickton uttered.

"'Why have I done the things I've done?'"

"I didn't!"

"If you aren't asking why, then I am scared for you," Fordy said. "Then you are beyond help. You are beyond ever understanding yourself. And you are beyond anyone ever understanding you. You are that weirdo, if that's the case."

"This is way out of hand," Pickton said quietly.

"You're right. It's way out of hand. The train is picking up speed. You're going to be convicted and go to jail. The only question is, what kind of person are you? Because you're done on this. . . . They're going to keep going through your property and find more. This is over for you. This is over, Rob. This isn't going away. I know you just want balance. You were born into the pig farm. Deep down you probably loved it at one time.

"You know, when the cancer was in your mom, and it just ate and ate away and she got sicker and sicker and then died," Fordy continued. "That's what this lie is. It's a cancer. And you're the only one that can take care of that. You're the surgeon and you've got the knife in your hand—you've got to cut that cancer out. And you'll be asking, 'Why, why, why?'"

"You mean it's in the paper and everything else? I can't even go to the courthouse, or anything else."

"It's going to be hard on you. It's not going to be easy."

"I'm not going to get bail, or anything else."

"You'll be held in custody. You're in custody."

"Until I deal with this here."

"It's done. It's the only thing you can do."

21

"I'm telling you right now that you did kill some of these girls," Fordy said to Pickton. "And I'm telling you right now that you took them away from their families."

Fordy's demeanor had clearly changed. He had become more rough, and had begun outright accusing Pickton of the murders. He told him that the DNA evidence was the building blocks of the case, and that it would be the DNA evidence that would cause a jury to convict him of the murders of several of the missing women. Fordy told him again that Mona Wilson had been to his place. Fordy told Pickton that he did not view him as a monster, as someone who would "go out and hurt innocent little kids." He again said that the bloodletting on the mattress in Pickton's motor home was extreme, and the amount of blood loss that had soaked into the mattress would have rendered the person unconscious. He explained that experts had determined that the blood spatter on the wall had been caused from the impact of someone having been struck with a weapon of some type. By this time Pickton avoided looking at Fordy.

"This is not from a bloody nose," Fordy said.

"I agree with that," Pickton responded, still avoiding eye contact with his inquisitor. "Shit. I didn't do anything."

"You know what, Rob? You did. . . . This game of cat and mouse is over now."

Fordy reminded Pickton about the inhalers found on the farm, particularly the one found inside his trailer. Pickton said at one point that he had found it lying on the floorboard of a gray car. Fordy, however, told him that his brother, Dave, had told the police that the inhaler found inside the trailer had originally been found inside the glove box of a red car.

"What did you tell Dave?" Fordy asked. "Do you remember that? Unless Dave's lying."

"I never did, I never even told Dave," Pickton responded.

Fordy wanted to know if Pickton's response meant that Dave had lied to the police.

"No, I mean I don't think Dave really knows," Pickton replied.

"Dave's telling us that you told him," Fordy added.

"I told him I found it in the car," Pickton said. "I didn't tell him what kind of car. Yeah, that's true. And he presumed it's in a red car because it's full of clothes. We're always talking about a red car."

Pickton added that he might have seen a black purse inside the red car, in addition to the inhaler. When Fordy specifically tried to get Pickton to recall what he had done with the purse and what its contents might have been, Pickton said that it had been too long ago for him to remember.

"We're going back a long time here," Pickton added.

"Yes, we are," Fordy agreed. "We're going back right to when Sereena was killed. Sereena Abotsway. Obviously, you know that . . . was Sereena's inhaler."

"Sereena, who's that?" Pickton asked.

Fordy pointed to her photo on the large poster.

"That's obviously the inhaler that we recovered," Fordy continued. "It's dated July nineteenth. . . . That, as you know, was leaked out to the media. So you took the inhaler in and you . . . didn't take anything else in [from the car]?"

"I can't remember," Pickton said.

Fordy went back to the black purse, and asked Pickton if he had taken it inside his trailer.

"I don't know," Pickton replied. "I might have. . . . I'm going back a while here."

"Well . . . it's not that long. You're doin' a good job. Thanks. I appreciate that. So Sereena then disappeared on July nineteenth, that's the day she picked up her inhaler."

"It looked fairly new when I—when I—" Pickton said.

"It was brand-new," Fordy interrupted. "It was the same day she got it."

"Oh . . . really?"

"Which is probably why it makes sense. You thought it . . . was so expensive."

Fordy told him that he found it very interesting how Sereena's inhaler could be inside his trailer without her having ever been there.

"She hasn't been there," Pickton said.

"Yeah."

"I don't know her, really."

Fordy told Pickton that his DNA was mixed with Mona Wilson's DNA, and that Mona Wilson was dead, killed on Pickton's farm.

"I didn't do it," Pickton said. "I don't even know her, really."

"You're a liar," Fordy told him.

"Who's the other one?" Pickton asked, now wanting

to know the name of the other woman that he had been charged with murdering. "The one who left the bag there. She's not here," he said, motioning toward the poster. "Is she dead?"

"Yeah," Fordy said. "Sereena Abotsway. You're also charged with her murder, Rob."

Fordy pointed out her photo to Pickton again.

"She's dead! She's dead, too! She's dead! No way. No way." Pickton told Fordy that he had dropped her off at the bus depot, and that she was supposed to have come back to the farm that night.

"When did you drop her off?"

"Nine," Pickton replied. "Nine A.M."

"Where did you sleep?"

"In the trailer."

"Did you have sex with her?"

"No. I wanted to."

"What happened?"

Fordy insinuated that Pickton was lying by saying that Sereena Abotsway never left Pickton's property that evening, but Pickton reiterated his account of taking her to the bus depot. He said that he gave her a hundred-dollar bill.

"I feel sorry for you telling me these lies," Fordy said.

"I'm not lying. I'm not lying. I think we better call this off."

"You don't have to tell me anything. I understand that."

"You're telling me she's dead," Pickton stated.

"She's dead. And you know what? We haven't finished talking about the first girl."

"I didn't do that. I didn't. I'll tell you right now. I didn't."

"Who did?" Fordy challenged.

"I don't know anything about it. I don't. . . . I am

being honest. I didn't even go in the trailer. Just because it's on my property doesn't mean anything. I haven't been in that motor home for quite a spell. Not for quite a spell. The other girl with the black case. I drove her to the bus depot. Nine A.M. I'm not sure of the date. She's a French girl. What's her name? The one with the black bag."

"Is that the one you never slept with?" Fordy asked.

"I slept with her."

"Have sex with her?"

"No. She'll tell you the same thing. I dropped her at the bus depot. At Coquitlam station."

"Where'd you work that day?"

"I don't remember," Pickton answered.

There was a light knock at the door, and Fordy left Pickton alone in the interrogation room for a few minutes. During his absence Pickton sat there talking to himself.

"I can't believe this," Pickton said, still being videotaped. "No way. I can't believe this." He repeated himself several times while Fordy was gone.

When Fordy returned, he brought a copy of the latest edition of the newspaper and placed it on the desk.

"Here's today's paper," Fordy said.

"Shit," Pickton said as he looked at the headlines.

Fordy left Pickton alone for several minutes, giving him time to read some of the articles that had been written about him.

"Believe me now?" Fordy asked when he came back into the room. "That you're done? It's over. You're not getting bail. You're going to trial, jail—you may die there."

Fordy pointed out Mona Wilson's photo again.

"She died at your place," Fordy said.

"I didn't know her."

"Your DNA is with hers. It's over. You're done, done, done, like dinner—roast pork. You can cry wolf and people will think you've done them all. There's two camps here—one is you buried them whole, the others think you chopped them up, ground them. We'll find a tooth here, bone here, no matter what way you did it, they'll find it. Experts are going to get evidence."

"I didn't do it. I didn't know her, really."

"You look me in the eye and tell me that, and you're a dirty, rotten liar."

"You can think what you like. I didn't do it."

"It's not somebody else's DNA. It's your DNA. One person. Robert William Pickton. So you're done on this. And you can continue to lie, to hide behind lies, because that's what people do when they're scared. . . . They have hardly begun out there."

"They're not going to find nothing there."

"You're wrong. They've linked you with tons of them. And they're only two weeks into this investigation. I can't imagine how you feel—but you're done. You need to start looking at yourself. 'Who am I going to take down with me—am I going to take down Dave?'"

"Dave? What's he got to do with it?"

"As long as you lie, he's attached to the lie. . . . It affects him. People who trust you. People who may even love you."

"I want to go back to my cell."

"It's my duty to talk to you," Fordy continued, ignoring Pickton's request to be returned to his cell. "That's what I'm going to do. You don't have to say anything to me. Friends have told us you said a good way to get rid of a girl—"

"Who said that?"

"Lots of people are coming forward. The—the killer is one who's known to the girls, and has means of getting them to the area, and disposing of the bodies. You have all three. I'm going to show you a tape. Just a second. You're thinking, 'This is not good. People I thought were my friends are talking about me.' Your DNA and Mona's are together."

At one point Fordy brought out an audiotape and told Pickton that it was an interview that police had with one of his friends, Andrew Bellwood. The tape sounded scratchy and was difficult to discern what was being said at times, but enough could be clearly heard to implicate Pickton in the murders of prostitutes.

"He proceeded to tell . . . me how he was killing these hookers," Bellwood could be heard saying on the tape.

"He what?" Pickton asked as he reacted to what he had just heard.

"He reached underneath the mattress," Bellwood's voice continued on the tape, "and grabbed some handcuffs and a piece of wire, and he told me how he would get the hookers on the bed, and have them lay on their stomach, and reach their hands behind their backs and put them in handcuffs. And after he handcuffed them, he proceeded to strangle them with a belt or the wire. . . . Anyway, then he told me that after he killed them, he would take them into the barn and bleed them, gut them, and feed them to the pigs . . . and nobody could trace them."

"This guy's out to lunch," Pickton told Fordy. He also said: "Funny stories in there, aren't they?"

As he continued speaking to Pickton, Fordy placed a videotape of Scott Chubb into the VCR and played it.

"I don't know him."

"It's a tape of Dwayne Chubb."

"Who's Dwayne? That's Scott."

"We know him as Dwayne. You might call him Scott."

The audio was somewhat difficult to discern, but Pickton was able to hear Chubb telling the police that Pickton had told him that if someone wanted to get rid of another person, he would take a syringe and inject her with windshield wiper fluid and that the police would think that she had died of a drug overdose. Chubb also described how Pickton had said something about having to give a woman a lot of money.

"I got the impression from him that he thought women were just dirty rotten pigs," the man identified as Chubb said on the tape.

"What! *What!* Is that Scott?" Pickton asked, obviously shaken by the videotape.

"I guess you get the picture," Fordy said. "So you can spin the story—nobody's going to believe you. That's what's going to happen here. You and I know they're going to find things in the ground. The decision to tell the truth is yours—you're certainly not getting out of jail. So you are going to be done and sent away. You took Mona's life, and your DNA is with her DNA. When you say you weren't with her, that's a lie. Nobody likes a liar. I hope you're not involved with anything else, because I'd have been wrong."

Pickton sat quietly and said nothing. He picked up the photo of Mona Wilson again and looked at it.

"Do you know the right thing to do?" Fordy asked. "Be strong—for . . . the people you love and the people who came to love you."

"Scott Chubb," Pickton uttered, as if he had not heard anything that Fordy had said.

"He's going to give evidence."

"After everything I've done for him."

"Yeah. This case is getting better and stronger. The foundations of this case are DNA. Other things make it stronger. You're smart. You're no dummy. I know you're not stupid. These girls on the (Downtown) Eastside, they had families, too. They had mothers once, too. People that loved them, coddled them. Deep down inside, part of me wonders, because you say you like to help people, maybe you think these girls you helped. These girls aren't ones you'd want to marry—like Connie. But you took these girls away, Rob."

"I haven't killed anybody. Really."

"Have you killed any kids? Tell me you haven't killed any kids."

"No, I haven't. I told you I haven't killed anybody."

Fordy changed the subject and began talking about Pickton's mother again, reminding him of when she lay on her deathbed, and how she likely had been thinking about what she wanted for her son Robert. Pickton, obviously growing very tired, began yawning again, but Fordy was not ready to let up on him yet. He moved his chair alongside Pickton's and asked him how being charged with the murders of two women, so far, made him feel.

"Makes me feel sick," Pickton said.

"That feeling is not going to go away. I knew that before you told me. I've talked to lots of killers."

"I'm not going to get bail or nothing."

"No, you're not. You're absolutely not. If you want to make your mom proud, then you need to be responsible. Don't let your mother down."

At one point Pickton wanted to talk about the other woman he had been charged with murdering, Sereena Abotsway, and asked to see her file. Fordy pointed toward Sereena's photo, but told Pickton that he wasn't going to talk about her until they had finished talking about Mona Wilson. He asked for details about what had happened to Wilson, but Pickton again denied knowing her.

"You killed her," Fordy said. "This whole book is written except for your side of the story—why you did what you did. You're dying to tell me. I've talked to lots of people. They feel better afterward."

Fordy told Pickton that people would never know his side of the story unless he made a confession. If he did not confess, he said, the media would portray him however they wanted.

"So, where do I go from here? I go to court?"

"Go to pretrial and then you go to court, and to court, and court, and court, and then jail, and you die there. That's another thing. I hope you always wear a condom when you're there because there's STDs. I hope you know this is over. Train is on the tracks, and it gets heavier with each piece of evidence, and it's going to run right over you, Rob. I know you're smart. I know you're not some wacko, some crazy guy. I know that. You have made mistakes. There's evidence all over the place. You can't hide from it. I want you to tell me the truth. I want to understand you."

"I got to sleep on it for a couple of days."

"This pain that's inside your stomach is not going to go away. It's going to get worse. Right now, you got a disease and it's going to eat you up. It's going to crawl inside you like the cancer that killed your mother. You want to tell me. You want to talk about this. You're wondering yourself. Rob, you can't run from this. You can't hide. This is going to keep going and going. I want to understand you and what happened. I'm not going to judge you and I'm not going to hate you. I'm going to try to understand you. If there was a situation where you wanted to help girls speed up the inevitable, I'll understand. People aren't going to hate you."

"Murder? Charged with two?"

Another officer, Constable Dana Lillies, came into the room and told Fordy that he was wanted outside to discuss new evidence that had been found. When Fordy left the room, she sat down next to Pickton.

22

Constable Dana Lillies represented a more sympathetic and temperate approach in her attempts at obtaining information from Pickton, and she seemed to provide a bit of relief to the murder suspect after the intensive grilling he had gone through with Fordy. Pickton did not know it yet, but the questioning the he had undergone for the last few hours was not over yet—he still had to meet with the head of the Joint Missing Women Task Force, Inspector Don Adam. Even though he wanted to go back to his cell, he would remain in the interrogation room for several additional hours. They were putting him through the wringer, multiple times.

"It's a lot to digest," Lillies said in a relaxed demeanor that was intended to put Pickton more at ease—for a while. "Like I was telling you last week, this was going to happen."

"Did you find the bones I told you about?" Pickton asked.

During his first arrest nearly two weeks earlier, Pickton had told her about some bones that investigators would find on his property. He had drawn her a map, and said that crime scene personnel would determine that they were ostrich bones.

"Yes, your map was perfect," Lillies responded.

"And they were ostrich bones?" Pickton asked.

"Yes, we knew they would be. Like Bill was telling you, there's more evidence every hour. How are you feeling?"

"I can't feel my toes," Pickton said, looking down at his feet, clad only in socks.

"You don't feel your toes?"

Pickton muttered something unintelligible under his breath.

"It's a lot to be taking in," Lillies said somewhat sympathetically. "Could you sleep last night? Have you eaten anything since you've been in custody here? I brought you a sandwich."

"I don't like it."

"What would you like to eat, Robert?"

"I don't know. At this stage, do I deserve anything to eat?"

"Of course you do. You're a human being who's made mistakes. I'm not going to judge you."

"I'm dead before I start."

"You're not dead. You're a human being. You deserve that. We're not here to judge you. I told you that last week. I'm ready to listen to whatever you have to say."

"I should be on death row."

"I don't believe that."

"I'm finished. I'm finished."

"You know what, Robert," Lillies continued. "You come to a point where you have to deal with . . . what's happened. The best way to deal with it is openly and honestly. It's not the end of the world. . . . You're going to go on living."

"For what?"

"You have good qualities. I've been talking to people who know you."

"I'm over with. I'm finished."

"You do have good qualities. You do care about people, people have taken advantage of you. . . . You are going to jail, not back to the farm. . . . That will be difficult for you because that's your whole life, right? It's a huge change. It's a lot to take in, but you have to be strong."

"For what? Dying?"

"[For the] people who care about you," Lillies said. "Dave is your fiercest protector. He's beside himself right now. I think what's important now is to give the families some closure. They want answers. You have to give them answers. You can keep your mouth shut. But you could bring an end to this suffering right now. People out there are thinking you're a monster. They don't see the side that I saw, when we sat and visited for a couple of hours there. A human being, with good qualities."

Pickton kept telling Lillies that he was "dead," and she attempted to sway his mental attitude into realizing that he was at a crossroads in his life, albeit a very serious one. She tried to make him see that his lying and denial about what the police believed he had done was acting as a "poison" inside him, growing and festering with each passing hour that he continued to hold it inside. Pickton was not listening to her, however, and sat in the chair, shaking his head, saying that he was "dead."

"Well, my name is mud," Pickton finally said. "I'm locked up here forever. You tell me why I don't think that?"

"Do you want to tell me what happened, and see if it feels better?" Lillies asked.

"What's it matter? I'm dead."

"This was Mona, right? I really want to understand what happened with Mona. I do."

"I didn't do anything, really."

"We all know that's not the case, Robert."

"That's what they say now. . . . I'm nailed to the cross anyway."

"Like Bill was telling you, her DNA is all over that trailer."

"But I always been in there. I've been in there off and on, but I don't know anything about this here."

"I don't think Bill told you where," Lillies said, a more serious tone in her voice. "Your DNA was on the dildo, that was on the gun you have—and her DNA was on the tip of that dildo. That's where it was found."

"That doesn't mean I did it."

"Yes, it does. It does, Robert. . . . You're hurting everybody by denying it."

"There's a lot of people know I had the gun."

Pickton covered his eyes with his hands as Lillies continued speaking, telling him that she would like to hear what he had to say about the gun with the dildo attached to it.

"Will you tell me about the, ah, gun with the dildo on it?" Lillies asked.

"Well, I put that on there . . . in case I have to use it for . . . shooting boars," Pickton said. "I shouldn't be talking about this. It'll be in court anyways, right? It's gotta go to court."

"For shooting boars?" Lillies asked, attempting to get him to continue about the gun.

"Yeah, pigs."

"With a dildo on the end of it?"

"Yeah, I put it on there for a silencer, but I never used it."

"That sounds a little unusual. . . . So tell me, how did Mona's DNA get on the tip of that dildo?"

"I don't know."

"Yes, you do."

"See, I don't know her," he said, refusing to look at Lillies as she picked up the photo of Mona Wilson and showed it to Pickton.

"That's not what I asked, is it?" she said. "You probably don't know her. Her name is Mona Wilson. She was a prostitute, and you killed her. Now, whether or not you knew her isn't really the issue. The reality of the situation is that the evidence doesn't lie, the reality of the situation is that her blood is all over that camper, and it's mixed with your DNA. So whether you knew her, where she lived, who her parents were, whether or not she had children, that's not what I'm asking."

She handed Wilson's photo to Pickton, who placed it on the table.

"I don't know her," he said again.

"Robert, you and I both know that's not true," she said. "One of the things I know, knowing about the kind of sex you had with these women, that doesn't change the way that I see you. I still see the good in you. I see the Robert I sat and chatted with for a couple of hours. I still see Robert who saw his favorite calf slaughtered as a child. You have real feelings. I know you're going to do the right thing. I believe people become who they are because of what's happened to them. That's what I want to understand. We talked a lot the other day about your history and growing up on a farm. And I think anyone in the same set of circumstances would grow up doing the same things as you. Maybe if you'd been raised in the circumstances I was raised in, it'd be a different situation right now. I'm here to understand you. I'm not here to judge you."

"I'm never going to walk again," Pickton said resignedly. "I've got two charges against me, and more pending."

"You know, as I do, they're going to find more evidence," Lillies said. "Here's your chance to help people, including yourself. I think you have demons you're struggling with—by sitting there silent, you're letting them take over."

Lillies continued trying to convince Pickton that much of the evidence had not even been found yet, and that it was still forthcoming. She also told him that people had begun to come forward to talk about what they knew about his alleged crimes, and that many people would provide information before it was over.

"Are you hearing me?" she asked. "What are you thinking, Robert?"

"I don't know."

"What are you feeling?"

"I can't get over Scott Chubb in the machine there," he said as he motioned toward the VCR on the desk.

"You're surprised he came forward to us? Was that a nod? Yeah. What I think really sucks is a lot of people were using you to support their drug habits, and they burn you in the end. There's a tip line on the news and people are phoning that. All those things are coming through and being followed up on."

"I can't get over Scott Chubb."

"Tell me about Scott. You guys good friends? Tell me about him. I'm interested."

"I can't get over him. Who was speaking with him?"

"I'm not sure. Was that someone you worked with? I don't know the man . . . but we're getting lots and lots of phone calls from people like Scott Chubb."

"I think that was Scott Chubb," Pickton said again,

covering his face with his hands once more. "Scott Chubb. F***. I can't believe it. It's way out now."

"It hurts, doesn't it?"

"Scott Chubb, of all guys. Of all guys—him! What is he trying to do?"

23

When RCMP inspector Don Adam walked into the austere interrogation room on Saturday afternoon, February 23, 2002, where Robert Pickton was waiting for him with Sergeant Bill Fordy—who had returned for additional questioning after Constable Dana Lillies had finished with him—Adam noticed that Pickton looked tired, gaunter than ever, and he momentarily considered that Pickton may have been exhausted, due to all of the interviews that he had already sat through with Fordy and Lillies. He was obviously stressed due to the situation that he was in, likely because the noose, so to speak, was becoming tighter with each hour that passed. Adam greeted Fordy with a nod and a handshake as he entered the room.

"Hi, Bill," Adam said. "I'm just wondering if I should spend a couple of seconds with Willie. I don't think he's quite got the whole picture of what is going on here."

"Absolutely," Fordy replied. "Do you want me to leave you with him?"

Adam indicated that he did not mind if Fordy stayed, then greeted Pickton.

"Hi, Bob," Adam said. "Or Robert? Which do you prefer to be called?"

"Doesn't matter," Pickton quietly replied.

Adam introduced himself and shook hands with Pickton as he momentarily stood up. He motioned for him to remain seated, and attempted to make his presence with Pickton seem as amiable as possible.

"I have heard some people say you prefer to be called Robert," Adam stated matter-of-factly. "I knew you as Willie. I used to be stationed in Coquitlam back in the early 1980s . . . back in the days when . . . you guys were burying equipment and doing that kind of stuff."

Adam was referring to how Pickton and others had buried equipment and machinery that had purportedly been stolen and possibly fenced to Pickton and others on the farm. After reminding Pickton how he had first come to know of him, he settled on calling him Bob.

"Bob, I'm in charge of this investigation," Adam told him. "I'm a sergeant. And even though Bill's gone over some of this stuff with you, I think that maybe you need to hear the overall picture. I'm not going to spend a lot of time with you, but I want to just set things out, sort of make them crystal clear as to how this comes together."

Pickton sat quietly, listening intently.

"Okay, the first thing you need to know is this," Adam continued. "Right now, we can associate you to twelve of these women, and that's two weeks into the investigation. Twelve of them. Next you need to know is that relative to Sereena Abotsway, and I'm not a front-line investigator, right—I direct the guys. Relative to her, we have Linda Dick, who will state last summer that she met you and Sereena together and Sereena introduced you as Robert, and Sereena said you were going out to your farm."

Pickton began shaking his head no in disagreement.

"No, no, no, just wait and listen," Adam said.

Adam explained to Pickton that he had his people tracking Sereena Abotsway's moves during her final days. He said that he knew when she picked up her welfare payments of approximately $35 every three days, and that even though she was not very good with managing what little money she received, she always seemed to be able to get her asthma medication, which was dispensed in the form of an inhaler. He explained that he knew that Fordy had spoken with him about the asthma inhalers found on the farm, and how they were identified as having belonged to Sereena Abotsway. He depicted the inhalers as a major problem for Pickton.

"We have statements from people, including your brother, where you say, 'Yes, it was a shiny case, I brought it into the house,'" Adam stated. "Willie, that's gonna be the evidence, all right. 'A shiny case I brought into the house.' You discussed it with a whole bunch of people, and we have that. You can't move away—that's your position. . . . Willie, you need to understand something. That inhaler was not found by itself in your house. It was found in a tote bag belonging to Sereena Abotsway. Inside that tote bag are her shoes, her clothes, a needle, and on that needle is her DNA and your DNA, together. Okay?"

Pickton began shaking his head again in disagreement, but he said nothing.

Adam further described how the investigators had gone through Pickton's garbage, layers of it, that was situated right below a window of his trailer, and had found three additional inhalers belonging to Abotsway, bringing the total found on Pickton's property to four, and that each bore the dates when the dispensing pharmacy had filled them.

"Yeah, we got four of them," Adam emphasized. "All right, Willie, you need to understand you told a lie to try and justify how that inhaler got into your house. . . . Oh yeah, Willie. There's no point shaking your head. Just listen to me, so you know what the evidence is, in case you need to know where you are. Because only by knowing where you are, Willie, by knowing exactly how locked-in you are, will you realize how the lies are dragging you down like a stone."

Pickton began wiping his eyes to remove an occasional tear, and at times it seemed as if he was about to begin sobbing. But he held his composure and continued to listen to Adam.

"If you pick up a great big boulder, Willie, and step into a deep lake, what happens to you?" Adam asked. "You go to the bottom, don't you? And the lies that you've told, the little cover-ups you've tried to create, are stones that are going to carry you to the bottom, Willie. All right, so you need to listen to me, 'cause I am not here to lie, and Bill got a bit of the evidence confused . . . and it's not his intention to lie, and I'm gonna straighten up that confusion right here and now. 'Cause we are not here to lie to you about the evidence, and we're not here to exaggerate the evidence, Willie. We don't have to. Do you understand? So, where Bill has made mistakes or got confused, I'm going to straighten you out on that."

In an insistent tone Adam told Pickton that a jury would convict him of Sereena Abotsway's murder.

"You will be convicted of that, all right," Adam continued. "On the tote bag, Willie, is her blood. And, Willie, you are locked into all of your stories about finding that one inhaler. Not a tote bag with blood. Not extra inhalers in your garbage, not any of that stuff, Willie. You are completely finished on that case."

Following a brief pause, but without missing a beat, Adam began detailing for Pickton all of the evidence and witness statements that had so far been obtained regarding Mona Wilson. Pickton occasionally looked up, like he wanted to say something, but decided to remain quiet. He began to look beaten, defeated, and he instinctively knew that there was little point in attempting to refute Adam as he recounted the details of the case to him. There would be time for that later, after he had learned everything that the cops knew about him.

"Mona Wilson, that is a murder site inside that motor home," Adam said. "We have got tons of witnesses talking about you in that motor home. There are tons of them. I've got forty-five guys out taking statements, and they have been working day and night. I've got a roomful of statements, videos, Dictaphone taped statements—everybody talking about you. It is an army of investigators, and they are the best in the province and we are not making mistakes, Willie. It is coming down on you like an avalanche, and you've helped bring it down by your little stories."

At one point Adam launched into a tirade about how many of the witnesses who were providing information to the police were fearful of Pickton, but they were coming forward just the same. He indicated that as long as Pickton remained behind bars, it was likely that additional people would come forward.

"Mona Wilson, that's a murder scene, all right, no doubt about it," Adam continued. "There're drag marks, where you dragged her out of there. There's the fact that you've got the dildo with the gun and your DNA mixed with hers on that dildo. How do you think a jury is going to look at a dildo on the end of a gun, Willie, that has DNA of you and her connected with a murder scene? What are they going to think?

"It doesn't end there," he continued. "We've got the ID of Heather Bottomley, all right, another girl there. We got the witness statements. Your friend, he likes you, he talks about liking you. But he is not willing to sit by, Willie, when you murder somebody."

Adam had apparently been referring to Scott Chubb, who had worked for Pickton on the farm. Chubb, of course, had been an informant to RCMP constable Nathan Wells, a rookie officer, prior to Pickton's arrest. It had been Wells who had obtained a search warrant to look for guns on Pickton's farm, and in the end had found much more than he had expected to find.

"People aren't willing to stand by you when . . . they know you're a killer," Adam said. "And, you know, he talks about the needle with the windshield washer fluid."

"I don't know nothing about that," Pickton replied.

"You don't know anything about that," Adam said. "Well, Willie, I got bad news for you because inside your entertainment unit or whatever it is, a chest of drawers inside your trailer . . . guess what's there? A needle with windshield washer fluid. Yes, Willie, absolutely."

"I know nothing about that," Pickton said.

"Willie, tell me your story," Adam urged.

"I'm honest with you," Pickton insisted.

"Well, you want to know something," Adam continued, trying to break Pickton's calm demeanor. "I haven't even started . . . but you want to know how bad it is? Your brother, Dave, is talking to . . . two policemen he's been dealing with. He told them today, 'I know it's over for Willie, I know there are bodies.'"

Adam calmly explained to Pickton that his brother had implicated other people in the killings, including Dinah Taylor, who had lived with Pickton for a year and a half and was frequently seen in the company of many of the women who began vanishing from the Downtown Eastside region. He explained that people were saying that Pickton had killed all of the women, but that he had help disposing of their bodies. He told Pickton that people were going to come forward with that evidence. Adam attributed much of what he was explaining to Pickton to his brother, Dave. He said that he was also aware that Pickton was being blackmailed.

"Now, I don't know if your brother knows where the bodies are," Adam continued, "but he's . . . just gotta work out the final arrangements to give that up. Willie, maybe you didn't kill every single one of them, maybe Dinah . . . is involved in some of it, maybe you were getting blackmailed. We know that Lynn Ellingsen was blackmailing you. We know that. Do you understand?"

Adam told Pickton that if he had been used, drawn into the murderous scenario by others, perhaps even pressured by others, that he needed to explain it all so that everyone could understand. Otherwise, he might take the fall for everything alone when others might have been involved. He explained how Dinah Taylor had taken off when things began to heat up and went back east to the Indian Reserve of her people of the Ojibway Nation in the province of Ontario, and how he had sent RCMP officers out to find her. He described how the officers had gone to her mother and father's home and how they had helped convince her to cooperate with the investigation.

"She said that she had phoned you and tried to cook up a story with you about some sort of a duffel bag, that it came from some hotel, the Cobalt," Adam said. "She gave that up."

"That's true," Pickton said, not acknowledging the alleged story that he had fabricated with Taylor, but instead trying to say that the bag came from the Cobalt.

"Yeah, well, she did phone you, because she told us that," Adam said.

"That's true, it came from the Cobalt," Pickton said.

"No, no, no," Adam said, getting irritated. "She told our people that was a story you guys agreed to tell."

"No."

"Well, I'm telling you that's . . . where we are now, Willie. You need to understand this. Lynn Ellingsen, who was blackmailing you, is now negotiating with her lawyer to give you up right now so she doesn't go down for whatever her involvement was. Right now, her lawyers have called us and are negotiating."

Adam asked Pickton if he had ever heard of Paul Bernardo and Karla Homolka, and without waiting for him to respond, he explained that the couple killed young girls in Ontario. He said that Bernardo and Homolka were the first man-woman team in Canada involved in serial killings, at least as far as the police knew. He was attempting to draw a comparison between them and Pickton and possibly another woman, possibly two, to infer that Pickton may have had assistance luring the women out to his farm. He was, of course, thinking of Dinah Taylor and Lynn Ellingsen, and he let Pickton know that in an attempt to shake him up a bit more.

"Now running this file, Willie, I can tell you that I . . . don't know how involved, or uninvolved, Taylor and Ellingsen were with you," Adam said. "I know they were bringing girls out to you. I've got tons of evidence of that. I know that Ellingsen has talked about blackmailing you. She talks about coming in when you were skinning a girl, hanging on a hook."

"That's not true," Pickton said.

"Listen to me for a second, you know how bad it is. I know that you were angry against the girls. I know that you blame one of these girls for giving you hepatitis C, that's true, isn't it?"

Pickton did not respond verbally, but simply shook his head no.

Adam explained to Pickton that he had witnesses who would testify that Pickton had expressed his anger to them for contracting hepatitis C from one of the prostitutes, and that he was also angry over having been stabbed by Wendy Eistetter, indicating possible motives for why he had become a serial killer. Adam continued to urge him to come clean, and stressed that he needed to begin thinking about the long term and whether or not he wanted to be despised for the rest of his life. Although there were not any deals being offered to Pickton, Adam indicated that it would be better for him if he helped clear the air by showing the world that he was not really the monster that was being portrayed in the media. The implication was that if he showed some compassion and admitted to what he had done, people would not think so badly of him.

"What's in this for us?" Adam asked. "Why do we care? Two reasons, Willie. Number one is that I know these families. I met them, I know them, and I know that these ladies' lives went wrong. I know that you have nothing but contempt for them, and I know that in my life, before I got involved in this file . . . I would just ignore them. I wouldn't think about it. But I've met their families, and they didn't end up wanting their kids to be that way, and your mom and dad didn't want you to end up being a serial killer. Do you understand, Willie? That's not what we want for our kids."

Adam told Pickton that his brother, Dave, did not want to see him destroyed, in the media or otherwise. He was simply trying to understand. But, Adam said, there were others on the task force that believed Dave was somehow involved in the case.

"Half of my investigators think Dave is fully involved," Adam said. "They think that the two of you were involved. There's other people that think the Hells Angels are involved with you."

He paused for a moment and stared at Pickton as Pickton shifted nervously in his chair. Sensing that he might be getting somewhere with his prime suspect, Adam moved closer to Pickton.

"Willie, you know how big or how small this is, you know whether it's just you, you know whether it's you and the girls, and you know whether it was you and Dinah, you know whether it's you and Lynn, you know . . . Willie. You know whether it's you and Dave. But if you're looking for why you should deal with this thing, deal with it upfront, I can tell you a number of really good reasons. By explaining, giving people a chance to understand, is going to make a huge difference in how you are treated for the rest of your life."

Adam said it might make a huge difference in how he was viewed in a prison environment and, particularly, how he would be treated by the other inmates.

"You're probably going to be the biggest serial killer in Canadian history," Adam said, attempting to appeal to Pickton's ego. "You're going to be a very, very famous guy. You will have achieved something. You know you eluded police for years and years, let's face it. It's pretty amazing. But it's over. And you know what, Willie, you're a smart, logical person. Bill said it, [and] it's true.

The reality is that I believe you want to . . . make it a smart, logical choice as we deal with this."

Adam again urged him to explain whether Lynn Ellingsen and Dinah Taylor had been involved, and whether they were pressuring him in any way. Adam said that if they were fully involved, it would provide some explanation to how things had happened, and would provide some answers to his brother, sister, and many of the people he knew.

24

As the interrogation continued, Inspector Don Adam continued in his efforts to play on Robert "Willie" Pickton's emotions. His reasoning seemed to be that he could shake Pickton loose and get him to talk if he kept hitting at him, long and hard enough, often using things he knew about the people that Pickton seemed to care about. In one instance he told Pickton that he knew there were people who believed that Pickton hated his sister; and other people, Adam said, had told the police that Pickton's brother, Dave, treated him poorly and frequently yelled at him. Adam claimed to know that Pickton was hostile toward his brother, which caused Pickton to begin shaking his head no. He even reminded Pickton how his brother and sister had both accomplished more with their lives than he had, suggesting subtly that he resented them for having done so. It appeared that Adam attempted to rub Pickton's nose in the fact that he had difficulty leaving the farm life.

"You broke out of the farm once," Adam said. "When was that? What year was it that you went down south?"

"Seventy-four," Pickton replied.

"In 1974, did you take a bus?"

"I flew all the way down there."

"How did you choose that place?"

Pickton told him that he had become pen pals with Connie Anderson, the young woman that he had gone to see, and that they had gotten to know each other through writing. Pickton had been twenty-four when Connie, originally from Michigan, invited him to visit her in Chicago, where she was living at the time. Adam reminded Pickton that he had nearly his entire life ahead of him at age twenty-four, and that he should have taken the opportunity to break away from the farm when it had presented itself to him.

"Willie, that was your chance to get away, to step away from the farm, to step away from what it was doing to you," Adam said. "You know, Bill and I talked to a young guy who's a killer out of Chilliwack. And he was a young guy, his parents are dairy farmers, and what he talked about is the fact that the farm was a trap. His parents' health wasn't good, and every day from four in the morning until seven at night, he worked—until he dragged himself home to drop into bed, asleep. He couldn't take a holiday, because the cows needed to be milked, and he couldn't have a relationship because the cows and the work needed to be done. He was completely tied to that life, and it was like a noose around his neck, Willie, tightening, choking, choking the life out of him, choking the youth out of him."

Adam told Pickton that all of the work on the farm, with no time to play, had filled the killer from Chilliwack with anger because of how unfair it had been for his sister to go away to college while he stayed behind on the farm. Adam explained that as the killer's parents became older and more frail, his chances of escaping the farm life diminished until they faded away. "Do you understand why, Willie?" Adam asked. "In our lives we want options, we want to be able to meet somebody we care about. Not prostitutes, Willie. . . . We've got lots of statements from prostitutes about the fact that you turn them over and you have sex with them, but you never even look at them."

"Yeah . . . really never had no sex with them," Pickton replied.

"Pardon?"

"Never had much sex with them."

"But sometimes you did," Adam said. "I've got statements from them."

"The ones brought over and . . . those . . . ," Pickton trailed off, but Adam quickly picked up on his statement about "the ones brought over."

"And you had the girls bring them out right?" Adam asked. "Did Lisa ever bring out girls for you?"

Adam described her as a blond-haired girl that had been married to a biker named "Blackie." Pickton described her as nice, and said that he knew her as "Lee," but he denied that she ever brought girls out to the farm for him.

"We know that Dinah brought girls out, right?" Adam asked. "You . . . don't need to think about it, Robert. You know that's a fact—we know that, you know that. All right."

Adam reminded Pickton that the police believed that Lynn Ellingsen had brought women to his place, but conceded that they did not know whether Ellingsen and others had participated in any of the killings. He also reminded Pickton that the police knew that Ellingsen was blackmailing him and that detectives had statements from witnesses to that effect.

"You've told people that, and we've got those statements, and you know what, she is going to screw you again, like everything she's done to you, she is gonna screw you again, Willie," Adam said. "And that's one of the things you could stop. You choose to tell the truth here tonight, and that choice is yours. But you could screw her right back, because if you talk before she does, there's no need for us to make a deal with her. We could be down there arresting her later tonight if you tell the truth about what was going on, do you understand?

"Don't you get tired of being beat up by people, and abused and used, Willie?" Adam continued. "Aren't you tired of it? Isn't it time you did something . . . just for yourself? Don't let these people beat you up, make you into a monster, use you, walk away from everything they've done, laughing and—what?—selling their story to CNN, so they make money on it. You know how it goes. That's all in the palm of your hand."

Adam told Pickton that he should not allow all of the people who had been coming forward with information to make a fool of him, and advised him, again, to come clean, deal with his situation and tell the truth. He told him that the present time would be his opportunity to tell them *why* they would find bodies on the farm, and assured him that they would.

"If Dinah, like your brother says, has killed some of these girls, and maybe that's not true . . . but if she has, or if Lynn knew and was still bringing the girls out, which is what I think, and Dinah was, then don't let them make money and make themselves famous and make you look worse and drive you into the dirt, Willie. 'Cause you have the power right here and right now to put a stop to this, and you know all you gotta do is tell the truth. We sort it out, 'cause suddenly when you tell the truth, they have no more power to hurt you. They have no more power to make money off you, and they have no more power to make deals. 'Cause I'm telling you that's how it works."

Adam explained that Lynn Ellingsen's lawyer was negotiating a deal for her as they spoke, and emphasized how that could hurt Pickton's case. He reminded him again and again how Ellingsen had hurt him, and how she had blackmailed and betrayed him—and that she was preparing to do it again. By this point, Adam was displaying a demeanor to Pickton that made it seem as if he was pleading with him, almost begging him to tell him what had happened on the farm. At times it seemed as if he had Pickton's best interest at heart, which must have been an effort to work on Pickton's psyche to persuade him to incriminate not only himself, but others.

"You could have killed those two girls (Ellingsen and Taylor)," Adam said. "[But] you didn't, did you? Do you see what I mean? You could have, but you didn't, because you care about those girls. And now they have done this to you. It's not right, Willie. It's not right . . . that she blackmailed you. It's not right what they are doing. I'm holding out my hand to you. I'm offering you a chance to have some dignity, to walk . . . through this thing. To stop being used by people, to not let them win and you lose."

Adam would not let up on driving home the point that Pickton had been blackmailed, been made fun of and ridiculed by the women that he thought had been his friends at one time. He assured Pickton that his was a lost cause, that the evidence was being uncovered quickly, and that it spoke for itself. He said that the evidence, in only two weeks, was overwhelming, and that it was coming in so quickly that he had to bring additional personnel in just to help keep it organized. He said that even though he had written three notebooks of information over the past two weeks, he could not even keep the evidence straight himself. He compared it to an avalanche rushing down the side of a mountain and that it would be impossible for Pickton to escape its consequences. He also continued to play on Pickton's guilt, if he felt any, by telling him that the families of the murdered women would only be hurt more if he chose not to talk about his crimes. He said that it would take time for his people to dig up the murdered women, or what was left of them, and that alone would continue breaking the hearts of the numerous families and prevent them from obtaining some sense of closure in their individual cases.

Adam reminded Pickton that Dinah Taylor's family had been urging her to cooperate with the police, and although she had not gotten to the stage of having a lawyer negotiate for her, it would not be long before she began trying to cut a deal with prosecutors.

"Now that you're . . . in custody, she knows that you're dangerous to her, 'cause you know what she has done and you know what Lynn's done," Adam said. "So it's gonna become a race to see who . . . deals with things first. If you let them win . . . that's a mistake, you know. Dave knows it's over. . . ."

Pickton interjected at that point and told Adam that he had to speak with Dinah before he could do anything, apparently referring to telling Adam what really happened.

"To say what?" Adam asked. "Like Dinah, can I—is it all right if I go and show them the bodies?"

"No."

"Willie, look at me for a sec, okay?"

"I gotta talk to her anyways first."

"Well, you're not gonna be able to talk to her," Adam said. "All right. Our people are gonna be negotiating with her over the next little while, and they'll come to some agreement. Dave is saying all right . . .

that it's all going to be over, that there are bodies, and that you didn't kill them all. . . ."

"There are bodies?"

"That there's murder, been murders, and he said you told him. I think he wants to believe in some ways that Dinah killed some of these girls and that, for some of them, you've just helped get rid of the bodies. That is probably partially true, Robert, partially true. Well maybe, maybe it's not. Maybe it was just you couldn't tell your own brother you'd done this. . . .

"I know that you still . . . clearly have feelings for Dinah, don't you?" Adam continued. "Do you understand if Dinah has killed these girls, then she has to deal with that, do you understand that? Does that make sense to you? If she hasn't . . . then we need to know that, so we're not looking at her as a killer."

"Yeah, but I gotta talk to her anyways first, before I say anything," Pickton said.

"No. But . . . let's examine that for a second, Willie. Tell me why we should let you do that."

"Well, I'd like to talk to her."

"No, no, no," Adam said, becoming somewhat frustrated with Pickton's apparent simplicity. "I know, but—but let me ask you this. I mean, if you were a cop, why would you, why would you allow that to happen? If you were in my shoes? Why should I, as a policeman, allow two suspects to talk to each other?"

"Well, I am not a suspect anymore, am I?" Pickton asked after a brief pause.

"No, well, yeah, you're charged, you're—"

"There you are. So I'm not a suspect anymore."

"Well, you're still a suspect in all the other ones. Right?"

"It's gonna come out anyways, right? About myself, it doesn't matter."

"What's the point?"

"That's what I am saying," Pickton said.

"Well, then let's just deal with one step at a time," Adam suggested. "I know you care about Dinah. What about Lynn? How do you feel about her?"

"I think she is a nice person."

"Um-hum. Did you think she was nice when she was blackmailing you? Well, you didn't, did you? No one likes to be blackmailed. Come on, let's be honest with each other."

"Yeah . . . she—she did blackmail me . . . time and time over."

"She says it was because she walked in when you were skinning a girl."

"Yeah, right."

"Well, Willie . . . I'm telling you right now . . . we've got statements from other people saying you've done that. Willie, we've got people saying that you used to have sex with them when they were dead, that you were—"

"Oh yeah, right."

Adam reminded Pickton that he was only trying to make him aware of just how bad things were for him in an effort to clarify his situation, which seemed hopeless.

"You know whether you are the worst monster to ever come down the pike here in Canada"—Adam paused while Pickton laughed out loud—"or not, you know whether you've killed . . . fifty women or—or more."

Adam told him that Bill Fordy had not mentioned to him during his portion of the interview that the blood of eight unidentified women had been found all over his place, particularly inside his trailer, as well as the motor home. Additional evidence of that nature was likely to follow, he indicated. He explained that the investigators believed that the other blood, besides Mona Wilson's, that had been found inside the trailer was likely from other kill sites. He explained that the task force was actually moving a lab on site at the farm to process the evidence as soon as it was found, and that they had devised a method in which they could rapidly separate pig blood from human blood.

"They're gonna be moving into the slaughterhouse, Willie," Adam said. "I absolutely believe we're gonna find human blood in there. What about that? Where do we go then? When everybody's won except you, where do we go? When the deals have been made with the woman who was blackmailing you, when she's escaped her responsibility . . . you only get one chance, and if you want to let her win, get used again—I saw how you felt about being blackmailed. No one likes to be black-mailed, but for the moment, Willie, in your life, you have a chance to pay back. And if you choose not to, then the whore's just used you again. Because the real-ity is some of these guys who are talking about things that you've done, and there's lots of them . . . but the re-ality is, is that you may have things you can say about them, to even things up. But the only way you can do that is by telling the truth and by dealing with it. So you wonder what's in it for you, Willie, it's a chance not to get kicked in the chops again by these people. 'Cause the other side of it . . . you know, we all try and protect ourselves."

25

During one segment of Pickton's lengthy and exhausting interrogation, Inspector Don Adam asked him about Gary Ridgway, who was finally identified as the Green River Killer, whose victims in and around Seattle, Washington, were also prostitutes.

"He may be the only person in North America who's killed more women than you," Adam told Pickton. "Right now, we don't know who's killed more—whether it's you or whether it's him."

Pickton began to laugh, shaking his head simultaneously.

"Well, Willie, I don't know," Adam continued. "I don't have a crystal ball, Willie. I don't know whether you've been killing for fifteen years, or for ten years. Why are you laughing?"

"Just the way you said it," Pickton replied. "F***, that's a lot of people."

"Well, Willie . . . you've killed a lot of people," Adam continued. "Let me ask you a question—without you telling me the number. Do you know how many it is (that you've killed)? Just take your time and think about it. Do you know the number, or is it . . . you don't know anymore?"

"I don't know," Pickton said. "I don't know."

Adam told Pickton that he understood that he was lying to him because he was scared, afraid of being caught. But he emphasized the fact again that it was all over for Pickton, that *he had been caught*. Nonetheless, he decided to play with Pickton's ego for a while.

"You wanted to get away with it," Adam said. "And you did a damn fine job. You completely stumped the police, and basically made them look like fools. All right? And they're going to take a lot of heat for that, Willie, for why they didn't catch Willie Pickton quicker. You led them on a merry chase for years. When you're in prison, the other prisoners are gonna like you for that, 'cause you made the police look stupid. There you sat under their noses, every few months killing a girl, and they didn't have a clue. Willie, it's impressive. . . . You say to yourself, 'I'm a simple pig farmer.' Do you remember saying that? Well, you're not. What you've done is—it's horrible, all right. You understand that it's horrible, but it's impressive. You may well be the most successful killer on the North American continent. You know right now whether you are or not, because if you are up over fifty, you are. Now I wouldn't bet against you being over fifty."

Pickton did not say anything during Adam's speech about what a great killer Pickton was, but instead he sat there quietly, listening and taking it all in as he occasionally looked up at Adam. It seemed, at times, that Adam was getting through to him, slowly breaking him down. Whether or not he would obtain an outright confession from Pickton remained to be seen. He turned away from the approach of feeding Pickton's ego and tried another tactic.

"You know, Willie, if a doctor said to me, 'Don, you got cancer in your right arm,'" Adam said. "If he said to me, 'Well, I'm gonna chop your arm off.' Do you think I would want my arm chopped off, Willie? Do you think I would? But if I knew that if I didn't deal with my arm, if I knew that it was gonna turn into gangrene and I would die, then I'd . . . logically . . . make a decision that you know, I'm finished if I don't do this."

Adam drove home the point that Pickton had no bargaining power except to confess, and even that small chip was quickly disappearing. He pointed out that if Pickton decided not to talk, the investigation would continue "rolling" and the search would continue, leaving the victims' families having to needlessly wait for another year or more, living in uncertainty, before they knew the truth about what had happened to their loved ones. While the families waited, the task force would continue digging and sifting, finding DNA, teeth, hair, bones, body parts, and so forth. Pickton just sat there and laughed.

"You laugh," Adam said, "'cause I know you really don't care."

"I don't think you'll find anything," Pickton clarified. "You won't find anything . . . 'cause there's nothing there."

Adam told Pickton that he did not believe him, and said that he was being foolish if he could not see what the police were going to do on his farm. Adam calmly explained the millions of dollars that would be spent as investigators went over the farm with a fine-tooth comb, and that during the process they would find plenty of evidence to obtain multiple convictions against him. Adam conceded to Pickton that he did not know precisely when he began killing women, whether it started in the 1980s or later, perhaps in the early 1990s. He said that he believed that Pickton was "full blown into it" by 1997, and that it would not be difficult to associate him with twelve of the missing women right then and there.

Pickton just rubbed his eyes as he listened.

He reminded Pickton that blood soaked into the wood paneling behind the wallpaper in his trailer, and would "last there for five hundred years in that state." He said that they would pull off the wallpaper, just to see what was behind it. He also told Pickton that investigators knew that he had changed the carpet in his motor home, and that they had interviewed the person who changed it out.

Adam also conceded that not everyone who had been speaking with the police about the case had said that Pickton was a bad person. In fact, some people had spoken of good things that Pickton had done in his life. Despite the good side of his interviewee, however, Adam told Pickton that something had gone haywire somewhere along the way because, Adam emphasized, it was *not* normal to kill women. He was attempting to cajole Pickton into telling him what had caused his hatred toward women, and what had driven him to the point where he wanted to kill them.

"If you don't take the chance and the opportunity to try and explain things, then every good thing you've done in your life, all the things that your mother would be proud of, and your dad would have been proud of, are gone, are lost," Adam said. "If people can paint you, Willie, as just a . . . simple, evil . . . hideous creature, who not only probably killed all of these women, but maybe . . . would have sexually assaulted the kids that came around the park. . . . We know that you did nice things for some of the kids. You gave them riding lessons. . . . You were good to some people, weren't you?

Do you want people saying that 'well, so and so used to go over to Willie Pickton's—well, he probably had sex with her when she was a little girl.' He . . . was probably screwing little boys. You know, gee . . . the next story will be that you were near schools, stalking kids. That's how people are, Willie. . . . Take ownership of the mistakes you've made, but don't take ownership of everyone else's horrible thoughts. Willie, people are gonna be looking for answers, and if you don't give them the answers, they're gonna make up a thousand stories."

Adam explained how years earlier he had worked as a polygraph examiner and had become an expert at being able to determine whether someone was telling the truth or not. Pickton indicated that he did not know what a lie detector test was, so Adam explained it to him. He also explained how when someone looked him straight in the eye and told him the truth about something, there was a certain "ring" or believability to what was shown in a person's eyes. He told Pickton that he had not seen that "ring of truth" in his eyes when Pickton denied being involved in the missing women's murders. Adam also said that he would know it if Pickton told the truth about something, anything, and that sometimes, because of fear, people only told what they knew in small increments.

At another point Adam again mentioned the allegations that had been made about Pickton having sex with some of the women after they were dead, which Pickton denied, and indicated that it was understandable that he would not want to admit to such horrible things. He also said that people were beginning to make him out to be a "horrible creature" by saying that Pickton enjoyed torturing the women, and enjoyed hearing their screams and seeing the agony that he put them through, perhaps over many long hours.

If Pickton chose not to talk, Adam indicated that people would likely portray him as having done those things, and that was how he would be remembered. Anything good that he had done in his life, even if made public, would quickly be forgotten. He pointed out that some serial killers had done the types of things that Pickton had been accused of—such as torturing the victims and enjoying their agony—and wondered aloud why Pickton should not be portrayed in a similar manner. He explained that many serial killers exhibit a progressive and driven behavior, increasing torture, for instance, with each successive victim until things get very much out of control.

Adam asked Pickton whether, perhaps a year or so down the road after he had closed Pickton's case, he would have to begin looking for another perpetrator who had killed some of the earlier missing women, or would Pickton make a confession to clear many of the cases. Pickton indicated that Adam would have to look for another killer besides him. After seeing Pickton's reaction, he asked him whether a biker, a Hells Angel who knew Pickton and his brother, was involved in any of the killings.

"I don't know." Pickton shrugged.

"Or you don't want to say?"

"I don't know, but there [are] so many people involved in this, it's way over. Way over."

"Let me ask you this question, Willie," Adam continued. "Right now, we're lookin' at you and probably, maybe, three of the girls . . . bringing the prostitutes out to you. Are there other people? Is this bigger than we think?"

"I don't know."

"Willie, did you keep them alive and torture them?"

"Well, I shouldn't answer that question because I am not even in court yet," Pickton said after a short pause.

Adam told Pickton that everything they had said to each other, so far, would obviously end up in court, but he stressed the point to Pickton that they were past the point of whether or not Pickton had committed a number of killings. Adam insisted that Pickton had murdered several women and that he was obtaining the evidence to prove it. What he wanted to focus on now, Adam told Pickton, was whether or not Pickton had killed the women quickly and whether he had drugged them, perhaps so that they would not feel the pain inflicted upon them. Pickton would not respond to Adam's continued probing, at least not by providing specific information.

"I made my own grave," Pickton said. "Now I'm gonna sleep in it . . . for the rest of my life."

"I know," Adam said. "But I'd like to be able to look at the brothers and sisters and mothers and fathers of these women and, if it's the truth, let them know that it's not a situation where you kept them chained up and tortured them and—and reveled in their screams, that you did find a way of either choking them quickly and painlessly, and that they went fast. 'Cause that's important to them. . . . Did they go quickly, Willie? I know you gave them drugs. I know you bought lots of drugs for people before they went out there. Did you allow them to shoot up and—"

"I give 'em money for drugs or whatever, but the problem is . . . whatever they do with the money is up to them."

"Yeah. But . . . when everything is out in the open, are we gonna be looking at stories of days of torture and cutting their fingers off . . . their bodies while they're still alive? Is it gonna be that sort of a thing, Willie?"

Pickton shook his head no.

"Willie, only you can tell me how much these people suffered. . . . Did any of them stay alive for days? Hours?"

"I don't know," Pickton said. "I mean, we are going over our heads here."

"Why do you say that, Willie?"

"'Cause I'm not supposed to talk about it."

"When I talk to these families, how bad is this gonna be, Willie? Give me that. How bad is it gonna be?"

"How bad is what gonna be?"

"How bad is their deaths? Are they tortured? Are you a sadist? Do you know what that means?"

Pickton shook his head no.

Adam reminded Pickton of a conversation that Pickton had had with a younger policeman that Adam worked with during the investigation. The policeman had asked Willie what the best day in his life had been. Adam asked Pickton if he recalled his answer. When Pickton indicated that he did not, Adam recounted what Pickton had told the younger policeman, that the best day of his life had been a day in which he had slaughtered forty to fifty pigs. Pickton had said that he began the slaughter at 7:00 A.M., and continued until about 1:00 or 2:00 A.M.

"Do you remember that day?" Adam asked.

"Yeah, that . . . was a good day at work, but that's not the best day."

"One of the things that people say about you is you know the pig business. Is that true?"

"Um-hum."

"That you are good at slaughtering, you take pride in your work, you do it well."

"And do it clean."

"And you enjoy it."

"I do it clean."

"Willie, do you enjoy it?"

"I don't know if I enjoyed it or not. I just did it for a job."

"You know, Willie, I think there's a part of you that likes killing."

"Hum?"

Adam started in on the numbers again, wanting to know how many women Pickton thought he might have killed over whatever time period, which was still unknown, in which he had been active. Pickton, at one point, wanted to know what was in it for him if he talked and told Adam what he wanted to hear. He made it clear to Adam that he wanted to negotiate a deal to get the police off his farm, but it was not clear why he wanted them to leave. Was it because he felt violated having his property torn up in such a manner? Or did he fear that what they would find might implicate others? Adam told him without hesitation that he was not prepared to make any deals with him.

"The reason is this," Adam said. "I know there's going to be some full bodies buried in there."

"Well, I wish you luck," Pickton said.

"You're saying they all went to the rendering plant?" Adam asked.

"The rendering plant?"

"Well, wherever you took them."

Pickton asked again if the police would leave if he told them everything they wanted to know.

"You want me," Pickton said. "You got me already."

"Yeah, I got you," Adam agreed. "You're absolutely right."

After going back and forth with the reasons why Adam could not make a deal with Pickton, he finally told him that he could not make a deal with him because, if he did, their conversation would not be admissible in court. Pickton said that he simply wanted to help put everyone's lives back together, presumably meaning his brother's and sister's, and that was why he had wanted to make a deal.

"I know all the numbers and everything else," he said. "But that's neither here nor there."

26

Adam reminded Pickton that Pickton had told him and others that he was not a drinker and that he did not use drugs, making it only reasonable to presume that he must have been sober and clearheaded when he committed the murders. As such, Adam suggested that Pickton should not have any difficulty remembering how many victims he had killed. Pickton just looked at him for a few moments before responding.

"What do you want me to say?" Pickton asked.

"You know how many times you've killed," Adam told him. "I mean, every one of those kills is going to be a special moment in your life."

"Umm, no," Pickton said.

"How do you mean that? I don't even understand that. You mean, like, it's just nothing?"

"No, not really," Pickton replied. "Nothing. I don't know."

"See, I need to understand that," Adam said. "Like . . . when you killed these girls, was it a big deal to you? Or was it just like killing . . . one of the pigs? Or somewhere in the middle?"

"Um-hmm," Pickton said. "Well, I don't know. I don't know what to say, neither."

Adam asked him if he had ever killed a woman that he regretted killing, and perhaps whether he had thought afterward that he should have let her go. Pickton, however, would not respond to that line of questioning, and just sat there, in the chair. When Adam moved on to talking about his brother, Dave, again, and said that he had been talking about possibly taking a polygraph test, Pickton spoke up.

"He's not involved in anything. He's protecting me."

Pickton told Adam that other people would be charged with murder besides himself. When Adam pushed him for details, Pickton would only say that it would be a man—one other man.

Adam pointed to the photo board of missing women again, and asked Pickton how many of the women he recognized.

"How many could you reach out and touch?"

"I can touch them all," Pickton said as he pointed toward the poster.

Adam did not know if he was being flippant, or if Pickton meant that he had killed all of them.

"No . . . I mean . . . that you killed?" Adam clarified.

"You make me more of a mass murderer than I am," Pickton replied.

"Are you saying you haven't killed forty-eight?"

"Hmm?"

"But you've killed women who aren't on here, too," Adam said. "So . . . like you said, 'Don't make me more of a mass murderer than I am.' Agreed?"

"That's right."

". . . It's becoming clear to me that there [are] women that you have killed that aren't on here," Adam pushed. "You would agree with me on that. . . ."

"Umm, no comment."

"Why not? Why not just . . . tell me the truth?"

"Because if they're not there, I'm not charged for it, right?"

"Yeah, but what's the difference between two and twenty? . . . It makes no difference [with regard] to the sentence."

"I could say one hundred fifty, too, but it's not any truth involved in there, neither, right?" Pickton asked. "We're grasping for something that's not there. . . . These are the ones you're concentrating on?"

Pickton gestured toward the poster.

"Yup," Adam responded.

"Now, whatever other ones are not on there, I'm not charged, right?"

"That's right. . . . You're only charged with two that are on there. . . . You will be charged with more, obviously, right?"

"Oh, probably. Maybe."

"The DNA is pouring in," Adam said. "But you see, I got to tell ya, I'm sitting here thinking, 'Well, why am I even having this conversation with you?'"

"That's what I've been asking you," Pickton said. "Like I says, I'm the head honcho. . . . I'm the head guy."

"So without you, none of these murders would have happened—is that what you're telling me? Is that true? Or would the other guy that you haven't told me about—"

"No," Pickton said, interrupting Adam. "No . . . there'll be guns involved, too."

"How do you mean, guns?"

"Well, like I said, they'll be guns involved, too," Pickton said. "There will be at least one extra gun . . . involved."

"That you've used to kill a girl?"

"Mmm, um, on other things. That's over your head, like I said. . . ."

Adam told Pickton that investigators had developed information showing that Dave had picked up some of the girls and brought them out to the farm, which Pickton quickly denied. Whether it was true or not, Pickton had no way of knowing—it could have been a form of leverage Adam was using to try and draw out information about whether other people were involved. Pickton, however, swore that his brother was not involved.

"It's just you?" Adam asked.

"He, ah, just me?"

"Well, you . . . never been involved with the girls with him—"

"No."

"Even just sexually?"

"No, nothing to do with Dave."

"Willie, you didn't do a good job of cleaning up the girls' blood," Adam said. "Like, you got to agree with me."

"That's right," Pickton said. "I was sloppy."

"Yes, you were," Adam said, breaking into laughter. "That sums it up."

"That's what I am," Pickton agreed. "I'm sloppy."

"How could Dave not see that?"

"'Cause he's too busy," Pickton replied. "Let's leave it that way, there."

"With everything that was going on, how . . . do you think you managed to avoid getting caught for so long?"

"No comment."

"Come on . . . is it just bad police work, or . . . like what?"

"Carelessness on my behalf."

Pickton told Adam that if he and his task force wanted to dig up the entire property, they could go right ahead—but he insisted that if they did, they would not find anything. Pickton mentioned that he had heard that there were people making comments about mass graves being on the property, and Adam attempted to persuade Pickton to take investigators to such locations. His reasoning was that if Pickton could pinpoint mass graves, it would simplify things for the investigators and allow them to get off the property sooner rather than later, which was what Pickton had indicated he wanted. Pickton said that he would if he could, but he indicated that he could not because such mass graves did not exist on his property. Pickton told Adam that the reason this case was so difficult for the cops was because of their own "bad policing" for so long.

"Yeah, 'cause it took so long to catch you," Adam agreed. "You're right. I know a lot of policemen who feel bad for the families of these people. Did you ever think of quitting?"

"Yeah."

"Was it . . . that drive we talked about?" Adam asked, insinuating that Pickton was driven to kill by something inside him. "I would like to know, 'cause obviously someday I'll be sitting here with somebody else, Willie."

"Yeah, it'll all come out," Pickton said. "It'll all come out."

Feeling that he'd come a long way in getting Pickton to incriminate himself despite the fact that Pickton had not given up too many specifics, Adam continued to press on, looking for a motive. He asked Pickton if he had killed the women because of fantasies, and Pickton shook his head no.

"Anger then?" Adam asked. "You sort of said it was anger. Would I be right in saying, Willie, that you had reached the stage where you just no longer . . . really viewed these girls as being worth anything?"

"Um-hum," Pickton replied. ". . . I had one more planned, but that was—that was the end of it. That was the last. I was gonna shut it down. . . . I was just sloppy, just the last one."

"You were gonna do one more?" Adam asked.

Pickton said something, but it was unintelligible. Then he continued: "That was the end of it. That's why I got sloppy . . . because the other thing never got that far."

Adam was not sure what he meant by the "other thing," but he had what he needed—an admission of guilt, of sorts. He asked Pickton why he had not simply dragged the mattress out of his motor home, where he had killed Mona Wilson, and burned it. Hadn't he realized that there was blood underneath it, lots of blood?

"Sloppy, like I just told you," Pickton said.

Adam asked Pickton about keeping trophies of his kills, like many serial killers do, but he quickly denied doing so. He just brushed off all the things found inside his trailer and motor home—such as the inhaler, identification cards, clothing, and so forth—simply as having been "sloppy."

"Jesus, Willie," Adam said. "You must be kicking yourself."

"I know."

"All you would have had to do . . . is go through [everything] and clean up . . . and you'd still be on the street."

"I know."

"It must piss you off."

"I know."

Adam then explained to Pickton that there was "blood cast-off" on the mattress and other locations, caused by someone being struck or hit, possibly with some kind of blunt object. He was talking about Mona Wilson, but it was not clear whether he was baiting Pickton or if what he was telling him was based on conclusive evidence that it was Mona Wilson's blood that had been cast off from sustaining blows to her body. They had said earlier that much of the blood in the motor home had been Wilson's, but they indicated uncertainty about whom the blood on the mattress belonged to—being only two weeks into the investigation, things were happening and changing quickly as tests were performed and new evidence continued to surface on nearly an hourly basis.

"Hitting her?" Pickton asked, appearing shocked at the accusation. "What do you mean? No, no, no . . . you guys are way off the deep end."

Why did Pickton keep playing these games? Why didn't he just tell him how he killed her? Adam wanted to know, becoming frustrated again.

"Well, there's impact blood," Adam said. "There's blood that's cast off from . . . where she's lying."

"Umm-hmm," Pickton said.

"Well, how do you explain that then? I don't understand. . . . I know there's bloody palm prints in there, too. Was she trying to get away? I mean, clearly, you didn't choke her to death, Willie . . . because there's blood all over the place."

Adam asked him if he had used a hatchet or a hammer on the victim, and Pickton denied using either.

"Like, what?" Adam asked. "Tell me! Come on, man, I'm dying to know, for heaven sakes."

"Um-hmm."

"Share at least that much with me."

"It'll come out in the wash."

"Come on," Adam pleaded. "Come on, we sat here all night. You're dying to tell me. I can see it in your eyes."

"Um-hmm" was all that he would say.

"What did you use?"

"Sloppiness."

Pickton said that he was too busy working job sites to clean up. He did not specify the job sites or what the work consisted of, however. He also did not answer Adam when he asked him if he had killed Mona Wilson on a weekend or on a weeknight, and he was silent for a few seconds before saying anything.

"You're making me a murderer, more than I am," Pickton finally said.

"Well, no, I'm not," Adam argued. "You've made yourself a murderer. My suspicion is that with your memory, you probably know exactly what day, you know what time at night, everything. Let's deal with just that one, Mona Wilson, in the mobile home. Firstly, why take her to the mobile home? Like, why not do it in your trailer?"

"No comment," Pickton said.

"Just 'cause it was gonna be messy?"

"No."

"Was she living out there, or staying there?"

"No comment."

"Willie, come on," Adam pleaded again. "Give it up. Come on, you owe me that much."

"You're not gonna . . . ," Pickton began, and paused. "You've been thinking on this one, eh? You've been thinking on this one for a while. . . . You really must be doing your—your homework."

"I do tend to do my homework," Adam agreed.

Pickton began laughing out loud again.

27

"Okay, there's sort of three . . . sites, Willie," Adam said, referring to locations where women were murdered on the farm. "The motor home—so you killed Mona—"

"Let's work with the motor home," Pickton interrupted.

"Okay. The motor home—you killed Mona on the bed, right? We agreed, on the foamy [mattress]. But there's another . . . more blood, agree?"

"No."

"That's what happened, yeah," Adam disagreed. "'Cause, well, the blood tells the truth, right?"

Before Pickton could respond, Bill Fordy entered the interrogation room. He was holding a large photograph of Pickton's pig farm, taken from the air. Pickton's eyes gleamed when he saw it.

"Oh, that's nice," Pickton said.

"They've got a lot of fancy pictures of your place," Adam said. He gestured toward the motor home on the large aerial photo. "So let's talk about it and . . . how many girls died in there. Mona died on the foamy, all right?"

"No comment."

"Well, we just discussed that," Adam said. "So, how many other girls died in there? We have other blood trails of other victims in there."

"Why? What else you got in there?" Pickton asked.

"Ah, more blood, different . . . from a different person."

"So . . . how many girls in there?" Adam asked. He was getting tired, but he was not about to give up now. "One, for sure . . . this is one way we can test your truthfulness, Willie. If you're truthful with me and you go, 'Well, Don, you could find up to five different women's blood in there,' and we do find, then we can sit there and say, 'Okay . . . now we can start to believe what Willie says.'"

"Uh-huh."

"So my question is, how many?"

"I'd say two, probably two, maybe three," Pickton replied.

"Okay, so we've got Mona, obviously, right?" Adam asked.

"No. We've got nobody yet."

"Yeah, we do. We got Mona. Trust me. Mona's the one . . . with her blood. Did you use that dildo on her? It's got her DNA on the tip, it's got yours. You did, didn't you? Was she alive or dead?"

"Alive."

"When you used it, eh? Did you shoot her?"

"Shoot her?"

"Yeah, well, it's on the .22—"

"No. There's not holes through it. I put no holes through that," Pickton said, referring to the dildo on the end of the gun.

"But you might have taken it off and shot the girl,"

Adam theorized aloud. "Like, whatever you did caused a lot of blood."

"Um-hmm," Pickton said. "You did some of your homework."

"Why not just tell me?"

"What can I tell ya?"

"You're having fun playing cat and mouse with me here, Willie. True?"

Pickton did not respond.

"Let me ask you this question," Adam said at another point in the interrogation. "Was it hard to do at first, and then it just gets easier? You don't think about it as much, it doesn't make you feel bad afterward? Did you feel bad after them at first?"

"I don't know."

"Yeah, I think you do, Willie. . . . You know they infected you, they stabbed you, they used you, they stole from you, didn't they, Willie? And you lashed back, not at everyone, though. How come you spared some of them?"

"They're nice people."

"And so the nice ones you let go? . . . Willie, come on. We don't need to play games with each other. Are you just not quite convinced yet you want to tell me the details of the killings? Is that . . . it? Come on, tell me the truth. Are you still thinking, 'What's in it for me?'"

Adam turned the questioning back to Mona Wilson. He asked Pickton when he took her out to the farm and killed her—then told him that he believed it was sometime in November or December 2001. Pickton sat quietly for a few seconds, and was obviously relaxed and comfortable with Adam and his questions. He was leaning back in the chair by this time, and had his feet propped up on the desk.

"You're close," Pickton finally said.

"Come on, cough it up," Adam urged.

"You're close," he repeated.

"But you used the dildo on her when she was still alive, is that true?" Adam asked.

"Mm-hmm."

"Did she do anything to . . . send you into a rage?"

"No, she didn't want to have any sex," Pickton said. "She didn't want to do anything."

"So you—what?" Adam asked. "Did you just lose control of yourself?"

"No, no comment," Pickton said, laughing loudly again. "No comment at this stage. I'm already talking to you guys, but I'm not even supposed to talk to you, but that's neither here nor there. I'm nailed to the cross. . . ."

"Yeah, you are," Adam said. "That's true. . . . Do you remember where you killed the other girl with the inhaler?"

"No comment, again."

Adam, guessing, suggested that Pickton had killed Sereena Abotsway in the slaughtering area. He pointed out the slaughterhouse to Pickton on the aerial photograph that Fordy had brought into the room.

"Or was she dead by the time she made it there?" Adam asked.

"No comment."

"If you want me to believe that you haven't buried these girls whole . . . then . . . what you're telling me . . . is that ultimately you either took them into the slaughter area alive, or took them in there dead and disposed of them."

"No comment. . . . I already told you how many's in the trailer. Probably, maybe, up to as high as three in that . . . motor home. . . . That was as far as we got."

"Right," Adam said.

"Possibly," Pickton added.

Adam informed Pickton that he needed to leave the room for a few minutes, and asked him if he was getting tired. It was getting late, and Pickton had been in the interrogation room for nearly ten hours by that time. The cops had been sweating him all day, and he seemed to take it in stride. Pickton said that he was okay. However, his demeanor began to change noticeably at that point.

"Yeah, you seem okay," Adam said. "Frankly, you've got more zip in you now than I do."

"No," Pickton replied. "It's just I'm telling you right now because I'm nailed to the cross anyways."

"Why not give me everything then?" Adam asked.

"Why should I do that?"

"I guess if I said it would be the right thing to do, Willie, that wouldn't mean anything?"

"No . . . 'cause I gotta talk to Dinah first, I told you that."

"So the families of these people, the families of these girls—"

"That's not . . . my problem," Pickton said, interrupting Adam.

"But they're not—" Adam said, but he was cut off again.

"Shit happens," Pickton said.

"Well, you certainly sum up how you feel about it," Adam said.

Pickton tried to turn the conversation back to his offer of a deal, if he could talk to Dinah, and how it would free up the property and help the investigators with their workload. Adam, however, was not having any of it.

"I mean, I'm . . . nailed," Pickton said again. "What I'm saying is I'm freeing the property and taking a lot of extra work off your hands . . . ," Pickton said.

"You know something?" Adam asked. "I could care

less about the work. . . . My sole reason for being with you here is to try to do something for these families."

"Mm-hmm."

"All right," Adam said. "I know you . . . don't understand that, and I accept that—"

"Yeah, but the problem is, I'm nailed already—so, what can I do? Honestly, you tell me. What can I do?"

"Well, let me ask you a question," Adam said. "If it was your niece or nephew . . . what would you want?"

"If it was my niece or nephew?" Pickton asked. "They're at the wrong place at the right time. What else can I say?"

Adam mentioned that he and his investigators had heard about a thing called "blood sport" that had been occurring at the farm, and that other people had been involved. The so-called blood sport, Adam said, involved a number of people—a group—that would kill the girls. Pickton laughed at the suggestion, and even though he acknowledged that there were other people involved, *but* he would not say what they had been involved in, he refused to name them. Instead, he simply told Adam that he would "just take the fall."

Adam also asked Pickton if he or others had made any snuff films at the farm; to which Pickton responded that they had not made such films.

If Adam was not disgusted with his interview subject throughout the interrogation, he must have been by now. His revulsion and loathing of Pickton was beginning to show as he was having difficulty holding his true feelings in check. He was tired, and he was sick of the games that Pickton seemed to enjoy playing with him. He had tried to appeal to Pickton's good side, if he had one, and had failed. Sure, he had dragged bits and pieces of information out of the pig farmer, and had actually managed to get him to admit to some of the killings. But it had become clear to him by eleven hours into the interrogation that Pickton, like most serial killers, had no sense of empathy and was unable to put himself into the shoes of others, unable to see what they saw and unable to feel what they felt. Any sympathy that he had exhibited, such as the occasional tears and the wiping of his eyes, had been for himself, not for the victims or their families.

Pickton was a very basic human being, but at the low end, only slightly above the animals, which lacked the ability to reason, that he had slaughtered all his life before turning to humans. Like all normal humans, but unlike the lower animals, Pickton had the *ability* to reason, and he had free will. He simply chose to make the wrong choices and decisions, likely out of a basic need for instant gratification to satisfy some inner urge, or perhaps rage, that he chose not to reveal. "Monster" was probably too kind a word to describe him.

Adam sat down again, instead of leaving the interrogation room like he had planned, and told Pickton that his complete lack of caring about the women that he had killed was his business—but Adam could not understand him, no matter how hard he tried. Pickton tried to counter his remarks, but again Adam did not want to hear it.

"I respect them for worrying about their offspring," Pickton said of the victims' relatives, "and for worrying about where they're located, or where they are, or [whether] they're inside a cave, or here or there. Yes, I would be in the same position as they are. But at my stage right now, I haven't got nothing to say, at this stage. . . . The part that bothers me the most is you got the whole place tied up and my brother can't do anything. That's all I'm saying."

Adam told him that it was his job to sit there and try to see things through Pickton's eyes, and that he had to do that in order to try and move the case forward. He was giving Pickton a glimpse of how he really felt about it all, all the while trying to hold back—in the event he needed to talk to Pickton again later. But it showed that he was having a tough time with it, and Pickton could see it.

"I have to try to understand you," Adam said. "And I have to talk lightly about what you did, because otherwise I'm gonna shut you down and you won't talk to me. All right? But at the same time, I'm seized with the fact that while you and I are talking about this, as if it's so many, ah, used cars . . . [but] there are people whose hearts are being broken, and . . . well, I just want you to know how much it bothers me to have to sit here and act as if this is just a chess game."

"Do I get to go back to my cell?" Pickton asked.

"Yup. Let me talk to my people and I'm sure we can arrange that."

It was 9:47 P.M. when Adam walked out of the interrogation room and left Pickton alone for a few moments to admire the aerial photograph, which had been taken of his farm. A short time later, as he was taken out of the interview room, Pickton glanced at several boxes that had been stacked against one of the walls. Some were labeled *DNA evidence,* and others were labeled *Toxicology reports, informants, and surveillance.* Pickton did not know it, but they were there merely for show—each was fake. But seeing them would give him plenty to think about and, Adam hoped, might cause him to have a change of heart and divulge more about the killings than he had during the lengthy interview. He was led into the visitor's area of the facility, where he met for a short time with his lawyer, and afterward he was taken back to his cell. He seemed unusually upbeat as he walked into his cell.

Part 4

Down on Robert Pickton's Farm—Again

28

When Pickton returned to his cell after meeting with his lawyer, following the eleven-hour-plus interview with Fordy, Lillies, and Adam, he did not seem particularly happy, but he seemed pumped, full of life. His present state could have been the result of having relived—at least in his mind—during his interviews with the RCMP officers much of what he had done to many of Vancouver's missing women. Whatever the cause had been, he was not ready to go to bed yet and call it a day. He clearly was in a talkative mood, and he hadn't a clue that the person he shared a cell with was an RCMP undercover officer.

"What time is it?" his cellmate asked when Pickton walked into the cell.

"Ten," Pickton replied.

"At night? You've been gone all day. F***, they beatin' you up in there, or what?" the cellmate asked.

"Yeah, they nailed me to the cross," Pickton said, repeating what had become one of his favorite phrases. "They got . . . three or four murders on me already."

"Really?"

"It's too big," Pickton said.

"Huh?"

"It's too big," Pickton repeated as he sat down on his bunk. "I guess I'll never get out."

"Huh?"

"The rest of my life without parole. Without parole . . . ," Pickton said with a gloomy tone in his voice. "I can't believe this. . . . F***, they're sure putting me through the wringer . . . like a f***ing nightmare in hell."

"Yeah."

Pickton expressed his opinion about how unpleasant the "f***ing long day" was with the cops, and how the investigators had told him they were gathering a lot of evidence against him, enough to charge him with thirty or more counts of murder.

"They want me real bad," he said.

"Yeah?"

"Now I'm all over the paper," Pickton said, speaking in a hushed voice. "Made the headlines. *Whoo!* 'Pig farmer charged with murder, first degree' . . . right across the f***ing headlines."

"You're an all-star."

"I told them, I says, 'If I'm going to be charged, I [need to] see some of the films.' I says, 'I'll key the queue, I'll make you a bargain,'" Pickton said. ". . . But I told them that 'you're going to have to open your mind to me. I'll tell you what you're gonna do, you see.' And he says, 'You can't tell me that, you're not a cop.' I says, 'You're just as much cop as I am. . . .' I told them already, I says, 'I'm not the only one. If I go down, a lot of other people are going to go down.'"

"That's what you gotta do, right?"

"F***."

"You really f***ing have to be careful," the cellmate said.

"I think I might have buried myself, 'cause I'm a key holder," Pickton said.

"Ha, well. What are you gonna do?" his cellmate asked.

"'If you want me,' I says, 'you want me . . . it's not up to them to tell you, it's up to the judge,'" Pickton said.

Pickton told his cellmate that even though he believed he had the police confused, he did not believe he would ever be a free man again. He figured that he would be serving a life sentence without parole by the time he was convicted in court. He was not even sure how many murders he would be tried for—so far, it was two or three. He mentioned how he had beat the rap in the earlier case involving the stabbing of Wendy Eistetter, but this time he believed he was finished.

"This time I'm not gonna walk," Pickton said. "I won't even come up for bail. . . . They said no. . . . I haven't got a record. I'm clean."

"Nothing?" his cellmate asked.

"No."

"That's a bonus."

"I've got, ah, two murder charges, now," Pickton said.

Pickton heard the sound of the metal tray as his evening meal was slid under the door. He went over and picked it up. His cellmate had eaten earlier. It appeared to be beans again, and it did not look appetizing. As he had done before, he gave the coffee, which came with the meal, to his cellmate.

"That's [some] f***ing harsh shit," his cellmate said about the beans.

Pickton was hungry, however, and ate it all. He even sopped the liquid up with his bread, all the while talking between bites with his cellmate about his cellmate's charges.

"They got you for murder charges? Or attempted murder?" Pickton asked.

"Well, they got . . . the attempt. They got—I talked to my lawyer. . . . There's some more pending . . . a couple more f***ing things they've got on me," his cellmate said.

"But you're nothing like mine," Pickton said.

"I'm f***ing looking at some serious time if . . . they put things together," his cellmate said. "Do you know what I mean?"

At that point in their conversation, Pickton held up his right hand in the open position, clearly showing all his fingers and thumb, apparently to indicate five. He then quickly made the appearance of a zero with his thumb and index finger. He then pointed at himself and placed a finger on his lips, telling his cellmate to be quiet and not say anything. The effort to keep his cellmate quiet did not work, however.

"What's that? Five? Zero?" the cellmate said.

Pickton laughed quietly and put his finger on his lips again to shush his cellmate, then gestured toward the camera. He went through the motion again, this time using two hands—five fingers of his right hand and forming the zero with his left hand.

"Fifty?" his cellmate asked quietly.

Pickton nodded to indicate yes, with a broad, wicked-looking smile on his face.

"Ha, ha, f*** you," his cellmate said. "You're . . . shitting me."

"Camera," Pickton said, gesturing at the camera again.

Pickton's shushing of his cellmate and the fact that the camera was ever-present did not seem to stop them from talking. Pickton was doing an outstanding job of incriminating himself, even though he seemed to know better than to talk in the presence of the video camera.

"You, yourself? I've done a few of these," his cellmate said.

"Um-hum."

"I've done a few. Yeah, I've a f***ing few under my belt. You're full of shit, man, you're [messing] with me. . . . I remember the first one I did, the very first one, took a pickax. Do you know what a pickax is?"

"Um-hum."

"For cracking ice—"

"Yeah, I know what it is."

"Put it right in here," Pickton's cellmate said, pointing toward the back of his head. "There's . . . like hardly any mess, no f***ing blood, and f***ing hard to detect, eh. It takes the cops a while to figure out what the f*** happened to the guy."

It was clear that Pickton really did not want to hear or talk about what his cellmate had done, but instead wanted to talk about his own situation.

"I buried myself now," Pickton said.

"How?"

"Got me. They got me on this," Pickton said as he finished up his evening meal.

"No shit. Give me a break. What have they got?"

"I don't know, there's old carcasses," Pickton said.

"So, what have you got? You know what I'm saying?" his cellmate asked.

"DNA."

"F***!"

"Yeah."

"Come on, buddy . . . that's nothing. They can't finalize, though, if you've got a f***ing missing person. It's f***ing pretty hard to collect DNA on that."

"They've got DNA," Pickton said.

His cellmate, in an effort to extract additional information from Pickton, told him that the best way to dispose of something was to dump it into the ocean.

"Oh, really?" Pickton asked with a somewhat wily tone in his voice.

"Do you know what the f***ing ocean does to things? There ain't much left," his cellmate said.

"I did better than that," Pickton said, grinning again.

"No."

Pickton slid his meal tray under the cell door and sat down next to his cellmate so that, he believed, he could speak undetected.

"A rendering plant," he whispered, sniggering creepily under his breath.

"Hey?"

"A rendering plant," Pickton repeated.

"Ha! No shit. . . . That's gotta be pretty good, eh?"

"Mm-hmm."

"Can't be much f***ing left."

Pickton told the cellmate that he was caught because he was becoming sloppy toward the end.

"Really," the cellmate said.

"They got me—oh f***—gettin' too sloppy," Pickton said. ". . . I was gonna do one more, make it an even fifty," Pickton said.

Pickton's cellmate laughed.

"That's why . . . I was sloppy about . . . I wanted one more, make—make the big five-oh," Pickton said.

"Make the big five zero," his cellmate said, laughing. "That's f***ed. F***ing five-zero. F***ing half a hundred."

Pickton chuckled evilly at his cellmate's remarks, thinking, of course, that they had been made in adoration of his ability to kill forty-nine women.

"Yeah. Like you say, that's the best part . . ." his cellmate said.

"Everybody says," Pickton said, pounding his fist. "How many of those? Wouldn't tell 'em. . . . I wouldn't tell 'em."

Pickton told his cellmate how the investigators had asked him to talk about all his victims and how he had refused. He seemed proud that he had not given in to what the cops had asked him.

"You know, they got forty-eight on the list," Pickton said matter-of-factly as he talked about the official list of missing women as it appeared at that time in 2002. "You know the list has only got, like, only got half the people in there."

If what Pickton had just said to his cellmate was true, investigators would be hard-pressed to find out what had happened to the other half of the missing women on the list. And if Pickton had really killed forty-nine women, like he had said, but only half of those women were on the official list, who were the other women that he had killed?

"How does that all fit?" his cellmate asked. "That helps you."

"Yeah . . . but I think most of them, based on that f***ing . . . evidence, I think I'm nailed to the cross."

"Hmmm."

"But if that happens, there will be about fifteen other people [that] are gonna go down. Some will go down the tank," Pickton said.

"Yeah."

"I said they were my friends," Pickton said.

"Huh. Hey, between me and you, man . . . you look after it for yourself," his cellmate said.

"I thought they were my friends. . . . I seen in the interview . . . people . . . even says I filled the syringes up with antifreeze and you inject the stuff and you're dead in about five to ten minutes," Pickton said.

"*Hmmm.*"

". . . They got a lot of stuff on me," Pickton said. "That's only part of it. . . . They're gonna nail me to the cross."

Pickton told his cellmate that the cops had told him that if he had kept his act clean—that if he had not gotten sloppy—he would have likely gotten away with murdering Vancouver's prostitutes for a lot longer. He said he knew that was how they had gotten him—his sloppiness, and the guns that they had come to find.

"I made my own grave by being sloppy," Pickton said.

"Doesn't that just kick you in the ass now?"

"It pisses me off, no way," Pickton said. "You know it pisses me right off. . . . They just—they don't have nothing, but nothing. . . . Really pisses me off. I was just gonna f***ing do one more, make it even."

As his cellmate laughed about what he had said, Pickton began getting undressed in preparation for turning in for the night. He took off his jogging suit and began scratching as he gloated over his new celebrated status.

"Bigger than . . . the ones in the States," Pickton said. He was talking about the Green River case, which, he told his cellmate, the police had talked about during his lengthy interview. His cellmate agreed that Pickton's case was bigger than Green River.

"F***, it looks like you got the record," his cellmate said.

"It's big. It's growing," Pickton said. "They say they want to dig. . . . They want to dig . . . they're gonna dig for a year."

"That's unbelievable."

"Let 'em dig," Pickton said. "I told them already . . . 'No shit. Have fun. Play in the dirt.'" Pickton sniggered as he spoke. "'Teeth, we're gonna find fingernails, bones,'" Pickton said, indicating what the investigators had told him. "Mr. Sloppy. Sloppy at the end."

"F***, they're gonna burn your ass."

Pickton lay quietly on his bunk for several moments, staring up at the ceiling. When he spoke again, he told of how he had stumped the cops and had confused them during the interrogation. "But I sure racked their brains, I'll tell ya," Pickton said. "Now they didn't know what to say."

"You stumped them, eh?" the cellmate said, laughing.

"Oh, f*** yeah, I had 'em going," Pickton bragged. "I had them going. I was sitting in the chair and everything else. . . . I really had them going today."

Pickton had become even more boastful by this time. He told his cellmate that he had been in control of the interrogation. He said that he sat back in the chair and propped his feet up on the desk as he "screwed" with the investigators' minds. He told his cellmate that he had even told the cops that he was looking forward to additional interrogation sessions, hopefully sooner rather than later. His cellmate changed the subject at one point and steered Pickton back toward the number of kills he had made, playing on his ego by saying that Pickton must have the highest number of victims.

"Hmm. God . . . you're f***ing up there (in numbers). That's gotta . . . like you say, put you over the top," his cellmate said.

They talked about how many victims' lives the Green River killer had claimed, but could not seem to agree on an accurate number. When Pickton apparently grew tired of comparing himself to Gary Ridgway, he returned to the investigation that was occurring at his farm.

". . . They even took my—my linoleum off the floor," Pickton said. "Peeled it right off. Peeled all the wallpaper off the walls. . . . They're digging deep. They're digging real deep."

"Yeah, they're working hard."

"Real hard," Pickton agreed. ". . . Four I was sloppy with. I just couldn't finish it off, so I cleaned it up and that's it."

Pickton indicated that his plan had been to let things cool off for a while, then start back up again at a later date. "Then, then do . . . another twenty-five new ones," he said, laughing out loud.

It appeared to the cops watching the video monitors that Pickton was enjoying himself. Smiling broadly, he waved toward the camera on at least two occasions and said "hello" on another. Whether he knew that he was being recorded or not was not entirely clear. Because he had indicated to his cellmate to be quiet a few times, it seemed like he had been concerned about being recorded. On the other hand, he had been talking very freely, although in hushed tones, for quite some time, indicating that perhaps he thought that he was only being viewed in the cell, so that guards could see that they were still there and were behaving themselves, and not recorded. It was also possible that he knew that everything was being taped and he was providing inaccurate, misleading information, thinking that he could confuse the cops even more than he had already—at least in his mind, that is.

At one point Pickton and his cellmate began talking

about guns, and Pickton reminded him that it was because of guns that he had been caught. Pickton told the cellmate that he had a MAC-10, a compact machine pistol, as well as a "ten mil, a .45, and a .38." He said that he did not believe that the police had found his .38-caliber weapon yet.

"Guns. That's how they got me, f***ing guns," Pickton said.

"F***! Just a little thing like that, eh?" the cellmate said.

"They took the walls out of my trailer," Pickton said. "So I don't know if they found it. I got over a hundred rounds of each. . . . Forty-nine."

"Almost made it," the cellmate said as Pickton reflected on nearly making his kills an even fifty.

"I'm worried about it," Pickton said. ". . . All the way up to fifty. I haven't done fifty yet." Pickton began laughing again.

"Yeah, screws you, though," his cellmate said.

"Maybe that means that, maybe that, maybe it does show you that, before they made the list . . ." Pickton trailed off, obviously thinking aloud about the list of missing women, but he did not finish his thought, at least not verbally. ". . . Top of the world."

"Yeah, for sure. Oh, for sure."

"And pigs are baffled, the pigs are baffled," Pickton said.

"Are baffled?"

"Pigs—cops," Pickton clarified.

"Oh," the cellmate said, laughing. "I'm thinking you're a pig farmer. Don't mess with me here."

"Now they're going to dig in the manure and see if . . . the pigs shit out human remains," Pickton said.

"They wouldn't eat human remains. F***ing pigs don't eat that."

"I know that, but you can't tell 'em that," Pickton said. "They never seen nothing like this ever before. But they might have already got it. . . . They haven't charged me for it, so maybe they haven't. . . . F*** me. So close."

Lying on his back, with his hands folded across his chest, Pickton told his cellmate that he planned to mess with the investigators' minds again the following day. Then he expressed that it would be a relief to go to jail.

"Better than sitting in this shit hole," his cellmate agreed.

Pickton began fantasizing about being a celebrity in prison, how the other prisoners would congratulate him—particularly for giving the cops the slip for so long and for trying to confuse them after being caught. The other prisoners would be shaking his hand, awestruck by his very presence.

"'I can't believe it. I mean, I can't believe it. I'm with the pig man,'" Pickton said, imagining aloud how the other prisoners might react to him.

His cellmate told him that he would be signing autographs in prison.

For the next few minutes, Pickton wavered back and forth about how he would be able to cut a deal with the cops so that he would be able to speak with a person from Ontario. Although he never mentioned the person by name to his cellmate, he was, of course, referring to Dinah. He desperately wanted to talk to her about something of great importance to him, and he believed that he could convince the cops to allow him to do so. He believed that he was holding the winning hand, and that the cops would keep returning to him for more of the information they were so anxious to get. In the next breath his wave of confidence suddenly diminished and he was back to saying how "dead" he was, that the cops had the goods on him. He wanted to believe that he would beat this rap, but he knew deep inside that he was finished. If he ever killed anyone else, it would not be a woman.

At 11:30 P.M., Pickton told his cellmate that he was tired.

"Got a long day tomorrow," Pickton said.

"Yeah. Better get some rest."

"So close," Pickton said as he pulled the thin blanket up around him and fell asleep.

29

Within days of Robert Pickton's name being splashed in large bold print across the front pages of many of Canada's major newspapers, several relatives of at least seven of Vancouver's missing women came out publicly to question police procedures and how the investigation had been handled—or, in their opinions, mishandled. Several of the relatives had spoken up before and had voiced their opinions, to no avail. Now, however, it had become crystal clear that investigators had known about Pickton and his pig farm for more than four years, yet they had not focused on him as a prime suspect in the missing women. Now that knowledge was in all of the newspapers, including information that over the past several years police had received a number of tips about Pickton's pig farm and that several of the sex trade workers from the Downtown Eastside had gone there regularly to participate in Pickton's parties.

The boyfriend of Andrea Joesbury, Mohamed Khogaini, spoke to the media and said that the police had questioned him a few months after Joesbury disappeared. Joesbury, who was listed as the forty-seventh woman on the Joint Missing Women Task Force poster, was believed to have disappeared in June 2001.

"They talked to me and wanted to know if she went to Coquitlam," Khogaini said, demonstrating that the police at least suspected that there were some links to the pig farm at that time.

Joesbury, it was revealed, had been a friend of Dinah Taylor's. Taylor, it was publicly stated, had lived on Pickton's farm until December 2001, only a couple of months before his arrest, and it had been shown that Taylor was responsible for inviting a number of the sex trade workers to parties at Pickton's farm.

By the end of March 2002, the task force added thirty investigators to work alongside the eighty investigators and twelve forensic experts who were already working on the farm. The task force also revised its estimate of how long investigators might be at the farm—at first they figured it might take them a year to complete their work there, but now they were saying that it could take up to three years.

Also by the end of March 2002, the task force added the names of five more women to its list of missing females. However, one of the women was located within a few days, alive and well and residing in eastern Canada.

On April 3, 2002, Pickton was charged with three additional counts of first-degree murder for the deaths of Jacquelene McDonell, Dianne Rock, and Heather Bottomley. According to information that was released by prosecutor Michael Petrie's office, McDonell was believed to have been murdered sometime after January 21, 1999; Rock after October 19, 2001; Bottomley after March 21, 2001. Pickton, who appeared in the courtroom of Judge David Stone via closed-circuit television from the jail, was expressionless as the new charges were read to him.

* * *

As Robert Pickton languished in jail, the work at his farm continued nonstop. The digging and sifting of the earth continued at several locations on the farm, which had been turned, literally, into a major excavation site. Tim Sleigh, the CSI expert who had been involved in the search for evidence in the Mission area in 1995, following the discovery of the human skull that had been neatly sawed in half, had been working on the farm along with several other CSI experts. He had been kept busy searching for evidence and collecting incriminating items such as hair, blood, fingerprints, teeth, bones, and so forth.

Power failures had occurred on Pickton's farm as a result of the excavating equipment being used in the search for evidence, and at one point, on April 4, 2002, two months into the massive operation, Sleigh became concerned that the power outages might cause items to spoil, including potential evidence, in a number of freezers at various locations on Pickton's farm. Many items, including the freezers, had not been searched yet because they had been deemed a lower priority than some of the other areas, such as the slaughterhouse and Pickton's trailer. However, one of the freezers, located in a corner of a back room inside Pickton's workshop, had begun to smell, reeking of a horrible odor that resembled that of decomposition. Sleigh asked RCMP sergeant Fred Nicks to accompany him to the back room.

Before they could open the freezer to take a look inside, Sleigh and Nicks had to remove several heavy items from the freezer's lid. After setting the items on the floor, Nicks raised the lid a few inches and held it there, despite the strong, horrible odor coming from inside the freezer, while Sleigh looked inside, aided by a flashlight. He saw two plastic buckets lying on their sides, and noted that one of them had been partially inserted into the other. When he reached in with his hands to move the buckets so that he could get a better look, he quickly stepped back and asked Nicks to have a look and to tell him what he could see.

"Looks like a human head," Nicks said, trying to contain his revulsion.

Using his training as a CSI expert, Sleigh ordered that the freezer, as well as the entire back room of Pickton's workshop, be carefully photographed and processed before moving anything. It was the first instance in which the police had actually recovered human remains on Pickton's farm, and Sleigh wanted everything done strictly by the book. Once the preliminary work had been accomplished, Sleigh and Nicks removed the buckets from the freezer. The first bucket, the one that had been partially inserted into the other, had a label on it that said *Clout*.

Inside the first bucket was a human head, which had been cut neatly into two parts, sawed vertically from the front to the back, and it immediately brought back memories of Sleigh's earlier Jane Doe that he had examined years earlier in Mission. That head had been cut in the same manner as the one he had just found on Pickton's farm. Aside from the current mess that Sleigh was dealing with, the Mission location had been the only other crime scene in his career in which he had found a human skull that had been cut in that manner.

Sleigh noted that the head, however, was not the only body part inside the bucket—it also contained two hands and two feet. When he examined the second bucket, he found the same type of body parts: a head, which had been sawed neatly into two sections, and two hands and two feet. Upon closer examination he noticed that the top of the skulls—where the saw cuts did not quite reach—had been torn apart the rest of the way. Although Sleigh had examined human remains at numerous crime scenes over many years, he could not immediately recall a crime scene that he could label quite as horrifying as the one on which he currently worked. The discovery was merely the first of several such gruesome finds that would be unearthed.

Following DNA testing of Sleigh and Nicks's grisly discovery, the remains found on April 4 were identified several days later as those of Andrea Joesbury and Sereena Abotsway. Pickton had already been charged with the murders of Sereena Abotsway and Mona Wilson around the time of his interrogation because of the inhalers and other personal items of Abotsway's that had been found on his farm, and because of DNA linked to Wilson's blood found in the motor home and on items of clothing that were believed to have belonged to her. Now they added Andrea Joesbury to his list of charges, bringing the total to six. Inspector Don Adam was, of course, elated by the new findings and charges against Pickton, but two lawsuits, promptly filed by Andrea Joesbury's mother after positive identification of her daughter's remains had been made, dampened his outlook somewhat.

Joesbury's mother filed lawsuits against Pickton, as well as the local police, the province of British Columbia, and the federal government of Canada, seeking damages in the death of her daughter. In her suit, she alleged that the VPD, as well as the RCMP, had *willfully failed to properly investigate all information received, knowing that such willful failure to investigate would allow the killing to continue.* She also claimed that disposal of her daughter's remains was done *in a manner which denied them their human dignity and offends against public decency.* She further alleged that *the treatment of the remains of Andrea is a gross and willful violation of human dignity, is painful to family and has resulted in emotional trauma, distress and spiritual distress, which will continue indefinitely.* In her suit against Pickton, she sought *general, pecuniary, and punitive damages and costs,* and sought a legal declaration that the pig farm be held in trust for her and her family because the fact that her daughter had been killed there constituted a *permanent interment and spiritual site.*

A short time later, an attorney from Victoria, Denis Bernsten, announced that he was filing a multimillion-dollar class-action lawsuit against Pickton, the VPD, and the RCMP, seeking damages for relatives of the victims. The attorney's lawsuit accused the police of *willful negligent action* in their handling of the case, and said that deaths *may have been prevented.*

"All of these women were somebody's child," Bernsten said. "Someone loved them."

On May 5, 2002, Sleigh was asked to report to Pickton's so-called piggery, which was attached to the slaughterhouse, before it fell down due to all of the excavation that was going on. Workers, many of them archaeology students who had been trained to identify human bones, had been going through debris in one of the troughs that ran along the piggery's floor when they suddenly made another unnerving discovery embedded in pig manure. When Sleigh arrived at the location, he could see that they had found a partial lower human jawbone, which still held several teeth. Using a brush to clean it up, he noted that one of the teeth had a dental filling in it.

Two weeks later, following positive identification that the partial lower human jawbone had belonged to Brenda Wolfe, who was last seen in February 1999, a seventh count of first-degree murder was added to Pickton's list of charges. At least four of these women, it was noted, had been killed *after* Bill Hiscox had named Pickton as a likely suspect in Vancouver's missing women.

Meanwhile, some of the women's items found inside Pickton's trailer, which had likely been kept as trophies of his kills despite his denials to the contrary, were identified. A black boot found inside his bedroom closet had belonged to Andrea Joesbury, as was the black jacket found at the foot of his bed. A shirt found inside his closet, the task force determined, had belonged to Sereena Abotsway, and a leather jacket and two tubes of lipstick belonged to Brenda Wolfe. DNA had matched and connected the women in question with those items.

As Pickton sat in jail and watched the case continuously build against him, tabloids, both in Canada and the United States, began having a heyday with the details of the case that had been given or leaked to the media. One headline shrieked: 54 WOMEN FED TO PIGS! Whether any of the victims had actually been fed to the pigs remained to be determined, but it seemed like a distinct possibility since remains had been found inside the piggery. Nonetheless, health officials were compelled to issue warnings to the public that human remains may have been fed to Pickton's pigs, and the pigs subsequently butchered with their meat sold or given away for human consumption. There was also rampant speculation that human remains may have been ground up and mixed with ground pork used to make sausage. As a result pork sausage became a somewhat unpopular breakfast item in the area for some time to come, and citizens were repulsed and outraged over what they thought they may have eaten.

Two months to the day after the two buckets of human remains were found inside the freezer in Pickton's workshop, Sleigh and other investigators were unnerved again when they made another, similar discovery, on Tuesday, June 4, 2002, inside the slaughterhouse. Two more plastic pails were found concealed behind wooden structural braces between one of the main walls of the slaughterhouse and the pigpen. Sleigh and the others with him discovered a skull, sliced in two like the others, along with two hands and two feet. These buckets had been next to a number of other buckets that contained animal offal, the parts of butchered remains that are considered inedible by humans. The offal, also known as carrion, had apparently been prepared for removal and transportation to the rendering plant. The mess would have to be gone through just in case Pickton had mixed human remains in with the offal. Within a couple of weeks, the latest remains were identified through DNA as Mona Wilson's. Police guessed they would have been taken to the rendering plant on one of Pickton's regular runs, but he had been interrupted by his arrest and all of the police activity. Wilson's remains, as well as those of Abotsway's and Joesbury's, were likely part of what Pickton had been talking about when he had characterized himself as having gotten "sloppy."

Many of the cops, including Sleigh and Adam, found themselves wondering what Pickton had done with the women's torsos. Had he conducted a complete slaughtering operation on each of the women, including skinning and eviscerating them? If so, had he then cut the torsos into pieces and then, perhaps, taken the pieces and run them through a meat grinder? And if he had done that, what had he truly done with the ground-up remains? Fed them to the pigs? Mixed them in with ground pork? Perhaps a combination of both? The grisly discoveries raised more questions than they answered.

The discoveries also caused a number of police officers to voluntarily undergo psychological counseling and therapy.

30

By June 6, 2002, additional heavy machinery, which included two large conveyor belts, had been brought onto Pickton's farm to aid the numerous investigators, technicians, and crime scene experts who had been working there for the last several months. In addition to the police personnel, more than one hundred archaeology students used the equipment to sift through several layers of dirt. As the dirt was dug up from below ground level, it was placed on the conveyor belts and carried to screens, or sifters, where everything but dirt remained behind for additional examination.

About a month after Mona Wilson's remains had been discovered inside the slaughterhouse, the crime scene investigators dismantled many of the pigpen's half-walls that divided the stalls and removed a raised wooden platform, piece by piece. Amid a number of rat's nests that they had uncovered during the dismantling process, the investigators had also found fourteen hand bones, along with a green toothbrush. Tim Sleigh, who was overseeing much of the search for evidence, noted that one of the hand bones appeared to have knife marks on it, making it possible, even likely, that the hand, and whomever it had belonged to, had been hacked into pieces.

Upon further examination of the hand bones, it was determined that they had come from someone's left hand. Later, again through DNA matching, investigators determined that the left hand, or, rather, the bones that had once been a part of it, had belonged to Georgina Papin, who, it was believed, had disappeared in March 1999. The cops recalled that it had been Papin that Lynn Ellingsen had purportedly walked in on while Pickton was skinning her as she dangled from a meat hook. Even though they would not know it for quite some time, the hand bones would turn out to be the only evidence they would find showing that Papin had actually been to Pickton's pig farm.

During the entire crime-scene processing effort, where many things were going on simultaneously, a pathologist eventually examined the skulls that had been sawed in half and determined that Abotsway, Wilson, and Joesbury had died as a result of having been shot in the head. The pathologist also examined the half-skull from Jane Doe found in the Mission area, but there was no evidence of her having been shot. The other half of her skull had never been found, and if such evidence existed, it could very well have been inflicted on the missing half.

A tool mark expert was brought in at one point to examine the skull halves of Abotsway, Wilson, Joesbury, and Jane Doe. To everyone's astonishment, the expert was able to show that the bisections that had been performed on all four skulls were almost identical, even though one of them had been cut years earlier. Using a plastic skull as a model, the expert was able to show the tool marks and their paths. It was believed that the skulls had been bisected using a reciprocating power saw, a type of handheld saw frequently used in construction and demolition work in which the cutting is accomplished through the reciprocating action of the blade as it moves in and out of the power mechanism. Investigators had earlier found such a saw inside Pickton's slaughterhouse, but efforts to connect it to the bisected skulls failed. That did not necessarily mean that the saw found inside the slaughterhouse had not been used on the four victims; it only meant that investigators had been unable to conclusively show that the blade attached to it when found was the same blade that had made the cuts on the skulls.

At one point during the excavation process, Fox News reported that investigators had found bits and pieces of human remains inside a wood chipper on the farm, which, Fox said, police believed had been used to turn "the victims' bodies . . . into pig feed."

On August 21, 2002, one of the archaeology students who was working at the site of one of the conveyor belts saw an item of interest pass by in the dirt. When she picked it out of the dirt, the student saw that it was a partial jawbone that held three teeth. She promptly turned it over to one of the crime scene experts, who had it analyzed. When the DNA results came back several days later, the task force revealed that the latest partial jawbone had been that of Marnie Frey, who was last seen in September 1997. A pathologist who examined Brenda Wolfe's and Marnie Frey's partial jawbones said that it was possible that both had been bisected in similar fashion to the other victims.

In the same vicinity where Frey's partial jawbone had been found, students found two additional bones. They were later identified as a rib bone and a heel bone. The finding of those two bones turned out to be an astounding discovery that partially solved the mystery surrounding Tim Sleigh's Jane Doe—the DNA in both bones matched the DNA of his Jane Doe's skull. Although they still did not know Jane Doe's identity, or why half of her skull had been found miles away near the community of Mission, Sleigh at least finally knew that she had been one of Pickton's victims. He resigned himself to the fact that he would probably never know positively what had happened to the rest of her body, nor did it seem likely that he would ever identify her. Finding one of her rib bones and her heel bone on Pickton's property did, however, serve to move Pickton's killing timeline back to at least 1995.

Pickton was eventually charged with the murders of Georgina Papin, Helen Hallmark, Patricia Johnson, Jennifer Furminger, and Marnie Frey. Most of the charges were based on DNA analysis of blood, personal items, bones, teeth, hair—or a combination of the aforementioned—that matched the DNA that had been collected of the missing women, typically through the cooperation of their relatives.

By October 24, 2002, Robert Pickton's fifty-third birthday, the task force added four more first-degree murder charges to its growing list, bringing the total to date to sixteen. The latest victims for which charges were brought against Pickton were Heather Chinnock, Tanya Holyk, Sherry Irving, and Inga Hall.

Also on that same date, the family of missing Vancouver woman Angela Rebecca Jardine, twenty-seven, who was last seen in November 1998, was notified via e-mail that their daughter's DNA had been found on Pickton's pig farm. He was not charged with her murder, however, because the amount of evidence yielding her DNA was considered insufficient to bring forth charges. Jardine's case was similar in that regard to that of Sarah de Vries, whose DNA had been found several months earlier, but in scarce amounts. E-mail seemed like a terrible, insensitive method to notify a family that their loved one's DNA had been found on a suspected serial killer's pig farm, but for whatever reason that is how the notification had been handled.

The following day, October 25, 2002, a seller on eBay had put up a site asking for an opening bid of $9.99 for "Robert Pickton Dirt From His Pig Farm," posted under "Collectables: Rocks, Fossils, and Minerals." The seller claimed to be a local resident who had been to Pickton's farm. eBay.ca pulled the site from its offerings almost immediately before any bids had been made.

The tedious search for evidence at Pickton's farm continued for a full twenty months, until task force investigators wrapped up the massive excavation process on Tuesday, November 18, 2003. By that time the task force had seized hundreds of thousands of evidentiary items, 235,000 of which they had extracted blood, semen, hair, and other evidence from a methodical, if not mechanical, process of testing each item seized— many items more than once. Of the women that Pickton was charged with murdering, prosecutors were prepared to argue at trial that the evidence linked to those women was found within three hundred or so feet of Pickton's trailer. During their work on the farm, the police had also found mounds of buried women's clothing, some of it burned. Some of it had been found on Pickton's property, and some of it down the road on his brother's property. Although they had wrapped up the excavation of Pickton's property, there was still much work to be done.

By the time 2004 rolled around, government estimates of the costs associated with the task force investigation and the excavation of Pickton's property would likely exceed $70 million, in what had easily become the largest, most expensive serial murder investigation in Canadian history.

31

Many things occurred throughout 2004 and 2005 as Crown prosecutors worked through their massive case against Robert Pickton, methodically completing each item on their long agenda before they could bring what appeared to be Canada's worst serial killer to trial. Pickton was moved out of the RCMP's Surrey facility into the North Fraser Pretrial Center, a high-security remand center, in Port Coquitlam, as he and his attorneys did what they needed to do for the upcoming trial. When all was said and done, it would take months of pretrial hearings in British Columbia Supreme Court in New Westminster, nearly a year in additional legal wrangling, which comprised most of 2006, in which both sides were afforded the opportunity to present arguments on the admissibility of evidence, and yet another year to complete the actual trial.

In preparing their case against Robert Pickton, Crown prosecutor Mike Petrie, along with coprosecutor Derrill Prevett, had put together a string of witnesses and evidence unprecedented in Canadian criminal trial history. Although another dozen first-degree murder charges were leveled against Pickton in May 2005,

British Columbia Supreme Court justice James Williams, during the 2006 legal arguments, pared the charges to twenty-six and then divided those charges into two separate trials in the interest of moving things along at a more rapid pace. He also believed that two trials would be less confusing for the juries.

The first trial would be for the murders of Sereena Abotsway, Mona Wilson, Andrea Joesbury, Marnie Frey, Georgina Papin, and Brenda Wolfe. The legal arguments regarding the admissibility of evidence began on January 30, 2006, but they would not get to the voir dire proceedings, in which both sides are afforded the opportunity to examine potential jurors as to their integrity and possible preexisting prejudices before they are seated on a panel, until December. A number of publication bans were put into effect in Canada, resulting in a blackout of nearly all important news related to the case, in the interest that Pickton would receive a fair trial.

As an interesting footnote to an already very bizarre case, Robert Pickton, during that year of legal maneuvers, began a letter-writing relationship with Thomas Loudamy, of Fremont, California, a young man who corresponded with several convicted killers as a hobby. Loudamy, who used "Mya Barnett" as a fictitious name in his letters to Pickton, made two of the letters he received from Pickton public, he said, to help people learn more about a purported serial killer. The two Pickton letters, printed by hand in capital letters and with many spelling and grammatical errors, were dated in February and August 2006.

In one of his letters, he accused the police of lying and paying off witnesses to testify against him, and wrote that *the police got me as the fall guy* and *for that they look good, which is a joke*. He alleged that the police did not want to know the truth about the case but were *only interested in to charge any-one* [sic] *to get the heat off of their back*. . . . He suggested that the police should put up video surveillance cameras if they wanted to put *the right people behind bars* for the crimes he had been accused of committing, and said that *they are the fools*. Pickton also wrote that he was *brought into this world to be hear* [sic] *today to change this world of there* [sic] *evil ways*. . . .

Pickton quoted the Bible a number of times, and said that he was not of this world but was *from the past life*, the details of which, he claimed, would be in a book that he planned to write. In one instance he referenced Ephesians 5:5, to which he put his own take on defining the passage: *You can be sure that no immoral, impure or greedy person will in-herit the kingdom of God. . . . Don't be fooled by those who try to excuse these sins, for the terrible anger of God comes upon all those who disobey him*. According to the King James Bible, Ephesians 5:5 says: *For this ye know, that no whoremonger, nor unclean person, nor covetous man, who is an idolater, hath any inheritance in the kingdom of Christ and of God*.

Pickton's use of the Ephesians passage raised the question of whether Pickton might have used religion to justify his actions when he was writing to Loudamy, but it also raised an even more chilling possibility of whether he had been on a religious mission by killing prostitutes to help rid the world of "evil ways." His references to "whoremongers" and "idolaters" certainly seemed to indicate so, but then they could also have simply been the ranting of a lonely man seeking friendship wherever he could find it, since he had undoubtedly accepted the fact that he would likely never walk the face of the earth as a free man again.

Pickton also wrote passages commending Justice James Williams for his decision to reduce the count of murder charges against him and to split the charges into two trials. His words of praise for the judge seemed to have been written more out of his own self-serving wishes as opposed to the judge's legal justifications for making them.

They had to [sever the charges], they have no choice but to, if not there will be a whole lot of coart [sic] time waisted [sic] all for nothing in which there will be in need a whole lot of answers to many questions by the police and the R.C.M.P. when this coart case is over by the way of the public of when they find out that I am not in-volved [sic] at all. If the coart did not drop all these charges I could be in coart for at least two or more years and it really will be hard to keep a jury to-gether [sic] for so long.

He added that if Williams had not made the decision to split the charges, his case could end in a mistrial.

Pickton also took the opportunity to boast about what an important defendant he had become, and told his pen pal that he went to court in a convoy of three vehicles—one in front of him and another behind him—each with two sheriff's deputies for his protection. He said that there were also typically four additional deputies waiting for his arrival at the courthouse gates.

Time seemed to pass slowly in 2006 for Pickton, his lawyers, and the Crown's lawyers, but before year's end each side seemed to know how it would present its case to the jury. Petrie and Prevett, the prosecutors, would focus on the evidence tied to the six women whose murders Pickton was being prosecuted for in the first trial. Among the evidence that they would present were seven items with Sereena Abotsway's DNA on them, including a shirt and at least one of her inhalers; at least forty items with Mona Wilson's DNA; approximately eleven items with Andrea Joesbury's DNA; also three items with Brenda Wolfe's DNA. The excavation of Pickton's farm and the searches of all the buildings on it failed to turn up any personal items that had belonged to Georgina Papin or Marnie Frey, but at least five of the aforementioned items were found to have Pickton's DNA on them, as well as the victims'. The prosecution also planned to present, of course, much of the gruesome evidence found on Pickton's farm, and would call approximately two hundred witnesses to testify over the course of about twelve months.

Lawyer Peter Ritchie's defense team, led by attorney Marilyn Sandford and Adrian Brooks, would stress that investigators had been unable to conclusively tie Pickton to the buckets of body parts they had found on his property, nor could they say with certainty that the guns seized from the farm had been used to kill any of the victims. The defense contention was that Pickton had not killed any of the prostitutes that he was charged with murdering, and that he had not participated in any murders with other people. Furthermore, there was little DNA evidence, if any, that linked Pickton directly to any of the victims.

Jury selection finally got under way on Monday, December 11, 2006, and was expected to take at least two weeks to complete. It seemed that a major challenge would be finding people who would not have any difficulty sitting through a trial that would last a year. Another challenge that never seemed to present itself was how the presentation of such gruesome evidence and testimony would be viewed by prospective jurors. However, much to everyone's surprise, a jury was seated by the end of the following day.

Because the Crown intended to call more than two hundred witnesses, which could take many months to hear their testimony, the defense team requested that it be granted the right to present an early opening statement, right after the Crown had delivered its opening statement. Typically, the Crown would begin calling witnesses immediately after making its opening statement, and the defense would normally wait until the Crown had finished presenting its case before making theirs. Justice Williams ruled in favor of the defense, with no objections being voiced by the Crown, for the unusual procedural change. Williams noted that the court system had the discretion to allow such a change in procedure, and commented that allowing the defense to make its opening statement after the Crown's would be fair, given the circumstances of what would be a lengthy trial.

"The case . . . can quite readily be characterized as special or unusual in that it is anticipated that the trial will run in the order of twelve months," Williams said.

Williams also said that the benefit to the defense in being allowed an early opening statement would be that it would boost the jury's capacity to understand the evidence "in a meaningful way," and that it would allow the jury to "relate that evidence to a consideration of the issues."

Despite the Crown's willingness to accept the early opening statement by the defense, it asked Williams to impose three conditions on the defense, including that the defense provide an indication of the evidence it intended to present, that an advance copy of its opening statement be provided to the Crown, and that it not be allowed to present a second opening statement later on, after the Crown had rested its case.

Williams rejected the Crown's three conditions, but imposed an order requiring the defense team to provide the court with a copy of its opening statement for prior approval, in part to ensure that it did not "lapse into argument" at that time.

Satisfied that the preliminary issues had been resolved, Justice Williams sent everyone home until after the holidays. He set January 22, 2007, as the date that the trial would begin, allowing jurors ample time to get their personal affairs in order so that they could settle in for the trial that would last for a year.

Part 5

Trial

32

On Monday, January 22, 2007, the eagerly anticipated trial for Robert Pickton finally got under way in
the New Westminster courtroom of Justice James
Williams. Pickton arrived in a caravan of three police
vehicles amid a high level of security rarely seen in
New Westminster after a short drive from the North
Fraser Pretrial Center, where he had been held for
the past two years. Just like he had told his pen pal in
California, he was in the middle car. It was a few minutes before 9:30 A.M. when he was escorted inside the
building through a secure area. Even though Justice
Williams had declared that there would be no publication ban for Pickton's actual trial, there would be a
number of bans imposed later on, intended to protect
the identity of certain witnesses, particularly the undercover officer who had shared a cell with Pickton
shortly after his arrest. There was a media circus of
sorts outside the courthouse that resembled a feeding
frenzy in which reporters working for virtually every
media type, from television to tabloid, scavenged for
any morsel of information they could get, but the
media activity was not as heavy as had been expected.

As it was, there were approximately three hundred reporters and photographers present representing such media outlets as Court TV, BBC Radio and Television, the *Washington Post,* the *New York Times,* ARD television from Germany, the British Press Association, and *The Economist* magazine. Canadian television news and press agencies were also present, along with a number of technical and support personnel.

After Pickton had settled into the prisoner's box inside the courtroom, similar to that in London's Old Bailey, and the courtroom brought to order, Justice Williams admonished the jury of seven men and five women that some of the evidence they would hear would be shocking and disturbing, and cautioned them to avoid all forms of news coverage of the trial and to rely only on the evidence that would be presented in court.

"Where evidence is particularly distressing," Williams said, "there is concern that it may arise feelings of revulsion and hostility, and that can overwhelm the objective and impartial approach jurors are expected to bring to their task. . . . I ask each of you to deal with that as best you can. . . . You should be aware of that possibility and make sure it does not happen to you."

Crown attorney Derrill Prevett began his opening statement by telling the jury that the six women that Pickton stood accused of murdering—Sereena Abotsway, Mona Wilson, Andrea Joesbury, Brenda Wolfe, Georgina Papin, and Marnie Frey—were all drug-addicted prostitutes who frequently worked the streets of Vancouver's Downtown Eastside. He said that the Crown intended to prove that Pickton lured the women with drugs and money to his farm in Port Coquitlam, where "he murdered them, butchered them, and disposed of their remains" in a variety of ways. In addition to providing graphic details about the case to the jury, Prevett described how Pickton had admitted that he had killed forty-nine women but had wanted to continue with one more to make it an even fifty. Prevett also told the jury about Pickton's conversations with the undercover officer in his jail cell.

"During the afternoon and evening of February 22, 2002, Mr. Pickton and the undercover officer came to know each other," Prevett said. "The officer related his cover story to the effect that he was in custody awaiting transport back east to face outstanding charges for violent offenses. Mr. Pickton explained that he'd been arrested for two murder charges and that the police are looking at him for forty-seven others. In the course of telling about his past, Mr. Pickton repeatedly tells his cellmate that he believes he is 'nailed to the cross.' He also tells him he is being considered as a mass murderer—his words, you'll hear them. . . . In furthering his cover story, [the cellmate] tells Mr. Pickton that the police have him on an attempted murder charge and are investigating him for others as well. Mr. Pickton responds, 'But you're nothing like mine.' The officer tells him he is looking at some serious time if the police are able to put things together. Mr. Pickton then gestures with his hands, showing five with the fingers on one hand and a zero on the other. The officer asks, 'What's that? Five? Zero? Fifty, ha-ha.' Moments later, Mr. Pickton verbalizes what he had earlier gestured. He says, 'I was going to do one more. Make it an even fifty.'"

Prevett took the jury through a detailed outline of the gruesome evidence found on Pickton's farm, including the buckets containing the heads that had been sawed in half and the hands and feet of some of the victims, the revolver with a spent casing and a dildo attached to its barrel, the various finger, heel and jawbones, teeth, and so forth, and how DNA analysis had identified the six aforementioned women. He also explained that additional bones found near Pickton's slaughterhouse did not match anyone that the task force had listed as missing.

"These murders of these six women were the work of one man, the accused, Robert Pickton," Prevett said. "He had the expertise and equipment for the task. He had the means of transportation available and the means for disposal of their remains."

Prevett also explained that the jury would hear the interviews that the police had conducted with Pickton. He explained how the interview began with Sergeant Bill Fordy.

"Mr. Pickton . . . explains to Sergeant Fordy that his trade is a butcher, he butchers pigs, he has been doing it since he was thirteen years old and he describes roughly how he does it," Prevett said. "When you see and hear this portion of the interview, you'll see it's marked by the accused's denial. He claims he knows none of the women with whom he is being investigated. He states that he knows nothing and that he is just a pig farmer."

Pickton's account changed, however, later on during the interrogation, particularly when Staff Sergeant Don Adam took over the questioning.

"Staff Sergeant Adam asked him about the photos of women displayed on a large poster board, which has been brought into the interview room, and asks him, 'How many do you think you recognize? Like if you were free to talk right now, how many could you reach out and touch? No. But I mean, that you killed.' Mr. Pickton responds, 'You make me more of a mass murderer than I am.'"

Prevett explained that later in the interview Adam

suggested to Pickton that the reason he found himself in his situation was that he did not do a very good job when he cleaned up one of the girl's blood.

"You'll hear Mr. Pickton respond, 'That's right, I was sloppy.' Mr. Pickton goes on to say that bad policing is the reason why it took so long to catch him," Prevett continued. "Staff Sergeant Adam questions him about his motives for killing and whether he ever thought of quitting, and Mr. Pickton states that he had one more planned, but that was the end of it. 'I was going to shut it down. That's when I was just sloppy, just the last one.'"

Prevett said that Pickton told an RCMP officer: "I should be on death row."

Several members of the victims' families were listening from the gallery. As Pickton sat mostly expressionless in the prisoner's box, some of the family members could be heard sobbing as they broke into tears. It would be an understatement to say that the trial would be difficult for the victims' families. Dressed in a long-sleeved gray shirt, black denim jeans, and white running shoes, Pickton avoided looking at anyone in the courtroom, choosing instead to peer downward toward a pad of white paper on which he wrote, or printed, occasional notes. Members of Pickton's family did not attend the trial.

Among the details heard by the jury at the trial's onset were descriptions of the decomposed severed heads, hands, and feet found inside the five-gallon plastic pails, and how the women had died. Prevett described how Andrea Joesbury's head had been cut vertically in two, and that she had been shot in the right rear part of her head. The bullet had exited through her left eye. He described how her jaw had been cut up through the face to the top of her head, and how another cut had been made from the rear of her skull all the way to the top of the head. A fracture was present between where the two cuts nearly met, as if the head and skull had been separated the rest of the way manually, perhaps by hand—at least that was the presumption to be made from the description of the cuts and the fracture. One of her teeth had also been found inside the bucket.

The jury heard that there were differences in the manner that Sereena Abotsway's skull had been cut. Her skull had been cut from the rear of her head, up across the top of the skull to an area on her forehead, just above her right eye. Another cut had been made up through the center of her face to the middle of her forehead. She had been shot in the head near one of her ears. The .22-caliber bullet, which had been found in the bucket with her head, had passed through the brain and into the lower section of the skull. She had been decapitated between the second and third vertebrae. The information, not to mention the evidence photos, was not for the squeamish.

Prevett told the jury about the jawbone fragments of Marnie Frey and Brenda Wolfe, as well as the teeth and other bones, including Georgina Papin's hand bones, that were found on the property. He also described how investigators had found many of the victims' personal belongings in Pickton's trailer and at other locations on the farm, and how many of those personal items had yielded DNA from the victims. Prevett was adamant that the Crown would prove its case against Pickton.

When the defense team made its opening statement, Peter Ritchie told the jury that he and his team would vigorously disprove the Crown's case, and that they would contest the Crown's alleged facts of the case.

"The defense position in this trial is clear and it is that Mr. Pickton did not kill or participate in the killing of the six women he is accused of murdering," Ritchie said.

Ritchie asked that when the jury was afforded the opportunity to listen to Pickton in the police interview that they listen very carefully, not only to what Pickton said but to the interview in general.

"Don't forget that the Crown will be pointing you to ultimately only relatively brief courses of these very long interviews where the Crown is relying on significant words being spoken by Mr. Pickton, and that these words took place at the end of a very long interview. In addition, and I ask you to pay particular close attention to this, when considering the statements, the conversations that Mr. Pickton is engaged in with both the interview team and with the undercover police officer, pay particularly close attention to the evidence relating to his intellectual competence and close attention to his level of understanding. When you watch the videotapes, when you listen to them, pay close attention to what Mr. Pickton says and the manner in which he expresses himself. . . . When you first hear the statements, focus on these areas that I suggest may be of great importance in this case. Keep in mind what you hear through the course of the police interviews about Mr. Pickton's level of sophistication."

Ritchie contended that the picture that the Crown had painted of his client and the evidence found at the farm was not the full picture.

"It is the Crown's contention they can prove those facts," Ritchie said, "but at this stage it is only a contention that the Crown can prove these facts. . . . The evidence is unquestionably shocking and difficult for jurors to deal with, as it is for everyone in connection with the trial. I would ask that you approach your analysis of this evidence dispassionately and objectively. There is no question but that this evidence is difficult and disturbing."

Defense lawyer Adrian Brooks told the jury in his part of the opening statement that Pickton was innocent, and cautioned the jurors that any conclusions they may have already reached about Pickton's guilt or innocence were premature. He said there was much evidence to hear, and contended that there was also "reasonable doubt" attached to the case. He indicated that the defense would focus on Pickton's statements to investigators, as well as the ones he made to the undercover officer.

"The evidence that we are going to be calling in relation to those statements relates to Mr. Pickton's intelligence," Brooks said.

Brooks stressed that Pickton's own mother called into question the degree of her son's intelligence, which was one of the reasons she stipulated in her will that his share of the inheritance be held in trust until he turned forty years old. Brooks said that a psychologist would testify that he had performed an IQ test on Pickton, and from another psychologist who had analyzed aptitude examinations that he had taken in school.

"The school records will show you that Mr. Pickton repeated grade two, and that he went into the occupational program," Brooks said.

The defense would also refute the Crown's contention that a heavily stained mattress from Pickton's motor home had Mona Wilson's DNA on it, even though a lab technician had come up with those results. Brooks said that the defense would show that the stain on the mattress did not contain Wilson's DNA, nor, for that matter, the DNA of any other human. Instead, he said, the stain was "from the urea-formaldehyde line of products." Brooks said that the defense had an expert who would testify that the inside of Pickton's motor home was not a crime scene at all, but it was consistent with "intravenous drug use."

For three days, beginning January 23, 2007, the jury watched and listened to Pickton's videotaped interview with the interrogation team, including the parts where he said that he thought that the fact he was being investigated in Vancouver's missing women was "hogwash" and his insistence that he was being set up to take the fall for crimes that he did not commit.

33

The first witness called by the Crown was RCMP Inspector Don Adam. Adam testified that initially, prior to the Joint Missing Women Task Force being formed, the Vancouver Police Department had put together "Project Amelia" when they began investigating Vancouver's missing women—initially there had been ten women who had disappeared. However, by 1999, Adam said, the police had determined that nine of the women had only moved out of the area and were not actually missing. He said that the officers who were working on Project Amelia believed that the disappearances had stopped. Since no bodies had turned up, and because there was no evidence to indicate foul play, the investigators did not believe there was any reason to continue with the investigation. Their efforts, Adam said, had also been hampered by the fact that the DNA data bank at that time was insufficient. He confirmed the complaints from family members and others—including activists that were attempting to get the police to understand that they had a big problem that was not being adequately dealt with—that the police at that time had not been taking the disappearances seriously enough.

Adam said that by the time the Vancouver police had disbanded Project Amelia because they thought that the women had simply stopped vanishing, he believed otherwise—he suspected that the missing women, which consisted of more than the ten women investigated under Project Amelia, were homicide victims. After the RCMP and the VPD teamed up and formed "Project Evenhanded" under the guidance of the Joint Missing Women Task Force, which was after he had been asked to look into Vancouver's "stalled" investigation in late 2000, Adam and his team concluded that the numbers of missing women that they were dealing with in Vancouver simply did not exist in other locales.

"I concluded they were murder victims," Adam testified. "Unless they could be found, the evidence was that there was an ongoing serial killer active."

At one point during his testimony, Adam said that three other people besides Pickton had been arrested in connection with the homicides, two of whom were arrested prior to Pickton. However, he said, none of the three people had been charged with any of the murders.

During questioning by Peter Ritchie, it was brought out that Adam and Fordy had told a number of lies to Pickton during their interrogation. The jury heard that lies are sometimes used as an interrogation technique that aids an investigator in creating a relationship with the suspect.

"You said, 'I'm not here to lie,'" Ritchie quoted Adam as saying to Pickton in the interrogation room. "Was that a lie?"

"Yes," Adam responded.

Ritchie also elicited information from the witness that showed that the boxes in the interrogation room with Pickton were "props." He pointed out that the boxes labeled *Informant, DNA, Toxicology,* and so forth were either empty or filled with old binders or blank papers. Ritchie asked Adam if the boxes had been placed there to make Pickton think that his fate had been sealed.

"Exactly," Adam said.

It was clarified at one point by the Crown that lies told by investigators during an interrogation are admissible in court. Adam's testimony, as well as that of others, including Fordy's, took up much of the trial's second week. Also during that second week, the jury saw and heard the surreptitiously recorded videotape that depicted the damning conversations between Pickton and the undercover officer in his cell.

As the trial moved into its third week, RCMP corporal Howard Lew testified how he, as part of a team sent to Pickton's farm to search for illegal firearms, discovered evidence that incriminated Pickton in the missing women investigation. He described the items that he found inside the sports bag in Pickton's trailer: "Some novels, small running shoes, and a respirator with the name of Sereena Abotsway on it," Lew said.

He said that the name had not meant anything to him, but that Sergeant John Cater had recognized it right away and reported it to his superiors. The discovery resulted in aborting the firearms search, and literally catapulted the investigation to a new level. Cater later testified that the first weapon found on Pickton's farm was the revolver with the dildo attached to its barrel. It was during that search, the jury heard, that police found the sex toys, fur-lined handcuffs, and jewelry items in the headboard of Pickton's bed.

The trial's fourth week consisted of considerable testimony about blood evidence, particularly that found inside the motor home. A blood spatter expert delivered meticulous descriptions of how the blood evidence in the motor home was indicative of a lengthy attack that appeared to have started on the "passenger side, rear corridor area of the motor home" that concluded with a bleeding victim being dragged through the motor home. The expert, sometimes using photographs, said that he had found "cast-off" bloodstains, which occur when blood on an object or person is rapidly shaken off, as well as single blood droplets and transfer wipe stains. Transfer wipe stains, he explained, occur when a bloodied hand or other bloodied body part touches or is moved across a surface. He said that he had found cast-off stains on the walls, carpet, and the bed's headboard, and bloody handprints were found in the passageway from the sleeping area to the front of the vehicle. He said that he could tell that the struggle began in the sleeping area and moved toward the front of the motor home based on the direction of the blood droplets that were found on the floor and on the walls.

Because it had been shown that Pickton neither drank alcohol nor took drugs, defense attorney Brooks at one point elicited information that alcohol bottles, as well as a crack pipe, had been found in the motor home. It was obviously an attempt to open up the possibility that perhaps someone other than Pickton had used the motor home.

* * *

Later, Peter Samija, manager of the RCMP's forensic lab in the province of British Columbia, testified about the daunting task involved in collecting more than two hundred thousand samples from Pickton's property for DNA testing. He explained that the procedure involved in collecting such samples is very detailed, and that each item has to be carefully handled and labeled in order to ensure the integrity of the evidence. Samija described how CSI investigators, wearing latex gloves and masks, used tweezers to pick up items for later analysis, and cotton swabs were often used to extract potential evidence and placed inside sterile tubes and labeled. Much of their work also entailed the use of alternative light sources, such as black light, that could illuminate stains that might otherwise be invisible to the naked eye. They often used a grid pattern of search when using swabs to collect evidence to make sure that areas did not overlap.

Constable Daryl Hetherington testified how a number of officers had begun feeling ill early in the search for evidence, and that by the time they found the pails containing decomposing body parts, the human remains had begun to liquefy. She said that police had to use a strainer to separate the liquid material from the victims' heads and limbs.

Sergeant Tim Sleigh also testified about finding the body parts inside the freezer in the back room of Pickton's workshop.

"I saw a human head, hair, an ear, skin that was purpling, and what I believe was a jaw," Sleigh said. He said they had determined later that those remains were Andrea Joesbury's.

He described how the heads had been cut, and said that the flesh was by then in an advanced state of decomposition. He said that the remains found inside the second bucket in the freezer were not as decomposed as the first, and how investigators later learned that those remains were Sereena Abotsway's. Members of the jury had their own folders containing the crime scene photographs, and followed along as Sleigh and others testified.

At one point the defense team raised questions about the manner in which the search of Pickton's property had been conducted. According to defense attorney Marilyn Sandford, DNA from an unknown male had been found on the buckets in which the human remains had been found, and it was pointed out that other individuals were still under investigation in connection with the case. The cops provided swabs for DNA analysis to rule them out as contributors of the DNA.

On Thursday, March 8, 2007, Pickton's audio letter to a woman named Victoria, recorded in 1991, in which Pickton tells portions of his life's history, was played for the jury. Victoria's last name remained unknown at the time of the trial, as did her location—believed to be in a country other than Canada. The tape, which was just under an hour in duration, enabled the jurors to hear Pickton, in his own words, tell about his life as a child and some of the "stupid things" he did when he was growing up. Hearing the tape put a broad smile on Pickton's face as he listened to himself recount his life history and speak about happier times.

During that same time frame of the trial, jurors also

heard testimony of how the police had contaminated some of the evidence found on Pickton's farm, including the dildo on the end of the revolver. DNA from one of the police officers was found on the dildo, as well as on a hair clipper, and a plastic bag, apparently from improper handling. Jurors also heard how security on Pickton's farm had been breached on at least one occasion, in which a condom had been placed by someone on the roof of a vehicle on the property. The police confirmed that they did not know whether they had lost any evidence on the farm as a result of the security breach. Many items found in vehicles and in buildings on the farm, jurors were told, had been thrown away because the police considered the items debris and not worthy of seizing as evidence.

During much of the month of March, considerable testimony was given by members of the investigative team, and jurors were shown graphic photographic evidence of the remains of the victims, sometimes requiring brief recesses to give jurors time to compose themselves afterward. They also heard testimony from a crime scene technician that investigators had found clumps of hair, a condom, and various other items of evidence that had not previously been mentioned.

Jurors also heard testimony from Bill Wilson, the man who had discovered the skull in the Mission area in 1995 that had never been identified. Wilson, who had not previously been publicly identified, described how he had found the skull while selling wooden craft items along a roadside stand on Highway 7, a frequent activity that he engaged in. On the day that he found the skull, he said, business was slow and he decided to clean his car. He went across the highway to obtain water from the stream for that purpose.

"When I turned around, about forty to fifty feet away from me, was this object on the ground," Wilson testified. "I thought it looked like it was an old bowl because of the color, and I thought it looked like it maybe could have been an Indian artifact. Then I walked over and realized what it was."

Wilson explained that he did not report his discovery immediately because he had errands to run, and because he did not have a telephone at his home. He said that when he returned to the same location the following day, the skull was still there. He explained that he drove into Mission and reported it.

Under cross-examination by defense attorney Peter Ritchie, Wilson admitted that he had not initially wanted to get involved.

"But you had found it," Ritchie said. "Did it concern you that you had found a human skull? Did it bother you?"

"Of course, it concerned me," Wilson said, "but I had hoped it would have floated away, or however it got there, it would have left the same way."

As the trial moved into its eighth week, the jury was informed that they would hear testimony from a man named Andrew Bellwood, who, Derrill Prevett said, would testify that Robert Pickton had explained to him how he killed prostitutes. Although Bellwood's name had come up in connection with the case during Pickton's interrogation, it had not been mentioned publicly until the early part of the trial in January. His testimony at this juncture of the trial, now in April, showed that Bellwood had been a former employee of Pickton's.

Bellwood's testimony recalled an incident from 1999 in which he had been watching television with Pickton in his trailer when Pickton began talking about prostitutes and how he had lured women to his farm with offers of drugs and money. Bellwood described how Pickton had acted out in detail how he handcuffed the women during sex, and how he would strangle them.

"As he was telling me this," Bellwood testified, "it was as if he had a woman on the bed, as if it was a play. He was kneeling on the bed and proceeding to stroke the hair of a woman who was not there."

He explained that Pickton had told him how he would take the dead women into the barn, bleed them, gut them, and then feed them to his pigs, just like he had told the police on the tape that Bill Fordy had played to Pickton during his interrogation.

The defense team was quick to point out that Bellwood had received a number of "benefits" from the RCMP during the investigation, including $1,000 for an eight-day stay at a drug treatment center for Bellwood's domestic partner, and for paying his rent for several months. The defense also accused him of lying on several occasions.

"I most certainly wouldn't be sitting here today, after five and a half years, destroying my family's life, who are sitting at home right now and my kids crying over all the bad publicity, to sit here and not tell the truth," Bellwood told the jury.

34

As Robert Pickton's trial continued, the jurors were led through a demonstration by RCMP sergeant Tim Sleigh showing how investigators assigned numbers to the numerous exhibits in order to keep track of them. Sleigh also explained the process of how investigators identified fingerprints, and how the fingerprint identifications were verified by other officers. Sleigh often showed jurors photographs and charts that police used to identify fingerprints found at various locations on the farm, such as those of Pickton, his brother, Dave, and his friend Dinah Taylor, and how they confirmed them by comparing the prints taken from each individual.

The defense team elicited testimony from Sleigh regarding a right index fingerprint that belonged to Dave Pickton, found on a piece of cardboard inside a metal toolbox that sat atop the freezer in which Abotsway's and Joesbury's remains had been discovered inside the plastic pails. Similarly, Sleigh testified about how Dinah Taylor's fingerprints had been found at a number of locations inside Robert Pickton's trailer, such as the bed's headboard inside Pickton's bedroom, on a piece of paper inside the drawer of a nightstand, and on a formal letter from British Columbia's Department of Indian Affairs, regarding an application for entitlements, that bore Taylor's name. The jury was also told that Dave Pickton had been a subject in the investigation of the disappearances of Vancouver's prostitutes, and that he had not been named as a suspect in the case.

The jury had also heard testimony that Dave Pickton told investigators that Taylor had committed some of the killings and that she had been arrested as part of the investigation, but she had been released without being charged with anything because the police did not believe what Dave Pickton had told them about her.

Sleigh also testified that Robert Pickton's fingerprints had been found on a handgun that investigators located inside the same workshop where the freezer containing Abotsway's and Joesbury's partial remains were found. Sleigh said that a print of Robert Pickton's right ring finger was retrieved from a cardboard box that police had found sitting atop a table in the slaughterhouse, and that a print of his right index finger was discovered on the blade of a knife. Sleigh said that Pickton's fingerprints were also found on a syringe wrapper inside a garbage can outside his trailer, and told the jury that fingerprint evidence was significant because it verified that a person had "contact with an object, thing, or place," and, when present, determined if a person had access to a crime scene. Sleigh's testimony during this phase of the trial consisted simply of presenting the facts—except for what had already been stated, the significance of the fingerprint evidence was not elicited from the witness by either side.

* * *

Following several weeks of additional evidentiary testimony and presentation of exhibits, jurors heard extensive testimony from RCMP forensic laboratory employees who provided explanations about DNA, how more than 235,000 pieces of evidence had been collected from the farm and analyzed, and ultimately how approximately sixty items were linked to specific individuals, including four of the six victims whose murders Pickton was being tried for, as well as to Pickton himself. Several people who knew many of the victims prior to their disappearances also testified for the Crown and described how they had met the victims, as well as the last time that they had seen the women. Afterward, toward the end of May, testimony was heard from several people who knew Pickton.

On Tuesday, May 29, 2007, Gina Houston, described as a close friend of Robert Pickton's who was also known to bring her children to Pickton's farm, told the jury that Pickton once told her that up to six bodies were in his slaughterhouse. She said that she asked him on one occasion if he had killed any women on his farm and that he had replied, "No." She also recalled an incident in which Pickton had asked her to make a "double suicide" pact with him only days before his arrest in February 2002, purportedly because he did not want to go to jail.

Houston described an incident she had overheard involving a fracas with a woman inside Pickton's trailer during a telephone call between her and Pickton in December 2001. During her testimony, which often was tearful, Houston said that the woman's name was Mona.

"He told me he tried to do everything he could for her, but she didn't make it," Houston testified.

Houston said that Pickton had told her that the woman was in an area of his slaughterhouse where he had previously held cockfights. She said that Pickton had told her that there were perhaps six bodies inside the slaughterhouse. She also testified that she had seen prostitutes, including Sereena Abotsway, at his farm. Sobbing at times, Houston said that it was difficult for her to testify against her friend who, she said, had given her between $50,000 to $80,000 to help her maintain her drug habit and to pay her bills. She described Pickton as polite, gullible, naïve, gentle, and kind, and that two of her children referred to him as "Daddy."

Under cross-examination by the defense, Houston said that she might have actually heard the name Mona from news media reports at the time. She also said that a couple of days before Pickton's arrest in February 2002, she and Pickton had a discussion in which Pickton had purportedly told her that Dinah Taylor was responsible for Mona's death, as well as for the deaths of some of the others.

"You said to him, 'I know you didn't kill her—so, why don't we go straight to your lawyer tomorrow and I'll tell them what I heard on the phone that night,'" said Marilyn Sandford, one of Pickton's defense lawyers.

"Yes," Houston replied.

"You asked him, 'Did you kill any of them?' and he answered, 'No,'" said Sandford.

"That's correct," Houston said.

"Mr. Pickton said to you on the twentieth of February in the car that Dinah Taylor shot some of the girls," Sandford proposed.

"Not in those exact words," Houston clarified. "That she was responsible."

Houston described how she and Pickton had called Taylor from their car.

"Willie told me that she would do the right thing when she came back [from eastern Canada]," Houston testified. "He said she would take responsibility for what she said she would take responsibility for."

"Did he say anything else?" Sandford asked.

"[That] she was responsible for three or four," Houston responded.

Houston testified that she had seen Sereena Abotsway and Andrea Joesbury with Dinah Taylor, and that Taylor had become furious with someone named Andrea on one occasion, purportedly because Andrea had been paid more money for cleaning Pickton's trailer than Taylor had. Taylor had repeatedly said that she wanted to kill her. The judge cautioned the jury not to automatically presume that the Andrea in question was Andrea Joesbury, and said that the defense and the Crown would likely take differing positions on Andrea's identity.

When Houston testified about the purported suicide pact that Pickton had proposed to her, she said that he had mentioned a rope, a truck, or a train. Sandford, however, implied that it was possible that he had simply been talking about taking a trip.

"If he hadn't said rope, I would have thought that," Houston said. "You can't take a trip on a rope."

At one point Houston was asked to recall an incident that had allegedly occurred inside Pickton's slaughterhouse in which Pickton, Houston, Lynn Ellingsen, and several other people watched while Pickton butchered a five-hundred-pound pig. The Crown had said during opening statements that Ellingsen would testify that she and Pickton had picked up a prostitute in the Downtown Eastside area and had brought her to the farm, and that Ellingsen would say that she had seen Pickton butchering the woman later that night in the slaughterhouse. Although Ellingsen had not yet testified, the defense used the opportunity to elicit testimony from Houston that could be used to cast doubt on Ellingsen's statements when she did testify.

"She didn't see things the way other people did," Houston said.

Houston also said that she had seen Ellingsen on a number of occasions high from drug usage. Houston also agreed with Sandford's suggestion that Ellingsen could be "delusional" at times, which prompted an objection from the Crown and the jury being escorted out of the courtroom. When the jury returned, Sandford asked Houston again about the pig-butchering incident.

"She (Ellingsen) asked me if I had seen what she seen, and I told her something to the effect that it was just a pig," Houston testified.

Sandford questioned Houston again about the telephone conversation she said that she'd had with Pickton in which she had heard a female voice, a male voice, and others purportedly arguing.

"Willie kept saying, 'Stop that. Don't do that,'" Houston testified.

"You heard a woman scream, didn't you?" Sandford asked.

"Yes," Houston replied.

"He said, 'Oh, my God,'" Sandford offered, referring to Pickton.

"I'm not sure. He could have."

Following the telephone call with Pickton, Houston said, she sent her common-law husband, who was now deceased, to Pickton's trailer to determine what had occurred there. She said that he returned with mud on his clothing and a bite mark on the calf of one of his legs.

"It looked like human teeth marks," Houston said.

35

At another point in the trial, jurors heard testimony from Pat Casanova, a man who had not previously been mentioned publicly, except perhaps peripherally, in part because he had been a subject in an undercover police investigation. Nonetheless, Casanova had known the Picktons for many years and had spent many weekends butchering pigs at the farm. He was well-versed in pig slaughtering, and the Crown intended to show that the manner in which pigs had been slaughtered at Pickton's farm were similar to how some of the victims in Pickton's case had been butchered.

Under questioning by the Crown, Casanova testified that Pickton often shot pigs in the head with a nail gun, and afterward stabbed them with a knife and hung them up to drain their blood. He said that they typically were cut in half, vertically through the spine, and that a handsaw had been used for a number of years. Later on, however, he said, the handsaw was replaced with a reciprocating saw. According to his testimony, he had been held in custody for only a few hours. He denied killing any of the women, and said that he had never witnessed any of the killings. He also denied ever helping anyone dispose of any of the victims' remains.

Information brought out at trial about Casanova's perceived connection to the case raised questions, and at times it seemed like the revelations helped the defense's case instead of the Crown's. For example, a band saw that police seized from his property revealed the presence of human DNA, but in amounts insufficient to determine to whom it belonged. Casanova also testified that he did not have an explanation for how the DNA got onto his band saw. His DNA was also found at other locations on the farm, including inside the freezer in Pickton's workshop, and near a second freezer where human remains were also found. Although he said that he had never used the freezer where human remains were found, he admitted under cross-examination that he had placed pig carcasses inside one of the freezers prior to Pickton's arrest in February 2002. Although Casanova had been arrested in connection with Pickton's case and questioned, he was never charged with any crimes associated with the case.

A bit later, Scott Chubb testified for the Crown and repeated much of what he had told the investigators, including what Pickton had purportedly told him about killing "junkies" by injecting them with windshield wiper fluid. He also testified about anger that Pickton allegedly exhibited toward Lynn Ellingsen, who had been "costing him a lot of money," and he inferred that he wanted her harmed.

At one point during his nearly three days of testimony, Chubb was shown a poster board of photos of the missing women and was asked if he had seen Pickton with any of them. He pointed out Georgina

Papin's photograph and said that he had seen them in Pickton's flatbed truck parked at a strip mall in Port Coquitlam. Although he was unable to remember the date that he had seen them, he said that the woman had been wearing a baseball cap.

It was also pointed out that Chubb had been the person who had provided the tip to the police about Pickton's weapons, which had led to the search of his farm and, ultimately, his arrest. Chubb's memory was often hazy, and the defense lawyers seized the opportunity to question his reliability as a witness, as well as his credibility—in part because of the fact that the RCMP spent more than $25,000 to help him relocate under a witness protection program of sorts, and for paying for some of his living expenses after becoming a witness.

Chubb testified that he did not have anything to do in connection with the disappearances of the women, and said that he had not helped dispose of any bodies.

Lynn Ellingsen took the witness stand on Monday, June 25, 2007, and provided some of the more dramatic testimony of the trial as she recounted how she had witnessed Robert Pickton skinning a woman believed to have been Georgina Papin. Ellingsen, who had resided in a spare room in Pickton's trailer for several months, told of how she had walked into the slaughterhouse one evening and saw a female body dangling on a meat hook from the ceiling. She described the victims feet, which were at eye level, and recalled that the woman's toenails were painted red. She told of seeing blood and long black hair lying on a stainless-steel table near the body. Covered in blood, Pickton had been slicing an object, which she did not name, with a knife when he saw Ellingsen. She said that he forcefully pulled her over to the table and threatened her.

"I saw this body," Ellingsen testified. "It was hanging. Willie pulled me inside, behind the door. Walked me over to the table. Made me look. He told me if I was to say anything, I'd be right beside her. I told him, 'I wouldn't say a word—I promise.'"

She explained that the woman she had seen hanging in the slaughterhouse was a woman that they had picked up earlier that evening after cruising Vancouver's Downtown Eastside looking for a prostitute for Pickton to take back to the farm. She described how she had smoked crack that evening, and how Pickton had taken the woman they picked up into another room while Ellingsen went into her room. She also recalled how she had been awakened by a loud noise and had seen a bright light in the slaughterhouse next door, and the horror that she encountered when she went to investigate.

"This woman that we had picked up," she said, "at my eye level was where her feet, like her legs were. I seen red toenail polish. On this big shiny table, I don't know what it was, but it was lots of blood and, uh, hair, black hair."

Mike Petrie, the prosecutor, asked her if she had seen the person's face.

"Not her face," Ellingsen replied. "But it was her hair, like she had long black hair and that's what was laying on the table. . . . I just remember her toes."

"Was Pickton doing anything to the woman?" Petrie asked.

"There were knives with blood on them," she replied. "He was full of blood himself."

Responding to Petrie's questions, Ellingsen said that she had met Pickton through Gina Houston, whom

she had become acquainted with at a halfway house
where Ellingsen was living to get out of a violent relationship. Pickton eventually allowed her to move into
the spare room in his trailer, and paid her to clean it
on a somewhat regular basis. She said that Pickton
knew about her drug problems, and he helped her
acquire drugs.

The defense team made Ellingsen's known drug use
an issue regarding her competence as a witness, and
at one point Petrie, apparently in an effort to counter
the defense's efforts to discredit her, asked her to explain how the use of the drugs affected her mentally
and physically.

"It numbs you," Ellingsen explained. "It doesn't
make you see things that are not there. It doesn't make
you hallucinate. . . . I know what I saw. I did see . . . this
woman's body."

During a police photo lineup, Ellingsen picked
Georgina Papin's photo as the person she had seen
dangling from a meat hook inside Pickton's slaughterhouse. However, she could not provide the precise
date that she and Pickton brought Papin from the
Downtown Eastside to his farm.

After seven months of testimony, given by nearly
one hundred witnesses, the Crown wrapped up and
rested its case on Monday, August 13, 2007. Three
weeks later, Pickton's defense team began their effort
to prove their client's innocence by continuing their
attack on the credibility of the Crown's main witnesses. They would take nearly seven weeks to present
their side of the case. The defense strategy was simple,
yet powerful, and consisted primarily of sowing seeds
of doubt on the Crown's case against Pickton.

Bill Malone, one of Robert Pickton's friends and business associates, testified that he had witnessed visitors coming and going at Pickton's farm at all hours of the day and night—nearly nonstop. Those visitors, he said, included friends, employees, complete strangers, and a few thieves, and that due to a lack of security, all of those people had nearly unlimited access to Pickton's trailer. The inference, of course, was that any number of people could have committed any or all of the crimes for which Pickton had been charged.

The defense team also presented expert witness testimony to refute some of the Crown's earlier bloodstain evidence. One of the expert witnesses testified that it was his opinion that some of the stains that were previously identified as bloodstains were not even blood, but were, instead, various types of glue. A second expert witness testified that the blood found inside Pickton's motor home did not make that site one of bloodletting, and that whatever had occurred there had not necessarily been a fatal incident.

All in all, Pickton's defense team was well-organized and raised many questions leading to a defense of reasonable doubt. For example, if Pickton had actually killed the women, why had he killed them? The Crown had attempted to show that he had killed them because he was angry over having contracted hepatitis C from one of them, but their argument was weak and largely based on the interviews Pickton had with investigators after his arrest. Another important issue raised by the defense was why investigators did not find more DNA evidence that would tie him directly to the crimes—if he had, in fact, killed all of the women he had been charged with killing. After all, RCMP crime labs had received more than six hundred thousand exhibits for testing, and the defense contention was that more conclusive DNA evidence tying Pickton to the murders should have been found if he had killed all these women.

There was also the question of why there had not been more eyewitnesses, besides Lynn Ellingsen, to the actual murders and subsequent butchering of the victims, since there were so many people always coming and going at the farm. Lynn Ellingsen had been the only witness to actually see Pickton in action—and considerable doubt had been cast on her credibility. Had she really seen a woman being butchered? Or had she really seen Pickton butchering an animal, such as a pig? Or had she been so high on crack cocaine that night that she really did not know what she had seen? The defense had done a very good job of tearing apart the Crown's case against Pickton, which had mostly been a case built on circumstantial evidence.

The defense also had cast considerable doubt on Scott Chubb's testimony about Pickton, saying that a good way to kill junkies is to inject them with windshield wiper fluid. For starters, it was shown that aside from the windshield wiper fluid found in the syringe inside Pickton's trailer, no additional windshield wiper fluid was found anywhere on the farm. The defense also presented testimony from a chemist who said that it would take 150 syringes of the type found in Pickton's trailer filled with windshield wiper fluid to kill a person.

The defense team argued a number of significant points that refuted the Crown's theory that Robert Pickton lured prostitutes to his farm to kill and dismember them there, including the fact that there was no conclusive evidence that any of the women were ever inside his vehicle; the manner in which the women's bodies were dismembered was dissimilar to the way Pickton butchered pigs; the guns found on

Pickton's farm could not be conclusively shown to have fired the bullets retrieved from the remains of two of the victims; DNA linking Pickton to the victims' remains was minimal at best; and investigators were unable to match the saw blades seized from his property to the cuts found on the victims' partial remains. As the defense closed its case, lawyer Adrian Brooks argued that Robert Pickton was focused on exclusively by the police and prosecutors when there were several other possible suspects that could have been more closely investigated.

"Think about how all the evidence holds together and you will see the Crown has not proven its case beyond a reasonable doubt," Brooks argued.

Prosecutor Michael Petrie, however, argued that the evidence, taken as a whole, logically pointed to Pickton as the killer. He admitted that many of the Crown's witnesses were "unsavory," but he argued that their testimony should not be dismissed or thrown out.

"Let's have a reality check here," Petrie said. "This case is about the police finding the remains of six dead human beings, essentially in the accused's backyard. Could you accept for a moment that someone else snuck onto that farm with a bunch of body parts, bones, personal belongings? And somehow this real murderer got into Mr. Pickton's trailer and put the personal belongings of these victims there, all without him knowing about it? In my submission you're not going to entertain that bizarre theory."

The case was finally handed to the jury on Friday, November 30, 2007, with an admonition from Justice

Williams to "keep an open mind, but not an empty head. . . . Don't just talk, listen, too."

Following nine days of deliberations, the jury was unable to convict Pickton of six counts of first-degree murder. Instead, they had found him guilty of six counts of second-degree murder in the deaths of Sereena Abotsway, Mona Wilson, Andrea Joesbury, Brenda Wolfe, Georgina Papin, and Marnie Frey.

Prior to sentencing, Justice Williams heard victim impact statements from several relatives of the victims. Mona Wilson's sister described how Pickton's actions had totally changed her life, and that she now lived in fear because of how Wilson had been murdered. She said that she had lost considerable weight and had little interest in food now, and that she believed her sister would only rest in peace after Pickton received justice for what he had done.

Andrea Joesbury's mother described how the loss of a child was one of the most difficult things a parent had to experience. She said that the loss of her daughter had placed her and her family into a never-ending nightmare, and that the case itself had affected her health and her relationships with her family and other people. She said that the "gruesome, gory details" were something out of a horror movie and that such images plagued her. She said that her daughter's murder had forced her into seclusion, and that she now trusted no one. Stress and isolation, she said, had taken its toll on her, and she had felt suicidal at times. She said that tension and stress and "worrying about my other children fills my days."

Andrea Joesbury's grandmother described her family as "small" and "precious," and said that Andrea had been like her own child because she and her family had often helped Andrea's mother with Andrea's care because her mother had been ill a lot. She spoke of beautiful memories she held of Andrea, trips to beaches and parks, and how Andrea liked to dress up as a little girl. She talked of how Andrea wanted to return home, and that "she was ready to come back."

Brenda Wolfe's mother, daughter, and sister also told of how Wolfe's death, and the publicity surrounding it, had affected each of them. In part because of what she had read in the media about her mother, Wolfe's teenage daughter said that she had grown to hate her mother because she had believed most of what she had read about her, before realizing how much had been sensationalized. She said she wondered that if Pickton had not killed her mother, whether her mother would have come back to her. She said that she felt a lot of internal pain over her mother's death, and had turned to writing as a way to deal with it. She said that she knew that her mother was a good person, and did not deserve to die the way she did, and deserved to be portrayed in a more positive manner.

Wolfe's mother told of how the trial had been devastating and traumatizing for her, and that she harbored an anger within her that "reacts to fear, powerlessness, and pain." She said that the loss of her firstborn child, Brenda, had left a hole in her heart and in her soul "that will never close." She said that she wanted to know what happened to Brenda during the last hour of her life, and that "only the person who murdered her knows that and can tell me that."

Wolfe's sister described her as a "remarkable person" and "the most genuine person I have ever met." She said that Brenda's death haunted her "deeply inside," and that she felt scared when she thought about what Brenda went through.

After the victim impact statements were heard, British Columbia Supreme Court judge James Williams gave Robert Pickton the maximum sentence: life in prison, serving six life sentences concurrently, with no eligibility for parole for twenty-five years. British Columbia attorney general Wally Oppal said at a press conference that it would be unlikely that a parole board would ever release Pickton from prison.

Epilogue

On Monday, January 7, 2008, the Crown asked the British Columbia Court of Appeal (BCCA) to order a new trial for Robert Pickton on twenty-six counts of first-degree murder, citing numerous errors it believed were made by British Columbia Supreme Court justice James Williams, according to British Columbia attorney general Wally Oppal.

"The trial judge made an error in defining first-degree murder, and also in directing the jury on planning and deliberation, as well as excluding certain evidence that ought to have been admitted," Oppal said.

According to Oppal, the fact that the jury acquitted Pickton of the first-degree murder charges, but convicted him of second-degree murder charges, paved the way for a new trial on only the second-degree murder convictions—should the defense file an appeal on its own. The Crown's move seemed to be of a preemptive nature to ensure that Pickton would be retried on first-degree murder charges—should an appeal be successful.

"We think this is a proper case for first-degree

murder, and that's the reason the lawyers in the Criminal Justice Branch, as sort of a defensive, protective measure, are filing notice of appeal," Oppal said.

Called a "Crown appeal against acquittal," the filing would allow the Crown to argue that Pickton should not have been acquitted by the jury on the six counts of first-degree murder.

"We have always been of the view that there was planning and deliberation," Oppal said. "So if the matter is going to go to the Court of Appeal, our lawyers would argue that the planning and deliberations have been proved, and there should have been convictions for first-degree murder."

Meanwhile, the defense team appealed the verdict, as was expected, and urged that Pickton's next trial on charges that he committed twenty murders begin as soon as possible.

"We will be asking the second trial be scheduled as soon as it can be," Peter Ritchie said. "Our client is in custody and we want to get these cases heard as soon as we can."

Ritchie also said that he would not be representing Pickton at his second trial. Pickton's appeal lawyer, Gill McKinnon, however, said that the grounds for the appeal of the first trial were that Justice Williams should not have allowed the Crown to present "similar fact" evidence, such as the discovery of the Jane Doe rib and heel bones found on Pickton's farm, to be used in its efforts to convict Pickton of the murders of the six women for which he was being tried. The defense also argued in its grounds for appeal that the testimony of Lynn Ellingsen should not have been allowed, and that his eleven-hour interrogation tape with the police, in which he made incriminating remarks, should not have been admitted as evidence.

According to Ritchie, the appeals process will be complex and lengthy, and it could take up to a year and a half before it is even heard.

Meanwhile, the province of British Columbia holds a $10 million lien on Pickton's one-third share in the family property, which it held and used to finance his first defense.

"Our client gave everything he owned to the government in exchange for his defense," Ritchie said. "Our client did have considerable assets."

It is believed that Pickton's appeal will be heard by the BCCA sometime in 2009. At the time of this writing, however, a date had not been set and Pickton remained jailed as he awaited the outcome of the appeals process. There was also considerable uncertainty of whether he would actually be tried on the other twenty counts of first-degree murder.

Note to Reader

As a writer who makes a living out of studying and chronicling factual cases of murder and mayhem—admittedly a somewhat macabre occupation—it seems only fitting that I would cross paths with the bizarre, violent case of serial killer Robert William "Uncle Willie" Pickton. Because of my fascination and interest in what people like Pickton are made of, and what drives them to commit the horrendous crimes that they do, and because of my inherent desire to make certain that the victims of such depraved monsters are treated as fairly as possible when I write about them, there was little, if any, chance that a story such as this would slip past me. However, it's important that I make an ever-so-brief attempt to describe serial murder, what defines a serial killer, and the changes that have occurred over the past few years in the labels that are placed on such killers by psychology and law enforcement professionals. I don't profess to know all of the answers, nor will I attempt to cover everything there is to know about serial murder—and the killers who commit them—here. Most people by now already know what a serial killer is, and my job is to attempt to fine-tune the information that already exists. The story of Pickton's cruelty and inhumanity, in and of itself, takes up the slack without me having to completely reestablish what is known about serial murderers and their crimes.

According to the experts, the aberrant phenomenon known as serial murder has existed among mankind throughout history, although the degree of documentation of this type of murder has not been substantial prior to the last century. Despite the phenomenon's long history, however, experts on such murders will tell you that the numbers of incidents, or commissions of such murders, have never been as great as they are today. According to *Serial Murder: A New Phenomenon of Homicide*, a now somewhat-dated, but still very useful and valid, 1984 study of serial murder by Robert Ressler, formerly of the FBI's Behavioral Sciences Unit, and his colleagues, Ann Burgess, Ralph D'Agostino, and John Douglas, serial murder has climbed to "an almost epidemic proportion." Now, more than two decades later, these so-called "motiveless" crimes have come even closer to reaching epidemic proportions, with higher percentages of stranger-to-stranger murders than most sociologists, psychologists, and law enforcement professionals would have ever thought possible when they first began compiling statistics many years ago.

Despite the fact that some crime authors estimate the numbers to be in the hundreds, in reality there are likely only some thirty-five to fifty serial killers operating at any one time in the United States, according to the best law enforcement estimates currently available. Admittedly, this number even seems high, unless one looks at the total number of unsolved murders that occur in this region of the world each year and attempts to string them together by noting similarities. Indeed, those working in the various capacities of law enforcement expect the numbers to continue to move upward on the graphs, despite the advent of modern technology and better communication abilities and practices between law enforcement agencies in different jurisdictions, though not at the rapid rate that some so-called "experts" would have you believe.

But what is serial murder? And what is a serial killer?

The term serial murder was first referred to as "lust murder" by Roy Hazelwood and John Douglas in 1980, and it is generally accepted, albeit arguably, that Pierce Brooks, the mastermind behind the Violent Criminal Apprehension Program (VICAP) that is utilized by the FBI, and a true pioneer in the study of serial murder, first coined the term. No matter—the term is here to stay. According to Ressler et al., *Serial homicide involves the murder of separate victims with time breaks between each, as minimal as two days to weeks or months.* Ressler and his colleagues referred to these time breaks as a "cooling-off period." Because homicides involving multiple victims is gradually becoming more commonplace, and to facilitate an understanding of the aforementioned definition, it is helpful to differentiate serial murder from other types of murder, such as mass murder, which involves *four or more victims killed within a short time span,* and spree killings, which Ressler et al. defines as *a series of sequential homicides connected to one event committed over a time period of hours to days and without a cooling off period.*

When one employs these definitions, it can easily be seen that murderers such as Richard Speck, who, on July 14, 1966, broke into a peaceful Chicago town house and murdered eight female nursing students while engaged in a sexual frenzy after binding each victim (see *The Crime of the Century,* by Dennis L. Breo and William J. Martin, Bantam Books) would be classified as a spree killer; his blood fest was *connected to one event* and was *committed over a time period of hours . . . without a cooling off period.* Charles Whitman, conversely, would be classified as a mass murderer because he killed his victims within a short period of time while sitting atop a Texas clock tower. An example of a true serial killer can be found in John Wayne Gacy, who claimed thirty-three male victims in Illinois (see *Killer Clown: The John Wayne Gacy Murders,* by Terry Sullivan, with Peter T. Maiken, Pinnacle Books) over a considerable time period.

Henry Lee Lucas is another example of a prolific serial killer, who claimed to have killed at least 157 people, many of whom, according to Lucas, were murdered with the help of his "partner," Ottis Toole. However, it became difficult to establish precisely how many victims Lucas and Toole claimed, because Lucas attempted to manipulate the system by leading investigators from around the country on a number of wild-goose chases, only to later recant many of his confessions after obtaining favors for his disclosures.

It is important to note that most serial murders are sex-related; many of a serial killer's victims are nude when discovered, and evidence has shown that many such murders were committed during episodes of sadistic fantasy on the part of the killer. Ted Bundy, as well as Angelo Buono and Kenneth Bianchi, the so-called "Hillside Stranglers," are prime examples of serial murderers addicted to periodic bouts of sexually sadistic fantasy.

Dayton Leroy Rogers, who holds the appalling distinction of being Oregon's worst serial killer, was afflicted with such a cycle of sexually sadistic fantasy. In the Rogers case the evidence clearly showed that his crimes were sexual in nature and were driven by fantasy. This is in agreement with Ressler et al., who contend that serial murders are more often than not carried out within *the context of power, sexuality, and brutality.* Rogers's foul deeds were, without question, *clearly sexual and all evil,* and were committed because, despite being married and having a child, he got to the point where he could not achieve sexual gratification in any other way.

This was also true in the case of serial child killer Westley Allan Dodd, who claimed three young male victims and was planning his fourth murder when apprehended, and is true about the subject of the case at hand, Canadian "pig farmer turned serial killer" Robert Pickton. There is little question that the gratification experienced by such anomalies of nature is psychological, whether sexually motivated or not.

In the past many researchers—particularly those in the field of psychology—have used the terms "psychopath" and/or "sociopath" to place a label on those who have committed motiveless serial murders. Now, according to serial murder expert Dr. Steven A. Egger, those terms have become obsolete. Egger says that the preferred label is now "antisocial personality disorder," and that such killers "are not considered mentally ill or grossly out of touch with reality," but lack the ability to "experience love or empathy, due to family rejection and needs frustration." As such, Egger says, they are unable to "postpone drives for immediate gratification," which results in the ease with which they can rape and murder their victims without feeling the remorse that a "normal" person would feel about committing a crime against another human being.

Although the behavior exhibited by most serial murderers is ritualistic in nature, as Dr. Joel Norris so aptly pointed out in his writings, and whose crimes more often than not are of the stranger-against-stranger variety, it is important to note that not all serial murders are committed against strangers, and sometimes the investigators do not even know whether the killer and victim were strangers because of an inability on the part of the investigator, for any number of reasons, to establish the relationship—if one existed. On a more certain note, according to Norris and others, a serial killer's crimes are nearly always repeated within a framework of definite observable patterns, which, of course, form the ritual. In most cases these patterns rarely digress from crime to crime, although it has been shown that some serial killers make meager attempts to alter, veil, or otherwise disguise their modus operandi.

In almost all instances serial killers typically choose easy victims of opportunity, such as prostitutes, as in the Pickton case, as they troll city streets searching for prey, like an animal with a voracious, nearly insatiable appetite. Sometimes the victim will initiate contact with the killer instead of the other way around, as in the case of Gacy when boys and young men sought out employment with Gacy's construction business. Despite attempts to disguise their modus operandi, however, the ritual remains crystal clear in most cases and often includes bondage, torture, sexual deviancy, mutilation, dismemberment, and, of course, the eventual murder of the victim. Sometimes serial murder cases even involve cannibalism, as in the cases of Jeffrey Dahmer, Henry Lucas and Ottis Toole, to name only a couple. Simply put, the ritualistic behavior provides the framework in which the killer can carry out his or, in rare instances, her darkest fantasies.

When one studies the backgrounds of serial killers in more depth, it becomes easier to see that most, if not all, manifest what are now considered classic behavior patterns, or symptoms, of what has come to be known in law enforcement and psychology circles

as "episodic aggressive behavior," or their psychosexual offender cycle. Norris identified a number of
behavior patterns exhibited by serial killers that include some of the aforementioned ritualistic behav-
iors, including, but not limited to: wearing a mask of
sanity so that they can live and work among normal
people; compulsive behavior; a chronic inability to be
truthful; a history of serious assault; deviant sexual
behavior and hypersexuality; having suffered forms of
abuse as a child; a history of drug and/or alcohol
abuse; and committing extreme acts of cruelty to animals, to name but a few examples.

Norris also identified other patterns a serial killer
goes through during their ritualistic commission of
murder, including the aura or fantasy phase; the
trolling phase, in which he is searching for his victim;
wooing the victim; capturing the victim and carrying
out the murder; the totemic phase, in which the killer,
according to Norris, tries "to preserve the intensity of
the murder, to prolong the feeling of power and tri-
umph over their pasts by attempting to preserve the
body" by performing a ritualized dismembering of
the victim. Sometimes the killer cuts off the victim's
genitals, removes limbs, or decapitates the victim. At
any rate, when the killer has accomplished what he
has set out to do, he enters the final phase, known as
the depression phase, after which the vicious cycle
begins anew.

Dayton Leroy Rogers exhibited many, if not all, of
the aforementioned ritualistic phases of serial murder
that such killers act out. For example, Rogers always
started out in a fantasy state that involved bondage in
which he displayed the tremendous power that he held
over his female victims, all prostitutes, who had been
incapacitated by him. Official police files indicated that

he nearly always began his cycle by trolling high-vice areas of Portland, Oregon, where he wooed his potential victims with the promise of money—just like Robert Pickton, except that Pickton operated in Vancouver, British Columbia.

After Rogers had his baited victim securely in his vehicle, it never took long for him to begin exercising his power over her, the "capturing" phase of the ritual, after making them comfortable by drinking vodka and orange juice with his victim. Rogers's victims were nearly always bound, according to police and trial records that included testimony from some of his surviving victims. Sometimes his victims felt comfortable enough with him that they allowed themselves to be tied up, unaware that they would be seriously harmed, often murdered, during the game that they played with the sadistic monster. The bondage and power turned him on, elevated his mood, and became the springboard that hurled him further into his destructive mind-set and the murderous action that followed.

It often took Rogers hours to reach the apex of his sexual frenzy by torturing his victims. The torture he inflicted on his victims included cutting and biting the women's feet, breasts, and buttocks, and when he was finished, he would murder his victim in the most horrifying ways imaginable. Using a hacksaw, he sawed off the feet of several of his victims at the ankles, while, the police contended, the victims were still alive and conscious. When they went into shock and became unresponsive—or not responsive enough to satisfy his sick desires—from the unbearable pain and the knowledge of what was happening to them, he would either attempt other methods of torture in an attempt to bring them around, or he would end their lives and begin coming down from his sadistic psychosexual

high. He inserted what police believed was a machete
into the vagina of one victim, and ripped her up the
middle from her vagina to her sternum, again, police
believed, while she was alive and conscious. After fin-
ishing with his victims, Rogers would take souvenirs of
his kills, things like clothing and jewelry (some serial
killers take body parts), to aid him in reliving the
episode again and again within the confines of his tor-
mented mind. Eventually, however, after growing tired
of reliving what he had already done, and his blood-
lust no longer satisfied, Rogers's desire for a new
victim and fresh blood became uncontrollable and he
would become depressed. It was always within days,
or sometimes merely hours, before Rogers entered the
depression phase of his cycle during which the vicious,
murderous phases would begin all over again.

In many ways Robert Pickton's and Dayton Leroy
Rogers's murderous desires were very similar—except
Pickton, when all was said and done, had made Rogers's
actions look like child's play.

Most serial killers never take responsibility for their
actions, and often use manipulation and outright lies in
an attempt to shift responsibility for their crimes away
from them—even after being caught and convicted.
Like Rogers, David Berkowitz, the notorious "Son of
Sam" serial killer who terrorized New York in the mid-
1970s, exhibited many of the forgoing behavior patterns. While Rogers has steadfastly refused to speak
publicly firsthand about his crimes, Berkowitz has
openly discussed his case, even if only to attempt to shift
responsibility for his crimes away from himself. Like
Rogers, Berkowitz lived in denial of his crimes, at least
partly so. Despite his guilty plea in 1977, Berkowitz once
stated on *Inside Edition* that he did not act alone in the
shootings that killed six people, a statement that ap-

peared to conflict with the evidence. "I did not pull the trigger at every single (murder)," he said. Instead, he contended that he was part of an organized satanic cult.

Henry Lee Lucas was another serial murderer who could not be believed. While he confessed to having committed many, many murders, he later recanted most of his confessions and later told Dr. Steven Egger that he had never killed anyone. He told Egger that he had made the confessions because he wanted to make those in law enforcement "look bad."

The list of serial killers and their traits could, of course, go on and on. But it should be noted that perhaps one of the most important traits of such a murderer concerns that of the killer's motive. Serial killers do not typically commit murder for material or monetary gain, but go through the process sketched in this author's note almost solely for the desirability of the power and control it allows him or her to have over their victims. This is, perhaps, generally speaking, one of the primary reasons that a serial killer typically chooses victims from the lower walks of life, people such as prostitutes, the homeless, the elderly, and so forth, because they are perceived by the killer as lacking power and are less likely to be missed than, say, people who have reached a higher rung on life's ladder.

Robert Pickton appeared to have chosen his victims for that very reason—the disappearances of prostitutes and drug addicts would not quickly attract attention, nor would such disappearances, as it turned out, quickly attract the attention of law enforcement. Pickton chose his victims from Vancouver's Low Track area because he knew that it would take some time for the police to take an interest or otherwise catch on to what was occurring. Like most such killers, Pickton was cold and calculating, and over time became addicted to the power and control he realized that he could have over others.

Many serial killers often commit their crimes over large geographic areas, traveling from place to place through numerous law enforcement jurisdictions, thus making it more difficult for the police to connect a murder that occurred in, say, Pennsylvania with a murder that occurred in Mississippi. They investigate their respective crimes without ever being able to connect the dots, often resulting in a murder that remains on the books as unsolved. Robert Pickton, however, like Dayton Leroy Rogers, committed his crimes in a very limited geographic area (his pig farm), but nonetheless he managed to get away with the murders for an unusually long time before getting caught. In both the Pickton and Rogers cases, the killers chose victims that would not be quickly missed, except by friends and loved ones, and victims that could not easily be connected to them.

The wilderness of the Pacific Northwest makes a near-perfect backdrop for a serial killer to dispose of his victims' bodies with confidence that they won't easily be found, and perhaps that is one of the reasons that that region of the country has produced so many of these killers. Dayton Leroy Rogers liked to cluster dump his victims in the Molalla Forest; Ted Bundy scattered them here and there, before moving on to other parts of the country; and Gary Leon Ridgway, also known as the Green River Killer, liked to dump his victims in varied outdoor settings, often forests. Somewhat surprisingly, Robert Pickton picked up his victims in the same area of Vancouver, and murdered them *and* disposed of their remains in the same location—his pig farm.

Early on in the Pickton investigation, the police appeared to have initially ignored the concerns voiced by the victims' loved ones, some say for as long as twenty years, likely because of their particular lifestyle. At first, when the police finally began to see that an erratic pattern was emerging, they were simply baffled—in part (and in fairness to the police) because they had no corpses, no crime scenes, and no suspect to investigate. Because of the initial lack of clues, the police hadn't even *believed* that any crimes had been committed, a necessary first step to launch an investigation. By the time the massive case finally broke in February 2002, homicide investigators with the Royal Canadian Mounted Police suddenly realized that they were dealing with one of the worst serial murder cases in modern history.

By the time the police had formed a task force to try and catch the serial killer whose acts and numbers had already exceeded many of his Pacific Northwest predecessors, thirty-one women had vanished. By the time Pickton was stopped, it is believed that he was responsible for the disappearances and subsequent deaths of forty-nine women, and, by his own admission to an undercover cop, he had been planning on an even fifty, had he not become careless.

Robert Pickton has taken his place in the darkest annals of serial killer history, and he has arguably become perhaps one of the worst serial killers that the world has ever seen.